BAPTIST WHY AND WHY NOT

INTRODUCTION BY JAMES T. DRAPER, JR.
TIMOTHY AND DENISE GEORGE, EDITORS

BROADMAN
& HOLMAN
PUBLISHERS

Nashville, Tennessee

4212-53
0–8054–1253–0

Dewey Decimal Classification: 286
Subject Heading: BAPTISTS—DOCTRINES
Library of Congress Card Catalog Number: 95–20416

Unless otherwise stated all Scripture is from the King James
Version or personal translation

Library of Congress Cataloging-in-Publication Data
Frost, James Marion, 1849–1916
Baptist why and why not / J. M. Frost; Timothy and Denise
George, editors.
    p. cm.
With contributions by R. M. Dudley and others.
Originally published: Nashville: Broadman, 1900.
Includes bibliographical references (p.).
ISBN 0–8054–1253–0
    1. Baptists—Doctrines. 2. Baptists—Membership. 3. Southern
Baptist Convention—Doctrines. 4. Southern Baptist Convention—
Membership. I. George, Timothy. II. George, Denise. III. Title.
    BX6331.F69   1995
    286'.1—dc-20   95–20416
                                                      CIP

1 2 3 4 5 6 00 99 98 97 96

CONTENTS

Part II: Selections from *The School of the Church*

Part III: Miscellaneous Writings of J. M. Frost

General Editors' Introduction

The Baptist movement as we know it today began as a small persecuted sect in pre-Revolutionary England. One critic labeled them as "miscreants begat in rebellion, born in sedition, and nursed in faction." Excluded by law from the English universities, Baptists developed their own structures for pastoral training. They also wrote hymns, preached sermons, published confessions, and defended their beliefs against skeptics, detractors, and rival religious groups of all kinds. From the popular works of John Bunyan and Benjamin Keach to the learned theology of John Gill and Andrew Fuller, Baptists wrote with a passion and with a purpose. In time, a large body of Baptist literature was developed, writings that both reflected and contributed to the emerging sense of Baptist identity.

The Southern Baptist Convention (SBC) was organized in 1845 for the purpose of "eliciting, combining, and directing the energies of the whole denomination in one sacred effort, for the propagation of the gospel." This was an ambitious undertaking for the 293 "delegates," as they were then called, who gathered in Augusta, Georgia, and embraced this far-reaching vision at the founding meeting of the Convention. Through the years the SBC has suffered numerous setbacks and distractions—the Civil War, Reconstruction, the Great Depression, social unrest, denominational strife, and much more. But through it all God has graciously blessed Southern Baptists in ways that future historians will surely record as remarkable. By the end of the twentieth century, Southern Baptists had grown into America's largest Protestant denomination, a fellowship of some fifteen million members in nearly forty thousand congregations supporting more than nine thousand missionaries.

Drawing on this rich heritage, the Library of Baptist Classics presents a series of books reflecting the faith and vision of Southern Baptists over the past 150 years. We are republishing in fresh editions and with new introductions a collection of seminal writings. These works have proven their worth as classics among Southern Baptists in the past and still speak powerfully to Baptists and other evangelical Christians today.

The Library of Baptist Classics includes writings of pastors, theologians, missionary statesmen, and denominational leaders from the past. Some of them are popular, others scholarly in form. They include sermons, doctrinal treatises, missionary biographies, and an anthology of Baptist confessions, covenants, and catechisms. Most of these writings have long been out of print. We present them now in the fervent hope that the Lord will see fit to use them again, as He has in the past, not only to remind us of the great legacy we have received, but also to inspire us to be faithful shapers of the future under the lordship of Jesus Christ.

Timothy George and Denise George,
General Editors

Foreword

JAMES T. DRAPER, JR.

The year was 1916. The date was the last day of October. The *Nashville Banner* heralded "Death Summons Dr. J. M. Frost." The short paragraph that headed the article stated simply, "Identified with Sunday School Board Twenty-Five Years. Considered Greatest Living Baptist." The esteem and respect that J. M. Frost commanded is hard to exaggerate. He stood tall in stature and demonstrated gigantic influence on Southern Baptist life. The *Nashville Banner* article included these words: "In Dr. Frost's death Nashville loses one of its most worthy citizens and the church one of its most sainted members. In more than one way he contributed to the growth of the city and to the enlargement of the work of the church and at the time of his death was considered by many the greatest living man in the Baptist church."

Born in Georgetown, Kentucky, to a noted Baptist minister, Dr. J. M. Frost, Sr., he began his education and his ministry in Kentucky. In 1871 he graduated from Georgetown College, and his first pastorate was at Maysville, Kentucky. Later he served in Lexington, Kentucky, and also Selma, Alabama. He came to the Baptist Sunday School Board as its first General Secretary from the pastorate of the historic Leigh Street Baptist Church in Richmond, Virginia. His leadership has been accepted in numerous ways. Howard College of Birmingham, Alabama, conferred upon him the Doctor of Divinity degree. Later, he was honored with the degree of Doctor of Laws by two institutions, Georgetown University in Kentucky and Baylor University in Texas.

J. M. Frost was a man of strong convictions and courageous actions. He determined to please the Lord in his every thought and deed. Yet his humble spirit and kind deportment endeared him to all. He always acted graciously with those with whom he disagreed. He had the ability to honestly and clearly represent the beliefs of others, yet not be condescending or condemning in his judgment. He pointed out differences with others and always came back to the standard of the Word of God as the final authority.

Beyond all of this, he persisted in the face of overwhelming opposition. When he began to promote the establishment of the Baptist Sunday School Board, he was opposed by virtually all in positions of responsibility. In his own words, "practically all the Baptist papers of the South" opposed his idea. Led by the old, well-entrenched American Baptist Publication Society and aided by many of the finest and strongest leaders among Baptists of the South, the opposition was vigorous. J. M. Frost guided our Convention through that tumultuous time and brought about the establishment of the Baptist Sunday School Board with little animosity directed at him personally. He was a man of great diplomacy and tact; yet he had fierce determination that God had given him a word and resolved to be obedient to God. He stated his conception of the Baptist Sunday School Board very simply: "God touched me and I thought it."

It is fitting that a man of Frost's qualities should have edited *Baptist Why and Why Not.* He clearly articulated these issues and continually called Baptists back to the basics of reliance upon the Word of God. He used terms like "absolute inerrancy," "inspired," "infallible," "all-sufficient," "sole authority," "indispensable," "one standard," and others. He stated,

> We recognize at this point no room for division, either of practice or belief, or even sentiment. More and more we must come to feel as the deepest and mightiest power of our conviction that a "thus saith the Lord" is the end of all controversy. With this definitely settled and fixed, all else comes into line as regards belief and practice. Church relation and membership must be determined not by family ties nor business consideration, nor social conditions, nor personal convenience, but simply and solely by the teaching of the Word of God; and if conviction makes men stand apart, then better stand apart than prove false to one's highest self. The noblest and mightiest union is the union formed in convictions—none other is worth the naming.

It is upon this foundation that the Baptist Sunday School Board builds today. The unswerving devotion of J. M. Frost to the Word of God and to the necessity for teaching that Word through the churches is our vision today. His many books and articles continually demanded that the churches engage in what he called "teaching and training." That is still our assignment. We teach the Word of God and train our people to apply those eternal truths to their lives. To that end the Baptist Sunday School Board now offers more than four hundred different publications, with more than ninety million pieces distributed annually in more than 120 countries around the world. We are pursuing the vision that J. M. Frost gave us more than one hundred years ago.

We have included in this volume some of J. M. Frost's most challenging and searching writings. All of these together will give readers a firm grasp of the history we have inherited and the future to which we are directed. May God bless these pages in every way to convey these truths.

Introduction

TIMOTHY GEORGE

The essays published in this volume present a slice of Southern Baptist life at the close of the nineteenth and the beginning of the twentieth century. Since its founding in 1845 the Southern Baptist Convention had grown from a small struggling denomination into a major religious force in what some observers were then calling "the New South."

Progress had been slow and difficult, and Baptist work had been beset by many obstacles and crises, including the struggle over slavery, the ravages of the Civil War, the rigors of Reconstruction, financial duress, doctrinal dissension, and denominational infighting. These problems were by no means fully resolved in 1900, but Baptists in the South nonetheless approached the dawn of the new century with their eyes on the future, buoyed by the great progress which had been made and confident about the future. J. B. Gambrell, the Great Commoner from Texas, captured the spirit of the denomination when he said that Southern Baptists were a great people who had come to a great time.

During the first three decades of the twentieth century, the two key words for Southern Baptists were "efficiency" and "cooperation." In 1898, the SBC had appointed a Centennial Committee to review the work of the Convention and to suggest a better way forward for the future. In 1900, they issued their report which contained the following conclusion:

> Fifty-five years ago the Convention came into existence, and adopted a constitution declaring . . . that the purpose of the Convention's existence was "to carry into effect the benevolent intentions of its constituents by . . . eliciting, combining, and directing the energies of the whole denomination in one sacred effort for the propagation of the gospel." More than half a century has been spent, and the plan adopted has not yet enlisted one-half of our churches, nor one-tenth of our members. Is it not time to re-examine the plan which, after such a trial of its merits, has come so far short of accomplishing its avowed purpose? Is not this turn of the century a good time for earnest inquiry into our whole plan of work?

Several years later the Convention appointed a Committee on Efficiency which brought its report in 1914, urging the various boards and agencies of the denomination to remember "the unity of their common cause and the necessity of their cooperation with each other." Out of this concern an SBC Executive Committee was created in 1917.

Guided by leaders such as George W. Truett and E. Y. Mullins, the Convention soon launched the Seventy-five Million Campaign which issued in a systematic plan of missions giving known as the Cooperative Program. In 1925, the SBC met in Memphis and adopted the Cooperative Program which has remained the lifeline of mission support among Southern Baptists to the present time. In that same year the SBC also adopted its first Convention-wide confession of faith, The Baptist Faith and Message. These two acts—the acceptance of a common confession and the consolidation of denominational giving—propelled the SBC into a period of unprecedented growth and expansion. By 1995, when the SBC celebrated the sesquicentennial of its founding, it could claim a membership of more than fifteen million persons in forty thousand affiliated congregations jointly sponsoring nearly ten thousand missionaries through a Cooperative Program budget of some one hundred fifty million dollars.

Back in 1900 the numbers looked quite different. There were 646 messengers registered at the annual meeting of the Convention that year. The Foreign Mission Board reported 94 missionaries serving in six nations while the Home Mission Board supported 671 missionaries under appointment. Still, these figures represented a significant advance over previous decades. For example, in 1892, one year after the founding of the Sunday School Board, J. M. Frost declared that no more than one-half of Southern Baptist churches had Sunday schools. In the realm of theological education, the vast majority of Southern Baptist pastors had received no formal preparation for ministry. Until the founding of Southwestern Seminary in 1907, Southern Seminary in Louisville remained the only theological institution supported by the SBC.

With the coming of the new century, Southern Baptists prepared to face the future with renewed commitment and great expectations. This was also a time when leaders of the denomination felt the need to emphasize Baptist distinctives and denominational identity in the face of growing pluralism and increasing diversity across the religious landscape.

Part 1 of this present volume reproduces ten essays from *Baptist Why and Why Not*, a book edited by James Marion Frost and published by the Baptist Sunday School Board in 1900. Dedicated to "the Baptist brotherhood of the world," this/ book was a manifesto of Baptist unity. In the first paragraph of his introduction, Frost pointed to four Baptist distinctives which he claimed were universally held by Baptist peoples throughout the world. Baptists were together, Frost said, "in contending for the faith," by which he meant an unswerving allegiance to the great doctrinal principles of historic Christian orthodoxy. Furthermore, he alleged, Baptists also shared a common history and heritage, a single missionary vision, and a united advocacy for both civil and religious liberty.

If, in retrospect, this claim seems a bit overstated, we should remember that in 1900 Northern Baptists had not yet formed a separate convention (that happened in 1908), and the full flowering of the Fundamentalist/Modernist controversy was still two decades in the future. Baptists on both sides of the Atlantic were still inspired to extraordinary missionary labors by the example of such nineteenth-century pioneers as William Carey, Adoniram and Anne Judson, and Southern Baptists' own Lottie Moon. The Baptist unity Frost extolled was both theological and pragmatic, but it would not survive the hurricane-force winds of modernity which were just then beginning to be felt in places like Chicago, Rochester, and Louisville.

Richard M. Dudley had a long and varied career in Baptist life as editor, pastor, professor, and sometime president of Georgetown College. His essay on "The Distinctive Baptist Way: Our Reasons for the Separate Existence of the Baptists" calls for "an intelligent, candid, and loving discussion" of the Baptist way. While he champions freedom of worship, he also emphatically states that "religious liberty does not consist in the right to do as one pleases in religious matters." Dudley also recognizes that Baptists share with many other evangelical Christians a common commitment to the cardinal doctrines of the gospel. And, as significant as believer's baptism by immersion is for Baptist identity, Dudley refuses to accept even this ordinance as a rationale for the separate existence of Baptist congregations. Rather he claims that the "Baptist bedrock" is belief in "the supreme authority and absolute sufficiency of the Holy Scriptures."

Martin Luther, John Calvin, and other Protestants also accepted this principle, but were inconsistent in their application of it to church life. As Dudley puts it, "I am a Baptist because by the fundamental principle of Protestantism I am bound by the Word of God in all matters of faith and practice." While he was proud to be a Baptist, and indeed by conviction could be nothing else, Dudley also sounded an irenic note when he expressed the desire that his Baptist identity not make him "narrow, bigoted, and intolerant, but humble, patient, and loving toward those who differ from me."

T. T. Eaton picks up Dudley's theme in his essay "Why the Bible and Not Other Standards." In the style of a good three-point sermon, Eaton unfolds a triad of reasons for the Baptist adherence to biblical authority. First, it is the best standard. The Bible is a complete repository of moral truth, Eaton declares, and even when compared to the religious writings of non-Christian traditions such as the Koran and the Book of Mormon, the Bible proves itself superior in every way. Second, the Bible alone is authoritative. Eaton appeals to the verbal inspiration and infallibility of the Scriptures as a guarantor of their abiding validity and compelling authority. "We are bound to believe and do whatever the Bible says we must. 'Thus saith the Lord' is an end of all controversy." Third, the Bible tells us what our souls need. Here Eaton touches on a theme deeply rooted in Baptist piety: True reverence for God's Word will not issue in an ivory-tower theology or mere "head religion," but instead will permeate the heart and soul of all believers who make it a lamp unto their feet and a light unto their path.

When Eaton wrote this article, he was pastor of Walnut Street Baptist Church in Louisville and also editor of the *Western Recorder*, a Baptist periodical in Kentucky. One of the most potent and influential Baptist leaders of his day, Eaton played a major role in the ousting of William Heth Whitsitt from the presidency of Southern Seminary.

"Why Immersion and Not Sprinkling or Pouring" was written by Charles A. Stakely during his tenure as pastor of First Baptist Church, Washington, D.C. He later served as pastor of First Baptist Church, Montgomery, Alabama, for nearly thirty years. Stakely was a lawyer by training and was well known for his forceful preaching and clear, logical style. In this essay he maintains that baptism is "a specific, definite act, a well-designed, God-appointed act, a truth-proclaiming act, from which one cannot diverge and maintain the rite itself." Stakely argues that the baptismal mode of immersion is naturally superior to pouring or sprinkling. It is also, he claims, authenticated by the witness of Scripture and the historical precedent of the early church.

In the nineteenth century the mode of baptism was a popular topic for Sunday afternoon debates between different denominational leaders. Baptist apologists frequently engaged their Methodist counterparts on this issue since the followers of John Wesley were wont to allow their converts to choose whichever mode of baptism they preferred. Stakely reiterates the traditional Baptist view, pointing out that the Greek word *baptizo* means "to dip or submerge" beneath the water. If one is physically unable to undergo the procedure of immersion, then baptism could be omitted because of this exigency. However, under no circumstances should baptism be performed in a manner contrary to the clearly defined pattern of the New Testament.

N. B. Broughton's essay "Why Sunday Schools in Baptist Churches" is a passionate plea for every Baptist congregation to establish a Sunday school as an essential part of its ongoing ministry. Broughton himself was well qualified to make this appeal. A distinguished Christian layman from North Carolina, he was a leading advocate of Sunday school work in that state, having served as a Sunday school teacher and superintendent there for some forty years. Broughton defines the Sunday school as "that agency of Christianity to which is especially committed the teaching of the Scriptures." He sees the Sunday school as providing the basis for the evangelistic and missionary outreach of the church. In typical Baptist fashion, he argues that the Sunday school movement started by Robert Raikes in England was no novelty, but rather the restoration of a pattern of Bible teaching which went back to Jesus and the apostles themselves. In the early decades of the twentieth century Broughton's ideas gained wide acceptance across the broad spectrum of the SBC.

The Baptist Sunday School Board took the lead in the development of Sunday school work. By mid-century the creative leadership of I. J. Van Ness, B. W. Spillman, Arthur Flake, and others had converted the Sunday school from a "baby room" for boys not old enough to wear "long pants and standing collars" into a standard feature of Baptist church life touching every aspect of its outreach and ministry.

William Mercer Harris had served Baptist congregations in Georgia and Alabama before being called as pastor of First Baptist Church, Galveston, Texas, in 1896. His essay "Why Missionary and Not Anti-Missionary: The Theology of Missions" recalls a theme which had caused much confusion and division among Baptists in the preceding century.

From the founding of the SBC in 1845, Southern Baptists had been strongly committed to Reformed theology. The first two textbooks of systematic theology produced by Southern Baptists—John L. Dagg's *Manual of Theology*, and James P. Boyce's *Abstract of Systematic Theology*—had both reflected this perspective. Other leaders, too, such as Richard Fuller, R. B. C. Howell, and P. H. Mell, had not hesitated to preach strong messages advocating the sovereignty of God in salvation and the priority of grace in drawing lost men and women to repentance and faith. But other leaders carried these biblical ideas to unbiblical extremes. A hyper-Calvinistic movement arose among Baptists and divided many churches. The hyper-Calvinists emphasized the sovereignty of God to the exclusion of human responsibility. They also opposed Sunday schools, theological seminaries, evangelistic services, and organized missionary work.

While not responding to all of their arguments in this essay, Harris reminds Baptists that the Great Commission is still in effect and that Christians are obligated to share the good news of salvation through Christ alone with all peoples everywhere. As he put it somewhat quaintly, "The whole world as a lost unit is in the divine contemplation always." While not denying the sovereign power of God to call and convert the lost, Harris calls on Baptists to be faithful to the task God has given them in world evangelization.

Curtis Lee Laws also had no association with the hyper-Calvinistic, anti-missionary Baptists, dubbing them "the dupes of an erroneous exegesis." His article "Why Missionary and

Not 'Omissionary'" points to an even greater source for the lack of missionary commitment; namely, the sin of neglecting to do what we know we ought to do. Laws' essay is a good example of the kind of well-crafted, passionate appeal on behalf of missions which was frequently sounded in Baptist churches. In response to this kind of preaching, many Baptists, North and South, responded to God's call and sailed forth from the shores of America to form one of the greatest missionary forces in the history of Christianity.

Laws wrote this article during his tenure as pastor of the First Baptist Church of Baltimore. Later he became a leader among conservative Baptists in the North and is credited with coining the term "Fundamentalist." Sadly, as Northern Baptists were increasingly impacted by the growth of modernism and liberal theology, their vision for world evangelization dimmed. By the late twentieth century, the number of missionaries sent out from their ranks had dwindled to a trickle. For all their success, Southern Baptists could well follow this same pattern of decline unless they heed the clear warning of Laws' message.

John Priest Greene was a pastor and educator who served for more than three decades as president of William Jewell College in Liberty, Missouri. His essay on "Why Education by Baptist Schools" is a strong apology for Baptist Christian higher education. He warns parents not to send their young people to secular institutions where they will be instructed by "sneering agnostics." Greene contends that all teachers at a Baptist school should be godly believers, well grounded in the Scriptures, modeling missionary concern and moral living before the students. Greene wrote in an era when the founding purpose of Christian schools was clearly in mind and supported by most Baptists. Greene retired from the presidency of his institution in 1923. Since that time, institutions of Christian higher education have been drawn, almost inexorably, into the vortex of secularization, pluralism, and an antievangelical bias. Nonetheless, Greene's words still stand as a manifesto of concern for all who care about the spiritual vitality of the rising generation.

David M. Ramsey had a long and remarkable career as pastor, college president, trustee, denominational leader, novelist, and raconteur. As pastor he served some of the leading churches in the SBC, including Citadel Square in Charleston, Grace Street in Richmond, and First Baptist in Tuscaloosa. "Why Become a Baptist" is Ramsey's personal testimony. He grew up in "one of those orderly Presbyterian homes of a former day," but was led by conviction to be baptized as a believer by immersion and joined a Baptist congregation. The key factor in this transition was his "little red-back Bible with its oft-marked pages." Ramsey's essay is a good example of the importance Southern Baptists have given to the theology of experience. This emphasis has sometimes led to a neglect of more substantial theological and doctrinal foundations, but at its best it reflects the witness of the man whose sight was restored by Jesus in John 9:25—"One thing I know, that, whereas I was blind, now I see."

One of the classic hallmarks of Southern Baptist polity is the autonomy of each local congregation. In the struggle over Landmarkism, the SBC was forced to clarify the relationship between local, independent congregations and the general work of the denomination done through its boards and agencies. J. B. Gambrell's "Why Conventions of Baptist Churches" is an admirable statement explaining both the doctrinal and practical aspects of this relationship. Gambrell describes the various entities of the denomination as channels through which the individual churches do the work of missions, evangelism, education, and the like. "Boards are channels, not fountains. They are means, not forces. . . . To illicit, combine, and direct the energies of willing workers for the carrying out of the will of Christ is the function of the convention, and this it does, not by authority, but by persuasion and the influence of intelligent piety."

In order for the SBC and other general Baptist bodies to carry out their channeling function, Christian stewardship must be given a high priority within the churches. C. E. Taylor, sometime president of Wake Forest College, provides an exhortation to Christian giving in his essay "Why Use Money for the Cause of Christ." At the time this article was written, Southern Baptists were still laboring under the "society method," by which each mission entity made a separate appeal to the churches. The development and adoption of the Cooperative Program in 1925 provided a more systematic and greatly more efficient means of denominational finance and missions budgeting.

Part 2 of this collection comes from the volume by Frost entitled, *The School of the Church*. These chapters focus on the importance of Bible teaching within the life of the church, the character and convictions of the Sunday school teacher, and the furtherance of the gospel message through this means. These pedagogical principles served to establish the ministry of Sunday schools in many Baptist churches, which in turn gave a tremendous impetus to the growth and consolidation of the Southern Baptist Convention.

Part 3 of this volume contains selected writings by J. M. Frost, the first president (then called Corresponding Secretary) of the Baptist Sunday School Board. We have chosen these eleven essays from Frost's literary corpus because they show the breadth of his work as a denominational statesman, pastoral theologian, and Christian educator.

"How the Board Came to Be" is Frost's own personal, first-hand account of the pre-history and early beginnings of the Baptist Sunday School Board. Earlier efforts to establish a publication ministry for Southern Baptists had come to nought. There was much opposition both within the SBC and from Baptists in the North since the American Baptist Publication Society had long served the entire Baptist constituency. Frost's proposal for a new publications board came to him late one sleepless night when he awoke to a great "stirring" in his soul. Later he said simply, "God touched me and I thought it."

While God used many different people to bring about the creation of the Baptist Sunday School Board, from a human perspective there is no doubt that J. M. Frost was the key player and motivating force. His work is acknowledged on a bronze tablet which hangs outside the Founders Room at the Baptist Sunday School Board in Nashville:

Divinely led,
His faith conceived it,
His genius planned it,
His courage built it.

The "Need for Doctrinal Emphasis in Teaching" is largely taken from one of the annual reports made by the Sunday School Board to the SBC. Frost points out the important relationship between sound theology and Christian practice. One of the founding purposes of the Baptist Sunday School Board was to provide ongoing instruction and doctrinal reinforcement for the churches. Through his own writings Frost encouraged the renewal of doctrinal preaching and the systematic expository study of the Scriptures.

The one absorbing theme of Frost's life and writings was ecclesiology. Several essays in this collection show him dealing with various issues which would have been faced by any Baptist pastor of his day. He grounds the church in the thought of God and describes its mission in the context of the history of redemption. Again and again he refers to "the church and its one Book," displaying an unswerving loyalty to the authority of Holy Scripture. At the same time he fully recognizes the importance of confessions of faith. Baptists are a people of God with definite beliefs and theological commitments which we should never be ashamed to declare for all the world to see.

Frost's chapter on "The Church and Its Public Services" is a compelling portrayal of Baptist worship at its best. "Your Membership in the Church" and "The Church of Your Membership" describe two essential aspects of Baptist churchmanship. His short essay on "The Baptist Art of Living Together" is an appeal for Baptists to display Christian respect and consideration for one another and to join together in common missionary concerns even though they may differ on particular details.

Taken as a whole, the writings of J. M. Frost, together with the essays he collected for *Baptist Why and Why Not*, may appear old-fashioned or even irrelevant for Baptists who stand today on the threshold of a new millennium. But they reflect the kind of firm faith and deep conviction without which we cannot do the work of God for such a time as this. The times are different, but God's truth remains ever the same. Men and women are still perishing in their sins without faith in Christ. There are 1.3 billion people in the world who have never heard the name of Jesus. God's infallible Word remains the only safe guide we can follow in all matters of faith and practice. We still need desperately for the Holy Spirit to fill our lives and be the true teacher in our churches.

With our eyes on our risen, ascended, and coming Lord, and with gratitude for those brave Baptist pioneers who blazed the trail on which we walk, let us renew our commitment to be faithful stewards of the precious heritage we have received, to the end that the church may be edified, the lost won to Christ, and God glorified in ever-increasing measure.

PART I

Selections from
Baptist Why and Why Not

Introduction to
Baptist Why and Why Not (1900)

J. M. FROST

This book is dedicated to the Baptist brotherhood of the world. Baptists are one in contending for the faith; one in their history and in the heritage of their fathers; one in their purpose to preach the gospel of the grace of God among all nations; and one in their championship of liberty, civil and religious.

This unity is not marred but strengthened rather by the condition that the Baptist host is divided territorially, that the Baptists of England and of Canada, of the North and of the South, have each a separate organization for the furtherance of their work and the fulfillment of their missions. In this instance division is strength, and offers an opportunity for the cultivation of fraternity in the highest degree, and each may rejoice in the splendid achievements wrought by the others.

Baptists are a mighty host for God. According to statistics, their membership in the world reaches nearly five million, divided numerically as follows: In the South, as the constituency of the Southern Baptist Convention, 1,586,709; in the South also as the constituency of the Baptist National Convention (people of color), 1,561,030; in the other states of the Union, 1,006,682; in other countries of the world, 786,701.

By virtue of our fundamental principles, each person in these many millions has stood out before his own congregation individually, and for himself made confession of personal sin, declared his repentance toward God and his faith in the Lord Jesus Christ, professed to have been the subject of divine power, and to have experienced the working of divine grace; has been buried with Christ in baptism and raised again to walk in newness of life to the glory of God. Following the rule applied in such cases, and multiplying this membership by five, gives a Baptist population of nearly twenty-five million, a vast army indeed, standing everywhere for fundamental principles.

Baptists have put much of their strength into institutions of learning and sought in every way the advancement of education. Their school property in the United States according to the *Baptist Year Book* is as follows:

- 7 theological seminaries, valued at $2,660,873, with an endowment of $2,392,180, with 160,734 volumes in the library.

- 94 universities and colleges, valued at $20,534,982, with an endowment of $13,062,672, with 748,532 volumes in the library.

- 77 academies, seminaries, and institutions, valued at $4,191,917, with an endowment of $731,079, with 83,089 volumes in the library.

This makes a total of 178 institutions, with total property valued at $27,386,772, with a total endowment of $16,185,929, and with 992,345 total volumes in the libraries.

Next to the churches, Baptists have in their schools the greatest source of power for projecting themselves into the future, for spreading their principles throughout the nations, and for influencing the thought and literature of the ages. It is their purpose that Christ be honored in these schools and colleges, that the Bible be given enthronement as the Word of God, that learning in its highest and noblest forms be subservient to Christianity and find its supreme glory in the glory of the Cross.

Baptists have a distinctive faith, and yet hold much in common with people of other names; indeed, their faith is the most universal faith. All Christians hold the baptism of believers, but division comes by adding the "baptism of infants." All hold that immersion is baptism, but a wall of partition is made by the adding of "sprinkling or pouring." All hold that baptism is a prerequisite to the Lord's Supper, but the division comes by asking a violation of this principle. All believe in the Scriptures as the rule of faith, but some, insisting upon the authority of other things, stand apart from the Baptists. Our people are as stout as the stoutest in holding fast and true the great doctrine of election with its coordinate doctrines, and yet are nothing behind the most earnest in emphasizing the freedom of the human will, and in proclaiming the gospel as the power of God unto salvation to everyone that believeth. Baptists have a singular advantage in the completeness of their faith, which in its very roundness is touched, tangent-like, by the faith of others, so that they come into accord at many points both in belief and practice.

But notwithstanding the many and important doctrines which are common to all evangelical Christians, there are yet fundamental and essential differences, so that the creed of one is not the creed of others. While we may magnify and rejoice in the agreement between the several denominations, yet no good but rather harm will come if we ignore or even make little of the differences. It is far better to recognize these differences, and understand them as differences in our interpretation of the Word of God and to cultivate at the same time earnestness in searching the Scriptures with a persistent purpose to follow where they lead. We accept the Scriptures as an all-sufficient and infallible rule of faith and practice, and insist upon the absolute inerrancy and sole authority of the Word of God.

We recognize at this point no room for division, either of practice or belief, or even sentiment. More and more we must come to feel as the deepest and mightiest power of our conviction that a "thus saith the Lord" is the end of all controversy. With this definitely settled and fixed, all else comes into line as regards belief and practice. Church relation and membership must be determined not by family ties nor business consideration, nor social conditions, nor personal convenience, but simply and solely by the teaching of the Word of God; and if conviction makes men stand apart, then better stand apart than prove false to one's highest self. The noblest and mightiest union is the union formed in convictions—none other is worth the naming.

The *Baptist Why and Why Not* is a denominational work, presenting a comparative study of denominational creeds. The writers have set forth with fairness and ability what is believed by other denominations, and have put over against this by way of contrast the things which distinguish the belief of our people from the belief of others. "A Confession of Faith," as viewed and used by Baptists, whether individually or in their churches, is simply an expression of what they believe the Scriptures teach concerning the several points of doctrine and practice. It is only a declaration of faith showing who we are and what we are, somewhat as the flag floating above the steamer at sea shows its nationality. By this declaration of principles, and in the name of our God, we set up the banner that it may be displayed because of the truth.

All Christian people are alike in accepting the Bible for their creed—of course, but beyond this is a question of immense moment at this time, indeed at all times; namely, what do you believe about the Bible? What do you believe the Bible teaches? The different writers have written not only with marked ability, but also with entire freedom from controversial spirit, as that term is generally understood. It has been the one controlling aim not to offend, but to instruct; not to confuse, but to discriminate; not to depreciate others, but to set out and emphasize the things which are believed among ourselves.

The *Baptist Why and Why Not* is not only doctrinal, but also eminently practical. Going beyond the sphere of doctrine, it sets out also almost the whole round of church life and Christian activity. It pleads for missions. It pleads for denominational schools as the highest form of Christian education. It pleads for the denominational paper and literature. It pleads for Sunday schools in all our churches as fostering the mightiest elements of power. It pleads for the exemplification of the noblest principles God ever gave to men. It can hardly fail to meet its purpose of being an effective "campaign book," giving emphasis to the faith of our people, and furtherance to all our denominational interests.

This book is meant to be a power, and a power it will surely be, in defense of the faith of our fathers, the faith once for all delivered to the saints. It is the Bible truth shining through the brain and heart of this generation out into the future, to illumine the pathway of our people in the years to come. In sending it forth on this, the first day of January, in the year of our Lord 1900, the Sunday School Board of the Southern Baptist Convention ventures the hope that it will find its way into many homes and everywhere prove a power for usefulness, to establish the kingdom of Jesus and hasten the day of His coronation.

January 1, 1900

CHAPTER ONE

The Distinctive Baptist Way: Our Reasons for the Separate Existence of the Baptists

R. M. DUDLEY

In the year 1879, I attended, as fraternal messenger from the Southern Baptist Convention, the Anniversaries of our Northern Baptist brethren at Saratoga, New York. At the same time and place was held the meeting of the General Assembly of the Presbyterian Church. I remember, as a pleasant incident of that occasion, a visit of the Reverend Dr. Jessup, Moderator of the Presbyterian General Assembly, to a meeting of his Baptist brethren. Being invited to speak he urged upon them the importance of greater devotion to the world of foreign missions (Dr. Jessup himself a foreign missionary). Failing in this he asked the Baptists what reason they could give to God for their separate existence as a denomination. The interrogation of Dr. Jessup chanced to be in a line of my own thinking and stirred me up to the question afresh. What reason is there for the separate existence of the Baptists as a denomination? Why should we have our separate churches, ministers, colleges, boards, missionaries, and societies? Why not merge our existence and enterprises into those of our fellow Christians of other denominations? This is a question that will apply to others as truly as to us. But we are responsible for our own existence and must give answer for the same to God and to a generous public whose sympathy and support we desire.

I wish there could be an intelligent, candid, and loving discussion of this question by every one of the denominations of Protestant Christendom. The public has the right to demand of each one of the different sects, upon the penalty of withholding sympathy and support, a reason for its separate existence. As to ourselves, we recognize the justice of the demand and will offer our answer. Let the people hear and judge of the strength of our plea.

Not a Good Plea

The first reason that would arise in the mind of an intelligent, free people would likely be: This is a land of religious liberty, and if the Baptists wish to maintain a separate existence, no one has the right to object. According to this the right to our separate existence lies in the fact that we wish it.

I desire emphatically to deny this right and the principle upon which it rests. Religious liberty does not consist in the right to do as one pleases in religious matters. Government cannot hinder my being a Baptist. This is true, but it is very poor logic to say that because government has no right to interfere with my religion, therefore I may do as I please.

The exercise of religious liberty is subject to two very important restrictions:

1. It must not run counter to the will of God. Christ said, "Go ye therefore and make disciples of all the nations, baptizing them into the name of the Father and of the Son and of the Holy

Ghost; teaching them to observe all things whatsoever I commanded you." There is no liberty of man that can supervene this law of the risen Lord. In accordance with this the apostle writes: "As free . . . using your liberty . . . as servants of God." "To this end was I born and for this cause came I into the world, that I should bear witness unto the truth," said the Lord. "The church is the pillar and ground of the truth." There is no room left for the exercise of my individual preferences in the kingdom of Christ. Others may claim their right to a separate denominational existence on the ground that this is a land of religious liberty, but God forbid that Baptists should urge this poor plea.

2. Again, the exercise of our religious liberty must not interfere with our duty to our fellow men. Brethren, I solemnly avow that in the present religious condition of mankind the needless multiplication of denominations is a crying sin against humanity. The great bulk of the human family are without the knowledge of the true God and Jesus Christ whom He has sent. Think of this, and then look at this typical town. It has 1,500 inhabitants. There are in it six or seven Protestant denominations. Each has its own house of worship, minister, and services. These represent thousands of dollars every year. Yet the people who attend services might be easily gathered into one house of worship and served by one minister. Before the bar of reason and conscience, the remaining five or six with the attendant cost must stand as a needless expenditure of labor and means, for which I believe God will hold men responsible.

The needless consumption of men and means in this way is today more than enough to supply the destitution of our country. In our own state it is more than we all have ever done to give the gospel to the heathen. If we had all the men and all the money that we need for Christian work at home and abroad the case would be different. But how does it stand? Here are six or seven men to supply a population of 1,500; and in China or India there is one minister to four or five million. Needlessly to multiply denominations because we wish to, while the bulk of the human family is dying without the knowledge of Christ, is folly and wickedness. It is rebellion against the last command of

Christ, and argues an indifference to the perishing souls of man. Again I say, with increased emphasis, God forbid that Baptists should justify their separate denominational existence on the ground that this is a land of religious liberty and no one has the right to interfere with us.

Recognition of Unity

In the further discussion of this subject, it would be an injustice not to recognize the substantial unity that exists among the various Protestant denominations upon many of the cardinal doctrines of the gospel. I need mention only the divinity and messiahship of Christ, His atoning death, His resurrection, ascension, and mediatorial reign, the office of the Holy Spirit, the inspiration of the Holy Scriptures, the necessity of repentance and faith, the general judgment, and the rewards and punishments of the future life. I gladly recognize all this and rejoice in it. While not agreeing about everything, I praise God that there is so much about which we are agreed. Someone may say: "If there exist this substantial unity, why let minor differences disturb you? Let each go his way as he thinks best and all live in peace." In answer we ask, does not so great unity demand that we strive after complete unity and escape the many and grievous ills of having so many different sects? If we differed about the things upon which we are agreed and agreed only upon the things about which we differ, then truly we would be compelled to say, "Let each go his way and live in peace." But since there exists so great community of sympathy and thought and effort among us, why should there be six or seven Protestant denominations in a town of a few hundred inhabitants? There should be an intelligent, candid, and loving discussion of this subject.

Getting a Better View

I wish now to clear the subject of a serious misapprehension. The Baptists are often charged with dividing Christendom upon a bare ordinance, and that one of the externals of religion. We are charged with building up a denomination upon the shallow and narrow basis of a mere rite; with filling the air with our cries about the little thing of how much water is to be used in baptism. We are charged with separating ourselves from others by the arbitrary restrictions that we have placed around the table of our common Lord, and with bigotry arrogating to ourselves a wisdom and sanctity superior to others. These are the characteristics that are supposed to mark the people called Baptists.

Even among many Baptists this subject fails of an intelligent understanding and therefore of a correct and proper statement. Ask scores of Baptists what is the difference between their own and other denominations and the answer will be: Baptists believe in immersion. This is a correct answer as far as it goes, but it is a very imperfect and shallow presentation of the truth. Or perhaps the answer would be: Baptists practice close communion. This again is correct so far as it goes, but as a full and fair answer to the question it is superficial and misleading.

Even intelligent Baptists are sometimes very careless in the statement of the fundamentals of the denomination. Dr. Gotch, the president of a Baptist College in England, says in the *Encyclopedia Brittanica*, perhaps the most splendid monument of learning in the nineteenth century, "The Baptists as a denomination are distinguished from other denominations by the views they hold respecting the ordinance of baptism." To proceed from so high a source this statement is a marvel of shallowness and carelessness. I demur to the statement of the venerable Dr. Armitage in the *North American Review* for March, 1887, that the distinguishing difference of the Baptists is "in the demand for a positive moral change wrought in the soul by the direct agency of the Holy Spirit as an indispensable qualification for membership in the churches." And what shall I say of that popular and useful little book from the pen of the venerable Dr. Pendleton, "Three Reasons Why I Am a Baptist?" A truce to all these brethren, honored and beloved as they are, but in the statement of the fundamental distinction of their denomination they need to go deeper and lay bare the broader foundation that the full truth may be known.

At the Very Base

The fundamental principle of the Baptists is their belief in the supreme authority and absolute sufficiency of the Holy Scriptures; and their separate existence is the practical and logical result of their attempt to apply this principle in all matters of religion. This is the bedrock on which the denomination rests. And we do not come down to the true foundation until we reach this. I will show you by the shortest of short methods that the statements of Drs. Gotch, Armitage, and Pendleton come short of the full truth. Ask Dr. Gotch why the Baptists believe in immersion, and he will tell you because the Scriptures teach it. Ask him if some other way would not do as well and his reply would be, "We have no right to alter any of the plain and positive commands of the Bible." This brings us to the bedrock truth stated just now.

In the same way you ask Dr. Armitage why Baptists believe in a converted church membership, and he will tell you that it is because the Scriptures so teach. But why not admit to the church all who belong to the same family and nation? The answer would be, "We have no right to go beyond the teachings of the Scriptures."

If you ask Dr. Pendleton why he practices close communion, that is, why he restricts the invitation to the Lord's table to baptized believers, there is but one answer that he would think of giving you: The Bible teaches us that the Supper was ordained by Christ, and He has taught us in His Word that only baptized believers are to approach it, and that we have no right to go contrary to His Word.

Let us look a moment at this principle and its importance. A father says, "Son, do this." But his son does something else. When asked about it he says, "Well, I thought that what I did was as good as what you told me to do." A master says to his servant, "Do this." But he does something else and when asked about it replies that what he did was altogether more convenient and withal more proper. Such a course of conduct in a son or servant when deliberately settled upon is a direct arraignment of the wisdom and authority of the father or master. Baptists say that in matters of religion there must be absolutely nothing like this. God's Word is the supreme and infallible rule for our guidance. We must not go contrary to it in any article of belief or in any duty enjoined. It is no partial revelation. By it the man of God is thoroughly furnished unto all good works. This is the fundamental position of the Baptists, and every peculiarity which characterizes them is the practical outcome of this principle.

This is the ground on which the Protestants of the sixteenth century planted themselves, the ground on which Luther stood in his great struggle against the Church of Rome. When he stood at the Diet of Worms in the presence of the emperor and the dignitaries of the Church and State and was called on to recant, his reply was, "I am bound by the Holy Scriptures: my conscience is held by the Word of God. Here I stand; I can not do otherwise. God help me. Amen." In accord with this is the justly celebrated saying of Chillingworth: "The Bible, the whole Bible and nothing but the Bible is the religion of Protestants." Baptists say that the decrees of Popes, Councils, Assemblies, Conventions, or what not are of no authority save as they are sanctioned by the Word of God. Traditions are worthless save for their historical or probative value.

This Principle at Work

And let me show you how it is that this fundamental principle has led to the separate existence of the Baptists and to the peculiarities that mark their denominational life.

1. Take, for example, the question of baptism. Luther said that the primitive baptism was immersion and that the primitive practice should be restored. The Baptists said the same thing and, following out their belief, immersed all who came to them even though they had been sprinkled before. Strange to say for this, Luther hated the Baptists hardly less than he hated the Catholics. Calvin said that the word "baptize" means "to immerse," and that it is certain that immersion was the practice of the primitive churches, but that in this matter the churches ought to have liberty.

Here now are the points of agreement and the points of difference between the Reformers on the one hand and the Baptists on the other. They all agreed that immersion was the practice of the primitive churches. Luther and Calvin thought that they were at liberty to practice another form; the Baptists said they ought to do what the Master commands, and that we have no liberty to change a positive ordinance which He has ordained. Here the work of separation begins. The issue was not as to what the act of baptism is, but whether we have the right to change it. Before the court of the highest scholarship of the world it has never been an open question as to what the true baptism is. It really is not now, as it was not in the time of Luther and Calvin. The question is about the right to change it, and it is not that Baptists think too much of one form above another.

I am frank to say for myself, that if it were a matter left to our choice whether we should immerse or sprinkle, while immersion is a beautiful and significant ordinance and sprinkling is a meaningless ceremony, still I would give up immersion rather than divide Christendom on a mere rite: I say if it were left to our choice. But it has never been left to our choice. And when others say that they will change the ordinance, the question between them and us is, not what is the true baptism but whether there is any right or authority to change it.

Baptists do not yield their position about baptism because it is the surface indication of a great underlying principle. Principles are of use to us because of the guidance they afford us in practical life. What honor or consistency is there in avowing a principle and then denying it in our daily conduct? We see how it is then that the peculiarity of Baptists upon immersion results from their fundamental position. They must be peculiar or they must give up the principle that the Word of God is our supreme and all-sufficient rule.

2. Take the Baptist peculiarity upon infant baptism. They refuse to practice it or to recognize it, because the Scriptures afford no warrant whatever for it. Luther's struggle here was great. He saw that the Bible says nothing in favor of infant baptism. The question with him was: Shall we give it up as our prin-

ciple requires? In fact, infant baptism had gained so great a hold upon the public heart that Luther feared the consequences of his radical and penetrating principle and hence modified his position and said, "The Word of God does not forbid it and so I will retain it." Zwingli was hesitating and perplexed and failed at last because he did not have the courage of his convictions. The Baptists said, "We will stand by the principle. The Word of God does not authorize the baptism of infants but only of believers." Here the work of separation is still going on and upon the same principle, namely, the supremacy and sufficiency of the Holy Scriptures.

The question of the baptism of infants was simply the surface indication of the underlying principle. The opposition of the Baptists to infant baptism was also strengthened by the vicious error that lay under it: the doctrine of baptismal regeneration. Infant baptism had its rise in the mischievous idea that anyone dying without the waters of baptism went straight to the flames of torment. This is one of the palpable facts of history. Baptists are sometimes charged with making too much of baptism. In the light of history the charge is ludicrous. One of the peculiarities of the Baptists is their opposition to those who, in times past, made so much of baptism as to contend that without it newborn infants could not get to heaven. If you will suffer the remark I will say that the Baptists are the only people who have never made either too much or too little of the ordinance of baptism. They make no more of it and no less of it than the Scriptures require.

3. Take the peculiarity of the Baptists respecting the Lord's Supper. They believe that it is the Lord's ordinance, not theirs, and that they have no right to make any other use of the ordinance than that which the Lord has ordained. He tells us that it is to show forth His death till He comes; and that it is to be administered only to baptized believers. We do not profess to be better, wiser, holier, or in anywise above others except in our rigid adherence to the terms that He has ordained for the government of this ordinance.

Suppose that a citizen of the English government should undertake to vote at one of our elections for president of the United States. The judges of the election would be compelled to refuse him. He might claim to be a more intelligent man than any of the judges, of better social position, of greater wealth, of truer knowledge of American institutions. Still they could not allow him to vote because he was unnaturalized. It would involve a violation of their solemn oath if they should allow him to vote. Pity 'tis that sometimes the administrators of human law have more respect to a strict obedience to its requirements than do the administrators of the divine law.

Standing by the Principle

I am not a Baptist because Baptists practice restricted communion, or immersion, or refuse infant baptism. I am a Baptist because by the fundamental principle of Protestantism I am bound by the Word of God in all matters of faith and practice. I believe in immersion not because I believe in one act above another but because the Bible teaches it; so of close communion; and so of the rejection of infant baptism. For these peculiarities as peculiarities I care nothing at all. Indeed I am sorry that we are peculiar in these matters. But these peculiarities embody an underlying principle in religion that is more important than reputation of life itself. And to surrender these peculiarities is to surrender that principle. And if an honest adherence to it and an honest endeavor to practice it bring odium upon us, let us have the manliness to bear it. To seek odium is detestable; to run from the post of conscience, or of duty to avoid it, is cowardly and traitorous.

And let us give our principles our hearty sympathy, our earnest prayers, our cordial and liberal support. To what better cause can we devote our time, our energies, our means, ourselves. As a group of Christian men and women were standing on the shore gazing after a ship going out to sea and on which a number of missionaries had embarked for foreign lands, one of the group enthusiastically exclaimed, "That is what ships were made for, to carry missionaries to the heathen."

If I am a Baptist and I am proud of it, I want that it shall affect me not in the way of making me narrow and bigoted and intolerant, but humble, patient, and loving toward those who differ from me, and hearty, generous, energetic, and persevering in the use of my time, talents, and means for the furtherance of the good cause. Let us show our devotion to our principles, not by boastfulness and arrogance, but by a watchful attention to the needs of the cause we love. Thus shall we best show to men our fidelity and zeal; and thus best help the truth in its onward march to complete and final victory.

CHAPTER TWO

Why the Bible and Not Other Standards

T. T. EATON

Why the Bible and not other standards? There are three reasons, either of which is decisive.

The Bible Is the Best Standard

We are often told to "accept the truth wherever found, On Christian or on heathen ground," and the inference is implied that there is some truth on heathen ground not found on Christian ground. But no one has ever ventured to name any such truth. The simple fact is that whatever religious truths may be found in other sacred books or in works of philosophy, these same truths are found in the Bible, and here they are free from mixture with errors.

Ethics knows nothing higher or nobler than the moral teaching of the Bible. Amid all the wonderful progress of the race during the more than 1,800 years since the last book of the Bible was written, not the smallest addition has been made to biblical ethics. No moral truth has been discovered beyond what is contained in the Bible. And the same is true of all other religious truth. If any man thinks some new religious truth has been discovered since the Bible was completed, he has only to attempt to produce it, and he will be convinced. What we must believe, what we must be, and what we must do, are set forth in the Bible with a clearness and a completeness found nowhere else. Not a doctrine, nor an aspiration, nor a duty is omitted.

Testimonies from Great Thinkers

Here are a few testimonies from great thinkers who will not be suspected of any bias in favor of the Book:

- Fichte says of the Bible: "This ancient and venerable record contains the profoundest and loftiest wisdom, and presents those results to which all philosophy must at last come."

- Renan says of the Gospel of Matthew: "All things considered, it is the most important book in the world;" and of the Gospel of John, he says, "It is the most beautiful book in the world."

- "In the Bible," says Coleridge, "there is more that finds me out than I have experienced in all other books put together. The words of the Bible find me at greater depths of my being, and whatever finds me brings with it an irresistible evidence of its having proceeded from the Holy Spirit."

- Professor Huxley said of the Scriptures: "By what other books could children be so humanized and made to feel that each figure in that vast historical procession fills, like themselves, but a momentary space in the interval between the two eternities and earns the blessings or the curses of all time according to its effort to do good and hate evil."

The other standards offered are other sacred books, like the Vedas, the Koran, the Book of Mormon; and the Church; and reason.

Vedas, Koran, Book of Mormon. All other books are weak in comparison with the Bible; and the great superiority of the Bible to these books being admitted by all who are likely to read this chapter, there is no need of arguing the point at length. A simple comparison of the lands where these other books are regarded as standard with the lands where the Bible is most believed in will convince the most skeptical.

The Church. The church derives its authority from the teaching of the Scriptures. And the church—using the term in its broadest sense, to include all bodies of confessing Christians—has ever taught the inspiration and authority of the Bible, although sometimes claiming the right to interpret it for the people. The meaning of the Scriptures, however, was ever the important thing. Ecclesiasticism has assumed to take charge of the Bible and to dole out its teaching to the people, but ecclesiasticism has never denied its authority. Often, as in the case of the Pharisees, the Scriptures were made "of none effect," but like those Pharisees, ecclesiasticism admitted them to be the highest authority. The result of withholding the Bible from the people and of filtering its teachings through ecclesiastical channels are manifest in Spain and Italy.

Reason. Shall we turn to reason? Then whose reason? Shall we seek to be guided by the reason of the wisest and best? Who will select these for us? Those most generally recognized as the wisest and best bow before the Bible. But reason will not avail us. The most it can do, in the most favorable conditions, is to save us from error; it cannot lead us to truth. The philosopher Kant, in his *Critique of Pure Reason*—the highest authority on the subject—says, "The greatest and perhaps the sole use of all philosophy, of all pure reason is, after all, merely negative, since it serves not as an organon for the enlargement of knowledge, but as discipline for its delimitation, and instead of discovering truth, has only the modest merit of preventing error." Professor

Huxley, in the *Nineteenth Century* for February, 1889, quotes and endorses this utterance of Kant.

John Ruskin quotes and commends the following language of Thomas Carlyle: "Perceptive reason is the handmaid of conscience, but not conscience hers. If you resolve to do right, you will do wisely; but resolve only to do wisely and you will never do right."

In a letter to a friend, published in the London *Christian*, Herbert Spencer said, "In my earliest years I constantly made the foolish supposition that conclusive proofs would change belief. But experience has long since dissipated my faith in man's rationality."

None of these men quoted can be charged with bias in favor of evangelical religion. They are the very ones to whom those who exalt reason as a standard naturally turn. It is manifest, therefore, that reason is not to be made a standard in religion. George Eliot has well said, "When you get me a good man out of arguments, I will get you a good dinner by reading you the cookery book."

The Bible Alone Is Authoritative

The second ground for taking the Bible rather than other standards is that it alone is authoritative. It is the only one we are under obligations to accept. The Bible alone speaks "with authority and not as the Scribes." The Protestant Rule of Faith as given by Dr. Robert Watts is as follows:

A. "That the Scriptures of the Old and New Testaments, to the exclusion of the apocryphal books and tradition, contain all the extant Word of God."

B. "That they furnish the only infallible rule of faith and practice."

C. "That the rule contained therein is complete, embracing all that man is to believe concerning God and all the duty that God requires of man." [1]

All through the Bible its authority is asserted. Paul argues for the plenary inspiration of Genesis (12:7) when he writes to the Galatians, "He saith not and to seeds as of many, but as of one and to thy seed, which is Christ" (3:16). Here the argument turns on the use of the singular rather than the plural. Jeremiah called "the roll," the "words of the Lord" (36:6). Jesus quoted Deuteronomy as infallible, and as settling the questions raised by Satan, saying in reply, "It is written" (Matt. 4:4, 7). Our Lord affirmed the infallibility of Psalm 82 by quoting from it and saying, "The Scriptures cannot be broken" (John 10:35). Indeed He argued the infallibility of the clause from the infallibility of the Scriptures containing it. These are but samples.

Jesus and His apostles ever treated the Old Testament as fully inspired and hence of absolute and final authority on all questions treated of in its pages. Peter tells us, "For no prophecy ever came by the will of man, but men spake from God, being moved by the Holy Ghost" (2 Pet. 1:21). And the apostles are put upon a par with the prophets (Eph. 3:5). Paul claims inspiration for the words he writes (1 Cor. 2:4, 13), and he enjoins that his epistles be read to the churches as Scripture (Col. 4:16). Peter calls the words of the apostles "the commandment" of the Lord (2 Pet. 3:2), using the strongest Greek word in the vocabulary for authority. And Jude exhorts us to "contend earnestly for the faith which was once for all delivered unto the saints."

It is not that men were spiritually elevated above their fellows so that with a broader and clearer vision they could instruct their fellows in spiritual things. It is not that certain seed thoughts or basal principles were communicated to men, which were to be expanded and developed along with the spiritual life of the ages, changing as circumstances might require—so that what is a correct statement of doctrine in one age is incorrect in another. Truth is not a system of "fluent and fluxions," such as Newton discussed. Truth cannot change. If two and two did not make four in the time of Abraham, they do not make four now and never will make four, while if they do make four now, they always did and always will. No possible change of circumstances of development of mind can have the slightest effect on the truth. So the

Bible is God's Word to the world; His message to mankind was delivered through chosen messengers, but delivered "once for all." It is not subject to addition or development or modification of any kind. It is the absolute and final authority in all questions of faith and morals. We are not bound to believe or do anything because Buddha, or Mahomet, or Shakespeare, or Goethe, or Spencer says so. While we are bound to believe and do whatever the Bible says we must. "Thus saith the Lord" is an end of all controversy.

The Bible Tells Us What Our Souls Need

The third ground for taking the Bible rather than other standards is that it alone tells us what our souls need. "Lord, to whom shall we go?" said the astonished Peter, "Thou hast the words of eternal life" (John 6:68). Dim and uncertain is the light of nature and of philosophy on the great questions of character and of destiny; so that Socrates, after thinking on these things as perhaps no other man has ever done, "felt," so his great disciple Plato tells us, "the need of some 'sure word of God' to guide us in the right way."

The Bible is not one of a class of books. It is unique in its theme, its power, and its authority. All other books are feeble in comparison. Scientific books tell us of matter, of force, of heat, light, and electricity. How feeble all this is in comparison with such utterances as "Let there be light," "I am the light of the world," and "All power hath been given unto Me." Books on political economy tell us of the laws of trade, of supply and demand, of how to develop the material resources of a country, and how to regulate taxation and the authority of officials. What are such things in comparison with the great themes of death, judgment to come, and eternity?

Ruskin tells us of the pictures fading away on the stones of Venice and the crumbling walls of Florence. With a few touches the inspired penman gives us a picture of love and duty, and the story of Ruth and Naomi fades never away from our minds. Probably the best book besides the Bible is Shakespeare, and the best thing in Shakespeare is *Hamlet*. But is not the sorrow of a dreaming boy for his foully-murdered father—for that is Hamlet—trivial in comparison with the grand drama of Job, where God and the angels are spectators, and Satan wrestles with faith in the torn heart of the patriarch?

In other books we find such truths as men can spell out with their observations and experiments, and such as they can guess out with their philosophy, but in the Bible we have the revelation of God to us, and the opening of heaven to our vision. Here we learn the remedy for sin. Here we are told how God can be just and the Justifier of him that believeth. Here we find the "words of eternal life." There is but one way of salvation and the Bible alone tells us of that. Nothing else but the gospel has ever changed a bad man into a good man, or ever can; while the gospel has done this in multiplied thousands of instances. "There is none other name under heaven given among men whereby we must be saved," and to be saved is our supreme necessity. Outside the Bible we can learn of God's power, of His wisdom, of His glory, but only here can we learn of His love and of His mercy. Only here can we learn that "Christ died for our sins according to the Scriptures." Only here can we learn of Him, whom to know is life eternal. Only here can we find the "sure Word of God" for which Socrates sought, and lay hold on the hope which "maketh not ashamed."

To take any other standard is to follow the creature rather than the Creator. It is to accept the thoughts of men as superior to the wisdom of God. It is to turn our backs upon the only light of the world and go out into that outer darkness that knows no morrow forever.

Diet of Worms

In the marketplace at Worms, I was profoundly impressed as I stood before the Great Luther monument. Surrounded by statues of his coadjutors, all fronting in the same direction, and rising on a pedestal in its colossal proportions, is the bronze statue of Luther. His right foot is firmly advanced. In his left hand he holds a Bible, on which his right hand rests clenched. The artist has seized the moment when the hero stood facing the Diet of

Worms to answer for himself. Looking into that calm upturned face I could almost hear from those parted lips the noble words: "Here I stand; I cannot do otherwise. God help me. Amen." Answering to this statue, across the ocean in the land where the Bible has been widest open, there stands a companion statue. It is the monument of the Pilgrims at Plymouth. On a lofty pedestal is a colossal statue of faith pointing with one hand to the open Bible and with the other toward the open heaven.

Other standards are composed of men's guesses, while in the Bible the great truths of God burn and glow with all the eloquence of heaven. And facing a gainsaying world it becomes us to plant ourselves squarely on God's Word—for we cannot do otherwise, God help us—and to point a sin-sick and guilt-blinded race to the open Bible and to the open heaven it reveals.

Notes

1. *Faith and Inspiration*, 86.

CHAPTER THREE

Why Immersion and Not Sprinkling or Pouring

C. A. STAKELY

Happily for us who are called Baptists our principles are marked by great simplicity. In the presentation of them no special ingenuity is required, and in their vindication there is no need of resorting to any process of explaining away the sources from which they are derived. They so lie on the surface of things that the unprejudiced reader can scarcely fail to see them, yet they are not superficial. So clearly are they imbedded in the truth itself, so unmistakably are they a part of the truth, that any candid look beneath the surface will find them amply confirmed.

In nothing else are we more clear-cut than in our position on the first of the two Christian ordinances, and at no other point in the statement and defense of our faith are we more entirely free from the necessity of artifice or indirection. With us, baptism is not in a mode, but in an act—a specific, definite act, a well-designed, God-appointed act, a truth-proclaiming act—from which one cannot diverge and maintain the rite itself. It is without the slightest reservation, but of course in perfect fraternity toward all Christian people everywhere, that we commit ourselves to the advocacy of immersion as against sprinkling or pouring, as the act in Christian baptism. And we rejoice to find ourselves more and more confirmed by every new appeal to the final authority no less than by the growing Christian scholarship of the world and the growing candor of those who represent it.

The question, Why immersion and not sprinkling or pouring? may be answered in the light of three considerations attaching to the former:

1. its natural superiority

2. its normalness as the act in baptism

3. its solitary position as the baptism of the New Testament

The Natural Superiority of the Act

On the supposition that immersion and sprinkling or pouring are valid modes of baptism, and hence that one is at liberty to make a choice between them, the former should be insisted upon for several reasons. In the first place, though not chiefly, it has the advantage of being universally acceptable. Whatever misgivings there may be in the mind of millions of Christian people touching the validity of sprinkling or pouring, there are absolutely none concerning immersion. The latter, it must be confessed, is greatly discredited in some quarters which witness every effort to break it down, but it is not absolutely rejected. No immersed person is ever required by any denomination of Christians to undergo sprinkling or pouring in order to baptism. The coin passes current universally, a fact which may someday become a stone in the temple of Christian union.

Of more importance is the consideration that in the act of immersion there is a gain on the dramatic, a legitimate, a necessary feature of baptism. Both in its nature and in its purpose, baptism is an acting out of certain truths or principles, and the more impressive it is made in the mode of its administration, the truer it is to its own genius and the greater influence it exerts over the mind of candidate and observer. To intelligent and reverent persons who are in sympathy with any of the high and holy ideas associated with baptism, immersion properly administered must be more impressive than either of the other acts. It is a solemn, meaningful performance; and, where all the conditions are favorable, it is beautiful beyond compare.

But more important still, it is a much better interpreter of the Scripture. We can handle the Bible better with immersion as our act in baptism than we can with sprinkling or pouring. There are many passages of Scripture back of the ordinance of baptism that were meant to be brought out in every administration of the ordinance, but some of them, yea most of them, it must be said, are exceedingly awkward in the hands of one who is sprinkling a candidate or pouring water on his head.

It has been openly deplored by many devout Christian thinkers not of our faith that much of Christian baptism—the baptism of the Bible, the baptism that was known by our Lord and His apostles—is really left out in the acts of sprinkling and pouring. "It must be a subject of regret," say Conybeare and Howson in their great work on the life and epistles of the apostle Paul, "that the general discontinuance of this original form of baptism (though perhaps necessary in our northern climates) has rendered obscure to popular apprehension some very important passages of Scripture." The reference to "northern climates" might have been omitted if the distinguished authors had kept in mind the custom of the Greek church which has consistently practiced immersion in northern Siberia and Alaska, the coldest countries in the world. In any case, they note the inadequacy of sprinkling or pouring to convey the whole content of Bible baptism, and in this they have the company of Dean Stanley, who wrote in the *Nineteenth Century* for October, 1879: "The change from immersion to sprinkling has set aside the larger part of the apostolic language regarding baptism and has altered the very meaning of the word."

Its Normalness as the Act in Baptism

It will stand to reason that three different acts that are equally acceptable as Christian baptism must be equally normal. But can this be said of immersion and sprinkling and pouring? Is it possible for anyone to claim it? On the contrary, nothing else is more generally and uniformly declared by church historians than that immersion was the normal baptism of New Testament times and indeed until a comparatively late day in the Christian centuries. "In respect to the form of baptism," says Neander, including the first three centuries of the Christian era, "it was in conformity to the original institution and the original import of the symbol, performed by immersion, as a sign of entire baptism into the Holy Spirit, of being entirely penetrated by the same. It was only with the sick, where the exigency required it, that any exception was made; and in this case baptism was administered by sprinkling."

"The usual form of the act was immersion," says Schaff, covering nearly the same period,

> as if plain from the original meaning of the Greek taken from the analogy of John's baptism in the Jordan; from the apostles' comparison of the sacred rite with the miraculous passage of the Red Sea; with the escape of the ark from the flood; with a cleansing and refreshing bath, and with burial and resurrection; finally from the custom of the ancient church, which prevails in the east to this day. But sprinkling also, or copious pouring, was practiced at an early day with sick and dying persons, and probably with children and others, where total or partial immersion was impracticable.

In the same line are Mosheim and Stanley and Kurtz, and church historians generally, though no one of them, as neither Neander nor Schaff, asserts that there was any known deviation from the observance of immersion actually within the period of the New Testament.

The Departure

It should be noted that when the departure came it was from immersion to the other acts and that these, at least at the time when we first come across them, were regarded as only a substitute for the former. Already in the second century the contest between principal and substitute had begun, as is known from the rule concerning baptism in the work called the *Didache*, or *Teaching of the Twelve Apostles:* "Having first uttered all of these things, baptize ("baptisate") into the name of the Father, and of the Son, and of the Holy Spirit, in running water. But if thou hast not running water, baptize ("baptisate") in other water; and if thou canst not in cold, then in warm. But if thou hast neither, pour ("ekkeon") water upon the head thrice into the name of the Father and Son and Holy Spirit." In other words, if the administrator could not baptize the candidate (which was to immerse him) he must pour water on his head. The earliest known instance of administration out of the usual way was in the case of Novatian in the third century, whose baptism was seriously questioned after his recovery from sickness during which it was applied. The substitute appears to have arisen in accommodation of infirm persons or persons in danger of dying, and out of a mistaken and superstitious view of the ordinance of baptism.

The Substitute Became Baptism

It should make little difference with us that afterwards the substitute became baptism in the popular estimation. No authority on earth could change its real character. Baptists cannot give it any countenance without some special authorization from the Lord Himself. Our Roman Catholic friends, seeing the manifest incongruity between the normal act in baptism and the widespread practice of its substitute, have made bold to declare that the church purposely changed baptism from immersion, it having been invested with the authority to do so, a position which no Protestant can well assume.

Its Solitary Position as the Baptism of the New Testament

But would the Lord invite His people to make a choice of modes of baptism that do not equally represent the ordinance? Is it not in the nature of a positive institution to call for precise observance, and is it possible that baptism which is such an institution, may, in the intention of its divine Author, be performed by one of several acts not equally normal? God is a God not of confusion, but of order. Now we reach our highest point: That which has shown itself to be the superior act in baptism, and also the normal act, is in addition the only act known to the Savior and His apostles, and hence the only one obligatory upon us. And in support of this our confident appeal is to the meaning of the enacting Word itself, to the examples of baptism given in the New Testament, to the figurative references to baptism therein contained, and to the New Testament symbolism of the ordinance.

It may have occurred to the reader ere this that it is manifestly absurd to speak of modes of baptism, though we have had to do it. If a person should stand up in one of our pulpits and read, "Go ye therefore and matheteusatize all nations" and then proceed to expatiate upon the different modes of matheteusatizing the nations, what would we think? We should want to know first what the word means in English, what duty or duties it commands in English, then we could listen to a discussion of the modes of performance. Now "baptize" is an anglicized Greek word, not a Greek word translated into English. What does it mean in English? If it means to sprinkle, we may discuss modes of sprinkling; if to pour, modes of pouring; if to immerse, modes of immersing; but we cannot in strict intelligence speak of modes of baptism.

The Greek word *baptizo* is found 175 times in extant Greek literature outside of the New Testament, before, during, and for three or four centuries after the Savior and the apostles, and in every instance it has the same general meaning. Whether employed literally or figuratively, it never deviates from dip, immerse, overwhelm, plunge, sink; and there is absolutely no reason why it should not be taken in the same sense in the New Testament. As the Greeks used it, and as they use it today, it was used by the Savior and the apostles.

What say the leading lexicographers on the subject? "To dip in or under water" is the pronouncement of Liddel and Scott, whose lexicon of classic Greek is as good as we have. Sophocles, in his exhaustive lexicon of Greek usage in the Roman and Byzantine periods, from 140 B.C. to A.D. 1000 gives "to dip, to immerse, to sink," adding "there is no evidence that Luke and Paul and the other writers of the New Testament put upon this verb meanings not recognized by the Greeks." Doubtless the very best lexicon of New Testament Greek in existence is Grimm Wilke's edited by Thayer; and in this, after the definitions "to dip repeatedly, to immerse, submerge," and some secondary and figurative meanings of a similar import, the learned author says: "In the New Testament it is used particularly of the rite of sacred ablution, first instituted by John the Baptist, afterwards by Christ's command received by Christians and adjusted to the contents and nature of their religion: an immersion in water, performed as a sign of the renewal from sin, and administered to those who, impelled by a desire for salvation, sought admission to the benefits of the Messiah's kingdom."

It is useless after such a showing as this to quote any example of the use of the word in Greek literature. The Greeks had words which meant to sprinkle and to pour, and they are freely used in the New Testament, but somehow they are never employed in connection with the ordinance of baptism; but the word and its cognates which always implied an immersion are the ones invariably used.

New Testament Examples

With this meaning of the word in mind, it is easy to understand how John baptized "in the river of Jordan" and "at Elim near to Salem because there was much water there," and how Jesus when He was baptized "came up out of the water," and how Philip and the eunuch "went down both into the water" and after the baptism of the latter, "were come up out of" it again. It is easy also to understand the meaning of every passage in the New Testament in which the verb *baptizo* or its corresponding noun is found in connection with these prepositions. And there is no reason for supposing the slightest departure from the common meaning of the word in the administration of baptism to the three thousand on the day of Pentecost. Distributing the three thousand equally among the apostles and allowing one minute of time for each candidate, the whole work would have been accomplished in four hours and ten minutes. Or, if the apostles had called to their assistance the seventy disciples mentioned in Luke 10, each administrator would have had only about thirty-six candidates to baptize. In our Baptist mission at Ongole in India in 1879, 2,222 converts were baptized by six ministers in nine hours, with only two baptizing at a time.

The figurative uses of baptism in the New Testament also become clear and even luminous under this meaning of the word. What could the Savior have meant by the question, "Are ye able to drink the cup that I drink of? or to be baptized with the baptism that I am baptized with?" or by the expression, "I have a baptism to be baptized with and how am I straitened till it be accomplished," aside from the thought of the overwhelming sufferings into which He was about to be plunged. "I would not that ye should be ignorant," said the apostle Paul to his brethren at Corinth, "how that all our fathers were under the cloud, and all passed through the sea; and were all baptized unto Moses in the cloud and in the sea," while the apostle Peter, in addressing the strangers scattered throughout Pontus and Galatia and other parts beheld a baptism in the picture of the ark emerging from the flood, "When once the long-suffering of God waited in the days of Noah, while the ark was a preparing, wherein few, that is eight souls were saved by water."

The Symbolism of Baptism

And when we turn to the symbolism of the ordinance with this meaning of *baptizo* in our thought there can be no question on the mind concerning what baptism was in the days of the New Testament. It symbolized purification indeed, but total purification, purification through the regenerating power of the Holy Spirit, purification always connected with its procuring cause in the Lord Jesus Christ, and so the believers' union with Christ in His death, burial, and resurrection. The element employed in baptism is symbolical, and the act is symbolical. The element is water and stands for purification, the act is an immersion, following in the nature of the case by an emersion— the one standing for a burial (which implies, of course, a death), and the other for a resurrection. Now neither sprinkling nor pouring will suit the case. Either of these could represent a partial purification, but it is a total purification that must be set forth; and neither of these could ever represent a burial and a resurrection.

Do the words of the Savior, "Except a man be born of water and of the Spirit he cannot enter into the kingdom of God," refer to baptism; and if so, how can that birth be set forth by sprinkling a few drops of water in the face or dropping a teaspoonful on the head? The figure is that of a delivery from the womb.

In his letter to the Romans the apostle Paul says: "Know ye not that so many of us as were baptized into Jesus Christ were baptized into His death? Therefore we are buried with Him by baptism into death: that like as Christ was raised up from the dead by the glory of the Father even so we also should walk in newness of life." To the Colossians also he spake in a similar strain: "Buried with Him in baptism wherein also ye are risen with Him through the faith of the operation of God who hath raised Him from the dead." And the apostle Peter: "The like figure whereunto even baptism doth also now save us (not the putting away of the filth of the flesh, but the answer of a good conscience toward God) by the resurrection of Jesus Christ."

What John Wesley says on the first of these passages, namely, that the apostle was "alluding to the ancient manner of baptizing by immersion," is said by nearly all scholars on all of them. The thought of a sprinkling or a pouring is so utterly incongruous as to be inadmissible. We must have enough water for a mystic grave, and we must effect in symbol a burial and a resurrection. If it be suggested, as sometimes it has been, that the Greek word cannot mean an immersion and an emersion at the same time, a reply is ready. The word means to dip as well as to immerse and may have generally had this meaning in the New Testament period. But it was not necessary for it to carry both meanings, the latter being implied in the purpose of the immersion. Still further, neither sprinkling nor pouring could have any advantage in such an issue. The Greek word could not mean to sprinkle and to cease to sprinkle at the same time, nor to pour and to cease to pour at the same time; so that if we should begin to do either we should have no authority from the Word itself to cease. It would be as agreeable to drown by remaining under the water in the act of immersion as to die of congestion of the brain as a result of an unceasing application of water to the head.

What Are We to Do?

Now with immersion as the superior act and the normal act and the sole New Testament act, what are we to do? Shall we join hands with those who say that it is sometimes impracticable, dangerous to health and life, indecent, inconvenient, and for these reasons set it aside for a substitute? Baptism is not a duty where it is really impracticable, and it should never be administered when it endangers health or life. The Father who instituted it, and the Son and Savior who submitted to it in His own person in order "to fulfill all righteousness," and the Holy Spirit who was present with approval and a blessing at the baptism of the Son, may be allowed to be the best judge of whether it is decent or not; and the question of our personal convenience should be allowed to be sunk out of sight, and that utterly, in the larger issue of an honest and loving and self-sacrificing loyalty to our Lord and Savior Jesus Christ.

CHAPTER FOUR

Why Sunday Schools in Baptist Churches

N. B. BROUGHTON

Let us consider two matters in connection with our Sunday school work as Baptists—first, several reasons for the existence of the Sunday school, and, second, some suggested methods for increasing its efficiency.

Why a Sunday School in a Baptist Church?

Because of What the Sunday School Is

We must acknowledge with regret that a great many persons have a very mistaken conception of the real nature of its work. They think that it is merely a place for the care of the children on Sunday morning, a sort of World's Fair "Baby Room." So widespread is this erroneous idea that in almost every community when boys get to wearing long pants and standing collars they think they are "too old to go to Sunday school." They accent in speech and thought the "Sunday" and forget that it is a "school." The Sunday school in truth is that agency of Christianity to which is especially committed the teaching of the Scriptures. If we fail to thoroughly realize this fact, we shall fail in our appreciation of its purpose and power.

Because We Need Such a Training School

More than any other denomination, we Baptists need a well-organized, well-equipped Sunday school in every church, indeed, in every mission station. We need the training that it will give.

As to Doctrines. This is emphatically true because of our very polity. A religious organization without the usual constitution and bylaws, book of discipline, or any such thing; a denomination calling no man lord, and without appeal to any earthly court, priest, or potentate; a people with but one book and that book the Bible; surely if we fail to "Search the Scriptures"—if we fail to teach God's Word, there can be no hope or expectation of our occupying that position which is our duty and privilege to occupy.

As to Giving. A Sunday school in every Baptist church, and that school given a proper conception of its true work, would soon supply us with a great host of trained, systematic givers instead of a multitude that no man can number that take pleasure in a freedom they claim to possess.

As Baptists we are today facing the great question of how shall we enlist all our people in the financial support of the cause of the world's evangelization? On every hand men and women are saying, "Here am I, send me," but for lack of means in the Lord's treasury, they are not sent. Organize a Sunday school in every Baptist church, give to that school the one work of teaching God's Word, of imparting His commandments, and we shall see such a quickening in the gifts of our people as has never yet been seen.

Because of Its Efficiency as an Evangelizing Agency

The Sunday school is the greatest of all the agencies given to the churches of Jesus Christ for bringing the world to God. This is true, in the first place, because it is a school, and there must be knowledge before there can be belief. There must be fact before faith. It is true, in the second place, because the material upon which it works is usually in the plastic state.

Daniel Webster once asked Thomas Jefferson the patriotic question, "What is to be the salvation of our nation?" After a pause, Jefferson replied, "Our nation will be saved, if saved at all, by teaching the children to love the Savior." Solomon's saying, "Train a child up in the way he should go, and when he is old he will not depart from it," today has the warrant of every century's experience that has passed since he said it. "Lycurgus," says Plutarch, "resolved the whole business of legislation in the bringing up of the youth."

Statistics gathered by associations and conventions show that more than ninety percent of all the membership of all our churches have come to us from the ranks of the Sunday school. It is further clearly established not only as to the organized church, but also as to our mission stations, that without a Sunday school we need hardly hope for increase, for progress, for conversions.

Because It Is Commanded

Some persons have an idea that the Sunday school is not a Bible institution, but is purely man-made. They say that Robert Raikes started the movement. There never was a more mistaken notion. Robert Raikes simply revived in England what had been in existence in Palestine before the time of Christ. Let us remember that preaching the Word is not the same thing as teaching the Word. The preacher proclaims the truth; the teacher examines it with his students by questions and answer. Both urge the acceptance—the preacher by general exhortation, the teacher by personal application. You can preach to trees and stones, but you can't teach them. The gospel is meant for people, and so the teaching of it (the work of the Sunday school) is commanded.

Commanded by Christ's Example. Christ was both preacher and teacher, and yet an examination of some passages in the New Testament will show us that His special, emphatic work was that of teaching. In Matthew 4:23 and 7:29 we find He went about all Galilee teaching in their synagogues as one having authority. In Mark 1:22 they were astonished at His doctrine for He taught not as the Scribes. Sometimes it was with one scholar, as Nicodemus or the woman at Jacob's well, and then again the crowd, as in Mark 10:1. He not only taught in the synagogue and by the seaside, but in the streets, as indicated by Luke 13:26. So important was this teaching work to the Master that He never let an opportunity escape. Even during the feast He went into the temple and taught, as in John 7:14, and early in the morning, as in John 8:2. When asked by the high priest of His disciples and His doctrine, He replied, "I ever taught in the synagogue and in the temple."

Commanded by the Apostles' Example. Among the first of the apostles to be persecuted were Peter and John, and reference to Acts 4:18 and 5:28, 42 shows that it was because of their teaching. In Acts 11:26 we are told that Barnabas and Saul conducted a school of twelve months duration, and as one of the results "The disciples were called Christians first in Antioch." And a further result was the qualifying of others who became teachers. This is the first account we have of what in this day we call a normal school, judging from the work that followed.

The apostle Paul, though a great preacher, relied very much upon teaching. In 1 Corinthians 4:17 he says, "I teach everywhere in every church." And he means by that the method of asking and answering questions, the only way that true teaching can be done. Refer to 1 Corinthians 14:19 and you see he urges the value of teaching with the voice. In 1 Timothy 6:2 Paul tells the young apostle to teach and exhort, showing that he recognized the value of both and that he did not regard them as one and the same thing.

To the Sunday school is committed this important work begun by Jesus Christ and followed up by His apostles, as to no other agency connected with a church of God.

Commanded by the Great Commission. As Baptists, the Great Commission, as recorded in Matthew 28:19–20, contains our marching orders. It naturally falls into three parts: making disciples, baptizing them, teaching them. The first is the mission work; the second, the observance of His ordinance symbolizing His death and resurrection; and the third, imparting His commandments. That is our work, and with us as Baptists the Sunday school is organized for obeying the last or third division of the Great Commission.

To conclude this part of our investigation, we Baptists need the Sunday school because of its efficiency as a training school for our denominational doctrines which we ought either to teach or abandon; because of its efficiency as an evangelizing agency, our command being to evangelize the world. And, lastly, because it is commanded in the Scriptures, indirectly by the example of Christ and the apostles, directly by the words of the Great Commission. We need it as a denomination. We need it as Christians. Being responsible for the use of the best instrumentalities possible, we cannot afford to be without it. Claiming to be followers of the Author of the Great Commission, we dare not be without it.

How Shall We Increase the Efficiency of the Sunday School?

Realizing the great value, the incalculable blessing possible to the Sunday school, the demand is upon us as Baptists to extend the work. How shall we do it?

By a Wide Reach to Interest the People

We organize all sorts of forces to reach the churches. We urge the importance of broadcasting our literature in all our homes. We hold mass meetings, institutes, and conventions to stir our people in behalf of missions. These are good, but have we not gone ahead of the foundation work and erected a structure that could not stand? In some communities there are many—in most communities there are a few—that deeply feel the great importance of a well-organized Sunday school. The work before us as Baptists is that of enlisting our whole people in this great work.

By the Whole Church Being Concerned for the Success of the Sunday School

Our most serious trouble as Baptists is not in getting a Sunday school organized in every church so much as enlisting the sympathy and cooperation of all the members. And to this work we believe we need first of all to address ourselves. The great majority of our churches are content with their ability to report to the association each year the fact that they have a Sunday school, giving but little thought or concern about the work committed to it or how that work is being done. In too many of the churches the Sunday school is almost a separate organization and is in all respects so treated. A closer relation is needed, and the more intimate it shall be made the more certainly may we look for an extension of the work.

By Organization for Increased Attendance and Better Methods

An inquiry in towns, cities, and country neighborhoods has revealed the lamentable fact that less than one-fourth of our population in the southern states, not including the larger cities, are outside of the Sunday school. We are not surprised with the condition in the large cities, but when these are left out, and our small towns, cities, and even country districts only are considered, the showing is cause for deep concern.

The cause for this is due largely to our want of systematic effort to change it. And this is all wrong. One of the very first things to be kept in our view in our Sunday school organization is that of reaching all the people. As Baptists we have made a great mistake in this matter. With a church organization so near the people our Sunday school should swarm with young and old.

House-to-house visitation, as observed by a few schools, if regularly and persistently pursued by all, would bring into our ranks such a multitude as we have not dreamed of. The people are all about us. We have come in a very quiet, orderly way but have not gone "out into the highways and hedges and compelled them to come in." The house that fails to do this will be empty. The house that obeys the command "may be filled."

An illustration of this comes to us as we write. A little over one year ago there was a Baptist Sunday school in the little town of P. with forty-five to sixty members enrolled. The superintendent of the school attended an institute that was held in a neighboring village, and during its sessions became deeply concerned for the extension of the work at his home. House-to-house canvasing was freely talked about at the institute, and on returning to the village of P. he at once organized this work in the interest of his own school. As a result of that effort, in less than one month, the little school of 45 to 60 had run up to 175, and soon to over 200. As a further but natural result, a revival of religion soon began in the church and over 150 persons professed faith in the Lord Jesus Christ.

Not only do we need to organize for largely increased numbers, but also for better methods of management and teaching. We must at once come to understand that the Sunday school demands the very wisest management and the most devoted and efficient teaching.

We are demanding these things for our day schools but we have sadly lost sight of their greater necessity for the Sunday school. And this accounts for so much of our work that is weak, unstable, not to say almost wholly wanting in attractive, holding power.

It was a great supper that had been prepared for those in the highways and hedges, streets and lanes—not a scanty, uninviting meal. There is abundance in the gospel out of which to provide such a feast that all may be fed. And when they have freely and joyously partaken they will come again.

We need the most efficient and godly members of the church for the officers and teachers of the Sunday school, men and women who realize something of the great possibilities of the Sunday school, and who will give of their time, their talents, and their means for its success. And we need organized methods for the training of these teachers. Just as a normal school, the Teachers' Institute and the Summer School are being established in all our states in easy reach of the day school teachers, so we must organize for the enlightenment and helpfulness of the Sunday school teachers and workers.

By Making the Sunday School Work as Part of Our Educational System

Not only are special chairs for technical education being added to private and state schools, but the same is true of our denominational schools and colleges; therefore it is not necessary that our boys and girls shall go away from home in order to be trained for preaching, teaching, dentistry, law, mining, milling, mechanics, etc. They can be trained in these various lines here in the South by the very best instructors. But how about Sunday school teachers? So far as we remember, not a school in the South, outside of our Theological Seminary, pretends to prepare students for teaching the Bible. A few of the schools have added what is called "A Course in Bible Study," or a "Chair of the Bible;" but not in one of these, so far as we know, do they pretend to instruct in the work of teaching the Bible. But some will say a person cannot teach what he does not know, and can teach if he knows what to teach. The last part of that proposition is a mistake. There are plenty of people who know much of the Bible and yet are not able to impart that knowledge. Many of these with a little special training would make splendid teachers in our Sunday schools. The truth is, for lack of training we have but few competent teachers in these schools. Once we realize the great possibilities of the work, we shall find preparation for doing it in the most efficient way possible being furnished in all our normal and pedagogical courses.

A Sunday School in Every Baptist Church

Yes, we need a Sunday school in every Baptist church and then from these churches we ought to plant one in practically every community of people throughout the world, and use every effort within our power to increase their efficiency, because in this God-given work is presented the opportunity for doing that personal work so necessary and so helpful to the development of the Christian and so indispensable in the work of winning souls for the Master.

CHAPTER FIVE

Why Missionary and Not Anti-Missionary: The Theology of Missions

W. M. HARRIS

Man comes into the world with an interrogation point stamped in fire on his immortal self which increases in the intensity of its brightness and warmth as the world and life with their mysteries and problems unfold before him. He asks questions about everything, and ought to. He asks, "Is God?" And answers, "God is." Is it probable that this God would have anything to say to His creatures along those lines of necessary knowledge upon which they can make no progress of themselves? It is. Has any man appeared in history who claimed to be the Word, the utterance of God? Yes, Jesus of Nazareth. Did He sustain Himself in this marvelous role? Did He live up to His great claims? Did He live a life worthy of the Son, the manifestation, the Word of God? He did. Could a man be an imposter or a lunatic and sustain himself in such a character? No. The verdict of the ages is "My Lord! and my God!"

To the man who has asked and answered these questions you come with another question. You say to him, "You are a follower of Christ, and you believe in giving His gospel to the whole world. Now, why? Why missionary and not anti-missionary?" And we are ready to answer.

Why World-Missionary and Not Anti-World-Missionary

Because Our Master Has Commanded His People to Be So

"All authority hath been given unto me in heaven and on earth. Go ye therefore, and make disciples of all nations" (Matt. 28:18–19).

During the session of the Southern Baptist Convention in Washington City, a smart man of the world remarked one day at the dinner table at my boarding house (the conversation having turned on the Convention and its work) that he "did not believe in foreign missions." I said, "You and the Lord Jesus Christ differ on that subject." I shall never forget the very peculiar way in which he laughed. And he did not say another word. It probably occurred to him that while it is the privilege of the American citizen to "differ," yet differing with Jesus Christ on missions, or on any other subject, is poor business. Since He has said, "Go and make disciples of all nations" why, of course, there is nothing to do but to "go" and "make disciples." If missions did not "pay," if not a single heathen ever believed, if all alike refused to become disciples, to go and teach would still be but to obey the command. No further reason for obedience to orders need be sought by a soldier than the fact that they are orders.

Because the World Is Lost and Jesus Christ Is Able and Willing to Save It While Nobody Else Is

A great many of us need to revise our notions of what it is to be lost. The common conception seems to be that to be in hell is to be lost. The true view is that to be in sin is to be lost. Sin is worse than hell and makes it what it is. Hell would not be the awful place it is if it were not for the sin that is there. And so Jesus came not to save people from a place called hell, but from a state of being and character, and a course of conduct called sin. "He shall save His people from their sins" (Matt. 1:21). It is sin that has cut the cable between God and man, and thus shut off from man that current of divinity in which alone is life, holiness, and peace; and left him to death, misery, and ruin.

Now, man is a sinner wherever you find him. The history of the world is the history of sin. On every page it is "writ large" that "man's inhumanity to man makes countless thousands mourn." Depravity is a historical fact as well as a Bible doctrine. Man in the record which he has made for himself has, with his own hand, written the verdict of his own guilt—he is a sinner. And he is, I repeat, a sinner everywhere; in Europe, in America, in Asia, in Africa, in Australia, and in the islands of the seas— everywhere, he has sinned against whatever light and law he has had, whether of conscience, reason, or revelation. Are not the Chinese sinners? If not, let me deal henceforth with the Chinese only. They shall not only do all my laundry work, but all my other work, and I should at once start for the Orient that I might spend the remainder of my days among them were it not that I am called to preach the gospel and my occupation would be gone in China. I could not preach the gospel there. The gospel cannot be sanely offered to anyone who is not lost. It is the gospel of the grace of God to condemned sinners.

The first thing we have to do toward getting one to receive the gospel is to persuade him that he is lost. Christ came, He said, not to call the righteous, but sinners to repentance. They that are whole need not a physician, but they that are sick. You would as well go to the jail and turn out a man who isn't there or get the governor to pardon one who has never been convicted, as to offer the gospel of Christ to any creature of God who is not a condemned sinner. The thing is unthinkable, absurd, and impossible.

The Question

But one says, "Can it be possible that God will condemn people for rejecting His Son, when they have never heard of Him?"

No, it cannot be possible. God will not condemn people for doing what they did not do. They are lost because they are in sin. To be in sin is to be out of harmony with God, and out of communication with Him, and to be so is to be lost. But this question about rejecting Christ brings up a popular fallacy for which the pulpit is largely responsible—that "unbelief is the great damning sin of the world." If people are condemned and eternally lost for rejecting Christ, then it is perfectly plain that if He had never offered Himself nobody would have been lost. Did Jesus endure all His sufferings that He might save the world from the penalty of rejecting Him? He could have stayed in heaven with the Father, suffering neither humiliation nor death, and done that. Really His death gives opportunity for rejecting Him, and so according to the notion at this moment under consideration, He not only suffered unnecessarily, but actually occasions that condemnation of human beings for rejecting Him, which would have been impossible had He never suffered.

No, unbelief is not the great damning sin of the world. It is not for the rejection of Christ that people are condemned, and finally cast into hell. Let us illustrate: You have pneumonia. You call in a physician. He prescribes veratrum and a blister. We will suppose for the sake of illustration that it is an infallible remedy. You reject the remedy and die. Now, you die because you reject the remedy, and yet it is perfectly clear that the pneumonia kills you. Sin is a great fact before there is any need of a Savior. It is a virus and fever of the soul. Jesus Christ is the only remedy. If you reject that remedy, or if it does not reach you, is not known, is not offered, you are gone. But it is the preexisting sin, the thing that made a Savior thinkable and needful, the disease for which

He is the remedy, that destroys you. Unbelief or the rejection of Christ is a sin and augments the already existing sin whose penalty is death.

The World: A Great Big Sinner

The world is a great big sinner. It is weltering in its iniquity. There is no part of it that is exempt. Man of every race and clime is a sinner. God is holy. By a law of spiritual affinity, God and the sinner cannot fraternize until there is a change. Hence ye must be born again. By the force of spiritual gravity everyone will go to his own place. The sinner's own place cannot be the home of the good, in the presence and fellowship of God. He is lost in his sins and must be saved from his sin. I do not know of anybody who is able and willing to do this except Jesus, and therefore I am in favor of telling sinners of every race, color, and clime about Him.

The Whole World as a Lost Unit
Is in the Divine Contemplation Always

It is contemplated by God the Father.

It is contemplated in His love. "For God so loved the world, that he gave his only begotten Son, that whosoever believeth in him should not perish, but have everlasting life" (John 3:16).

It is contemplated in His promise: "Ask of me, and I shall give thee the heathen for thine inheritance, and the uttermost parts of the earth for thy possession" (Ps. 2:8).

This same unit of a lost world that was contemplated by the Father in His love and promise is contemplated by the Son. It is contemplated in His death. "But we see Jesus, who was made a little lower than the angels for the suffering of death, crowned with glory and honor; that he by the grace of God should taste death for every man" (Heb. 2:9). "If any man sin, we have an advocate with the Father, Jesus Christ the righteous; and he is the propitiation for our sins: and not for ours only, but also for the sins of the whole world" (1 John 2:1–2).

It is contemplated in His great commission: "Go ye therefore, and make disciples of all the nations" (Matt. 28:19).

It is contemplated by the Holy Spirit who "reproves the world of sin, and of righteousness and of judgment" (John 16:8).

Now let us go back and trace the great connected thought in these passages of Scripture. When God the Father looked out from the depths of infinite love, He saw a world flying off at a tangent, crashing away into darkness, and making "sad discord" in the "music of the spheres." Seeing it, He pitied it; pitied this round, ruined unit of a world; loved it in the unity of its condemnation, in the entirety of its lost estate; and sent His Son after it to offer to bring it back to its place in the musical mechanism of the universe. He is looking at the same object when He makes the promise of the uttermost parts of the earth for a possession to His Son.

When that Son hung on the cross, when the black shadow of the Father's averted face fell on Him, when He cried, "Why hast Thou forsaken Me?"—that piercing shriek of agony that must have shivered the very atmosphere—when not a sympathetic voice reached Him from heaven or earth, or hell or any peopled planet, He bore on His lone heart the guilt of a race, the weight of a world—that same world that the Father loved. When He was going back to God it was into every part and to every creature of this same world that He bade His disciples go with the glad tidings of Himself.

Today the Holy Spirit is convicting the same world of sin.

We Are World-Missionary Because of the Believer's Unity with Christ

This unity is both legal and spiritual. And first it is legal. The believer has been crucified with Christ. Jesus is His other self. He has died for me and as me. I am one with Him on the cross, and from the cross on, forever. The believer went with Christ to the cross, to the tomb, arose with Him, ascended with Him, and is seated in Him today "in the heavenly places."

"Lord Jesus, are we one with Thee?
O height! O depth of love!
With Thee we died upon the tree,
In Thee we live above."

Several things grow out of this legal unity with Christ. In the first place, what is ours is His. Certainly, if He and we are not one, not a thing do we possess that does not belong to Him who is one with us. If followed out, this puts the coffers of Christendom at the disposal of Christ.

But, growing out of this same unity, what is His is ours—certainly, if He and we are one, not a thing does He possess that does not belong to those who are one with Him: "All things are yours," "joint heirs with Christ," "who hath been appointed the heir of all things." How marvelous the inheritance and the destiny of the child of God. How blinding the radiance of the glory that here unfolds to the astonished vision of the one who by faith and by the judgment of God has become identified with the Lord Jesus Christ!

But the very unity with Christ which makes us saved people at all, which makes His death our death, His life our life, His place our place, His wealth our wealth, makes His work our work. There is no escape from this for a Christian. It only remains to ask what is His work? And the answer is not in doubt—the world's evangelization.

I have said that the believer's unity with Christ is spiritual as well as legal. This spiritual unity grows out of the legal unity. It is said that a great astronomer saw in a moment of the inspiration of genius the plan of the universe, and exclaimed, in a sublime rapture, "I think God Almighty's thoughts!" The Christian is one who has come into harmony with the divine mind, and so thinks God's thoughts about grander things than the building of worlds and the organization of systems—about duty, responsibility, destiny, immortality, eternity; about humanity and divinity. And so he must come to take the Christ view, the divine view, of missions. It is a most glorious thing to agree with God.

Our Master's Commands

We are world-missionary in our faith, and trying to be in our practice, because our Master commands us to be, because the world is lost, because God contemplates the world always, because the evangelization of the world is Christ's work and His work is ours, because God has taught us to think some of His thoughts.

World missions include city missions, associational missions, state missions, home missions, foreign missions, as so many different departments of one great work. And in whatever department we labor, we should never fail to recognize its relation to the others and to the whole.

May God extend the horizon of every Baptist and every Christian until His vision sweeps the planet, and enlarge our hearts to take in the race.

CHAPTER SIX

Why Missionary and Not "Omissionary"

CURTIS LEE LAWS

Canon Wilberforce tersely put into four words the essentials of evangelical Christianity: Admit, Submit, Commit, and Transmit. To be a Christian, one must admit Christ, submit his wayward will to Christ's will, commit all the interest of his life to Christ's keeping, then henceforth to transmit, "to become the medium through whom the light and love of God shall be transmitted to others."

But all of these ideas may be put still more tersely into two simpler words: Come and Go. To be a Christian a man must come and go. Christ first says, "Come," and then He immediately adds, "Go." Who are to come? "Whosoever will may come." Who are to go? All who come. How many realize that both of these ideas are in salvation?

To accept Christ as a Savior is to accept Him also as Lord and to be obedient to His commandments. In thought we may discriminate between salvation and service, but in experience they are very close together. It is the common experience to express the capitulation of the citadel of the heart in the terms of service. This does not result from an arbitrary law, but from the fact that a Christian partakes of the nature of Christ, is "born from above." We are called into the service of Christ only after we are prepared for that service by regeneration. Then it is that we begin to represent Christ, to manifest forth His life and character. Conformity of life will follow transformation of character, just as transformation of character follows the new birth. This new activity is our function, not simply our option. It is a necessity springing out of our new relations. To be a Christian is to be like Christ, and to be like Christ is to have His Spirit, and He came to seek and to save the lost.

Home Church and Foreign Field

There is no distinction between work for Christ in the home church and on the foreign field. The man who loves one ought to love the other. The Rio Grande is not as broad as the Mississippi. From God's point of view there are no State Missions, no Home Missions, no Foreign Missions. These are but factitious divisions, the outgrowth of wisely-considered plans for the accomplishment of the greatest good in all the fields of missionary enterprise. The Spirit of Christ is the spirit of missions.

What Is an Anti-Missionary Baptist?

An anti-missionary Baptist then is an anti-Christian Baptist, and from all such may the church of Christ be delivered. And yet I am not able to persuade myself into believing that anti-missionary Baptists are insincere. They are, beyond a doubt, the dupes of an erroneous exegesis, and whatever be their culpability, they are not sinning against their consciences. I am not trying to shield them, nor to minimize their error, for I am persuaded that God will hold them responsible for their unenlightened state. And yet I believe that God will be more lenient with them than with that much larger class whom we are now to consider. If a man knows his Lord's will and does it not, he shall be beaten with many stripes. Ignorance does not excuse, but it may change the stripes from many to few.

The Omissionary Baptists

There are tens of thousands of Baptists, living in comparative ease, who do not contribute to any organized missionary work. There are tens of thousands more who think themselves too poor to contribute, but who waste their money upon useless, if not hurtful, indulgences. Certainly these cannot be called missionary Baptists. If you were to advise them to join the ranks of anti-missionary Baptists, they would have a fit of rage, for they will tell you that they are strong believers in missions. Some brother, unknown to me, has placed these folks together in a new denomination, and has felicitously named them "The Omissionary Baptists." Unlike the anti-missionary faction, they claim that they believe missions to be God's appointed means for the salvation of the world.

Ephraim is not alone in being a "cake not turned." Too many of our Baptists lack symmetry in their development. They lay much stress upon that clause in the Great Commission which says, "Baptizing them into the name of the Father and of the Son and of the Holy Ghost," but they seem to forget all about the first clause, which says, "Go ye and teach all nations." God requires obedience alike to both clauses, and surely if we claim to be Christians, we ought at least to try to do what our Master plainly commands. The fact that all the denominations have this "omissionary" contingent does not comfort me in the least. All of us believe that doctrine affects character, and that creed expresses itself in deed. Therefore, Baptists ought to be the best and most effectual servants of God in all the world. I am far more afraid of indifference than of antagonism. We would count it a crime to antagonize missionary enterprises, but we count it a mere peccadillo when men are indifferent. And yet the transgressing brother, whom I so castigate, may claim as near of kin the vast majority of us, who fail to measure up to our possibilities as stewards of the grace of God, who fail to do our whole duty as the representatives of Jesus Christ.

To Be Omissionary Is to Bring Ourselves into Judgment

It is well for us to study the teaching of the Master as to the sins of omission. In their experiences, too many Christians underestimate the heinousness of the merely negative, but the Master strongly emphasizes the truth that the sins of omission are as criminal as the sins of commission. In our prayers we confess that we have failed to do many things, but the confession is generally without poignant grief. The fig tree was cursed because of its unfruitfulness. It was not like the Upas tree, poisoning the birds that lodged upon it, poisoning those who took shelter under its branches, poisoning the earth about its roots. It was simply barren.

Dives did not treat Lazarus cruelly nor set his dogs upon him. He merely withheld from him what he might have given him. There is no evidence that he was wicked and cruel and sensual. Thomas Hood told of a rich woman, who in a dream was confronted with death, and who thus soliloquized:

> For the blind and the crippled were there,
> And the babe that pined for bread;
> And the homeless man and the widow poor
> Who begged to bury her dead,
>
> The naked, alas! that I might have clad,
> The famished I might have fed.
> Each pleading look, that long ago
> I scanned with heedless eye,
>
> Each face was gazing as plainly there
> As when I passed it by.
> Woe, woe for me, if the past should be
> Thus present when I die.

> The wounds I might have healed,
> The human sorrow and smart,
> And yet it never was in my soul
> To play so ill a part.
> But evil is wrought by want of thought,
> As well as want of heart.

Such was the experience of Dives, for his was the sin of omission.

The Sin of Omission

The five foolish virgins were not engaged in folly and sin. Their sin was the sin of neglect.

The man with the one talent did not squander his master's money in riotous living. He simply buried it, and thus kept it safe until his master's return. But how terrible was his condemnation!

The priest and the Levite did not add to the burdens of the wounded man. They got as far away from him as possible. They did not taunt him. They gazed straight ahead as they passed by. Yet they were criminals.

In God's sight it seems to be almost as grievous a sin to withhold the good as to do the evil. In the day when Christ shall judge the evil, He will say,

> Depart from Me ye cursed, into everlasting fire, prepared for the devil and his angels; for I was a hungered, and ye gave Me no meat; I was thirsty and ye gave Me no drink; I was a stranger and ye took Me not in; naked, and ye clothed me not; sick, and in prison, and ye visited Me not. Then shall they also answer Him, saying: Lord, when saw we Thee a hungered, or athirst, or a stranger, or naked, or sick, or in prison, and did not minister unto Thee? Then shall He answer them, saying, Verily, I say unto you, inasmuch as ye did it not to one of the least of these, ye did it not to Me. And these shall go away into everlasting punishment, but the righteous into life eternal.

Notice that He does not charge them with positive sins. He does not declare them cruel or unjust, He does not accuse them of dishonesty or lying, of theft or murder. It is "depart from Me ye cursed" because ye have not done. "Therefore to him that knoweth to do good and doeth it not, to him it is sin." In the light of this statement what will be the judgment of those who in their creed believe in missions, but who in their deeds neglect missions? If the Master cannot say "well done," what will He say?

To Be Omissionary Is to Imperil the Destiny of Millions

When we think of the millions living and dying without the gospel, our hearts must be of stone if we refuse to send them the Bread of Life upon which we feast. Robert P. Wilder used to say, "Religion is the only commodity, the more of which we export, the more we have at home." Instead of robbing ourselves by giving to missions, we increase our store. God help us to realize the worth of a single soul. We can never tell what we do for a soul that we bring to Christ, until we sound the depths of hell and scale the heights of heaven. We cannot calculate what the salvation of a soul means, for we cannot calculate what a never-ending hell means, nor what a never-ending heaven means. It will take all eternity to teach us the value of a single soul.

When polite and cultured Paris remonstrated with its favorite, Francis Xavier, because he meant to go alone and unarmed to a savage country, he nobly said, "If these lands had scented woods and mines of gold, Christians would find courage to go there, nor would all the perils of the world prevent them. They are dastardly and alarmed because there is nothing to be gained there but the souls of men. Shall love be less hardy and less generous than avarice? You say they will destroy me with poison. It is an honor to which such a sinner as I am may not aspire; but this I dare to say; that whatever form of torture or death awaits me, I am ready to suffer it ten thousand times over for the salvation of a single soul."

Shall we, with miserly niggardliness, clutch the Bread of Life while our brethren, over whom the Father's heart yearns, are starving?

To Be Omissionary Is to Fail to Glorify God

Christ said, "Herein is My Father glorified, that ye bear much fruit." It has been well said that we are to glorify God as the

ocean glorifies the sun. Stand upon the deck of a vessel plough-
ing its way through the surging sea. Behold the crests iridescent
with splendor, and see the ten thousand wavelets scintillating
like the facets of a rare gem. The dark and deep blue ocean has
been transformed into a kaleidoscope in which we behold an
ever-changing panorama of beauty. But whence cometh all this
beauty? Shining yonder in the heavens is the King of Day. In His
bosom is fire, in His eyes, light. The waves have not added to
the glory of the sun, but they have caught up and scattered forth
the radiant sunbeams, thus manifesting forth His glory and making His secrets known to all men. That is just how we are to glorify God. We cannot add to God's glory which is already
complete, but like the waves we can catch up the shining splendor of the Sun of Righteousness and manifest it forth unto the
world.

The humblest can be reflectors of God's glory. Perhaps many
around us will never see much of God's glory, unless they see its
dim and uncertain, but nevertheless real, reflection in our lives.
The Father's honor was very dear to the Son and He gave His
life to manifesting forth His Father's character. As the Father
sent Him, so has He sent us. Oh that the world might see the
character of Christ in our characters, and the love of Christ in
our love, and the works of Christ in our work.

The Credentials of Christianity

The credentials of Christianity are the characters of those
who have been transformed by the power of God. The clearest
vision that the world has of God is in the life of God's representatives. When the world shall see the Christ life in us, then will
the Father be glorified.

Beloved, if we neglect our present duty of worldwide evangelization, we shall bring judgment upon ourselves, condemnation
upon our brethren, and shame upon our God. If we are faithful,
we shall merit the "well done" of the Master, our brethren will
be brought to the knowledge of the Savior, and our God will be
glorified among the sons of men.

CHAPTER SEVEN

Why Education by Baptist Schools

J. P. GREENE

Because we are Baptists, we desire our children to be intelligent and useful Baptists. Is this not "sectarian," and even a little "bigoted"? Do we not thus deprive our children of the liberty of choice? I reply that we regard our faith as scriptural. So long as we believe this, we must desire our children to embrace it.

We do not prevent them from choosing their own faith, but rather encourage them to read the Bible and decide for themselves. We would, above everything else, have them make a decision, but would they not better be Baptists? The fear of "sectarianism" should not lead us to educate them in schools of other denominations. A preference for our own faith is reasonable and righteous. In particular the fear of "sectarianism" should not lead us to educate them in un-Christian schools.

Education in a Baptist school is a safeguard against narrow "sectarianism" and bigotry. Besides, I have no sympathy with the hue and cry against "sectarianism" heard in some quarters. Some of these broad, non-sectarian people are very narrow and sectarian in spite of their loud declarations to the contrary. We are Baptists from conviction, and intend to remain so till we get more light on a better way.

There are several good reasons why we should educate our children in Baptist schools.

It is a good thing to educate them in our own historical traditions. We have an honorable and even a glorious history, and our children should know it. We keep them in touch with our family history; why not also with our denominational history?

Every young American should get his college education in America, among his own people. It is a great mistake to take him abroad for his early training. So it is a mistake for a Western boy to go East for his college training. Let him get this part of his education at home, and go East or abroad for his university training. This will keep him in sympathy with his people, and he will thus get a better education.

A Baptist college is a center of denominational life. Our most noted names are associated with it. The portraits of these worthies adorn the college walls. It is good for our sons to breathe this historical atmosphere. They do not become vain, but they do gain a noble self-respect. A noble ancestry inspires us to noble deeds. What is more pitiful to see than the children of Baptists going about apologizing for being Baptists and seeking "social standing" in other denominations! Nothing but ignorance could lead them to do so foolish a thing. If they knew their own history, they would rejoice to belong to such a noble company.

In the college our young people become acquainted with denominational enterprises. Ignorance as to the general scope of our work for the Lord is the great obstacle in the way of our progress. To know the great things we have planned for the world is to get inspiration to work to accomplish them, hence the organized ways and means to enlighten our people. These enterprises will never prosper as they should until the church life is brought into intelligent sympathy with them. It is a most difficult undertaking, the instruction of all our people in the Lord's business. Life in our ordinary Baptist church is local, and often very narrow. The struggle for existence exhausts the time and energy of the members. They do not look out upon the broad, white harvest field, because they are absorbed in home interests. How can our young people look beyond these narrow borders? In many churches they are almost ignored. They have no specific work given them at home, and where they are the Macedonian cry never comes.

But the college is a center of denominational activity. All lines converge there. Books and papers abound in the library. Professors and students are alive. They are acquainted with the various enterprises, and are interested in all. From time to time secretaries of our Boards and returned missionaries visit the college and deliver addresses on their work. A new world opens before the students. Not only do they acquire knowledge of the work, but they also catch the enthusiasm of service. They realize for the first time that they belong to a vast army marching unto the conquest of the world. From that moment on, they are the ardent advocates and liberal supporters of all departments of the Lord's work. Who will reckon the good that our colleges have done for the cause of missions? Of course, we expect them to educate our missionaries, but this work is not so great as their diffusion of general missionary intelligence.

The college course is a good schooling for church work. Of course, our young people can learn to do many kinds of church work without going to college. I rejoice in all the efforts now being made to fit them for efficient service. Much good is being accomplished. But we shall reach a conclusion soon, and so will the young people, that this training is partial and inadequate. It cannot take the place of the college course. The young Sunday school superintendent or teacher will feel his limitations and wish that he had a thorough education. Perhaps a few of our young people cannot go to college, but most of them can, and they would if they were encouraged. A college education is cheap, especially in the West and South. Any able-bodied boy can work his way through college. And why would it not be a good thing for a church to help a good boy or girl in getting a higher education? Money cannot be spent to better advantage. Is there greater need in a church than a few intelligent and consecrated members—educated leaders in church work? Send the young people to college in greater number and see what rich benefits the churches will reap.

Suppose we should educate our children in un-Christian institutions. They would learn nothing of our denominational work, nor would such education fit them for work in our churches. Indeed, it would unfit them. If there were no other reason for education in Baptist colleges, this one is sufficient: the preparation of our young people for denominational and church work!

When we educate our young people in our own colleges, we secure their influence to our denomination. The college life decides many important questions. How old ideas perish and new ones rise in their places. Here the boy will perhaps find his life calling. Here he will form lasting friendships that will influence his whole life. Shall he be alienated from his own people? Everything in the Baptist college tends to holding him in the ancestral line.

It is a pity for a young Baptist, the heir of Baptist history and Baptist money, to drift away from the fold, and to squander his inheritance among strangers. It is a loss when he goes to another denomination, though we have no quarrel with him when he does it from principle. But when he goes into unbelief it is a real calamity! We desire to keep what the Lord has given us. We are not toiling and sacrificing for the cause of error. How many Baptist families have been broken up! How much Baptist money has been alienated! Gone to the use of the evil one! We have seen Baptist families and fortunes go to pieces, and there is no sadder sight! It is unnecessary, too. As a rule, this misfortune can be avoided.

Let Baptist parents bring their children up in the Lord, and educate them in Baptist institutions, and they will not depart from the faith. If they send them to school to the enemies of Christ, how can they expect them to follow the teachings of Christ? "Establish thou the work of our hands!" This is an appropriate prayer. It expresses a natural and pious wish. But we must build well. Hay, wood, and stubble cannot be established. They are poor building material. If we desire our children to continue in our faith, we must educate them in Christian institutions. The truth is, many Christian parents think too little of Christian education, and too much of money. A good Christian education is worth more to a boy than a million dollars!

How many Baptists believe this? In the infancy of our children, we should plan for their college education, and let them know that we expect them to go to this or that institution and that their education is to be their inheritance. Then if they depart from the faith, after a Christian training at home and in college, our sorrow will not be mingled with remorse.

Finally, it is absolutely necessary that our young ministers be educated in Baptist colleges. An un-Christian school would be uncongenial to them; besides it would not afford them the sort of training that they need. Other denominations might take them into their schools. But we could not expect them to educate our preachers, even if they could.

Young ministers as a rule are poor. God does not call many of the rich to preach. The poverty of these men is an appeal to us from God for Baptist colleges. He could call the rich if He wished, and save us the trouble of helping these poor men. "But is there not danger of helping them too much?" The Baptists have not yet approached the danger line in this respect. There is danger that we shall help them too little!

These young men must have college training, or cripple their influence. We dare not cast them off. God has given them to us, in their poverty and ignorance, and we must educate them. If we do not we shall betray our trust, handicap our churches, and dishonor our God.

Let us endow our colleges liberally and make education cheap for our preachers and for all our young people. No college can do good work and live without an endowment.

Even if our young preachers could get help in other schools, they would not get the sympathy they need. Why, in many institutions—in some calling themselves Christian—the divine call to preach is ignored and even ridiculed. Could our preachers find sympathy in such schools? Remember that these young men have gotten their consent to preach after much prayer and meditation. Some of them have passed through bitter struggles. They were not designated to the ministry by their parents, nor do they regard this calling as a mere profession. The hand of God is on them! Their hearts are tender and sensitive. Often they doubt their fitness for this holy calling, they are so poor and ignorant and inexperienced and weak. Can we compel them to go to a college where Jesus Christ is despised, or to one of another denomination where there is no special sympathy with their purposes? They would be miserable and discouraged—cut off from the tender sympathies of their own people. The Baptists would not be worthy of these choice young men if they did not provide congenial schools for them.

Young preachers also need to be educated in a spiritual atmosphere. While they are growing in knowledge they should also grow in grace.

Education alone cannot make a preacher. Piety is indispensable. The college life should be intensely religious. Students become eager in their pursuit of knowledge, and easily neglect spiritual culture. Even the most pious need incentives to greater piety, and encouragement to holier living. All Christian teachers and students will bear me out in this statement. Would it be wise, then, to educate our preachers in a cold, Christless atmosphere? Do you think that they ought to stand this test? They might. Could they grow in grace there? The tender plant may endure a great deal of cold, but the cold is not conducive to growth. Our preachers should grow in grace all the time. They should come out of college with glowing hearts as well as cultivated minds. A college that does not encourage and promote spiritual growth is not an ideal school for the lay-student, and certainly not a fit place for our young preachers.

The "New Learning"

Some of the friends of "the new learning" think that preachers should be educated in secular schools, away from denominational traditions, and among young men of other callings. There is nothing in this. We would as well take a child away from his family, and thus save him from family traditions. This is his family. God put him into it. Unless it is absolutely bad, why take him away from it? What is the matter with our denominational traditions? God gave us these preachers—they were begotten in these traditions. Unbelief is not producing any preachers, and therefore it is not competent to educate ours. We will try to take care of what God gives us!

Again in our own colleges there are many young men preparing themselves for other callings. Our preachers are by no means isolated. They have all the advantages of association with young men of other callings that they would have in other institutions.

These same people also claim that the secular schools are the best. This is not true. Christian scholars are numerous. Every branch of learning can show a long list of brilliant Christian teachers. But if the statement were true, it would be no argument for secular training. We should make our Christian schools better, the very best in the land. We have the money, and we can get the teachers if we will. But look at the work of these Christian schools. Their graduates are foremost among the best!

"But would it not be well to let our preachers get their college training in the secular schools, and then attend the seminary for their theological education?" This question is even now in the mouths of some Baptists. Well, our young preachers would not go to the secular schools, nor would their churches want them to go. This plan would force upon us an uneducated ministry. But if they should attend the secular schools, the result would be a cold, professional ministry which is worse than the uneducated. We do not want education unless we can have the right kind! Then what could the seminary do with such material? We must not forget that the college course is more important than the seminary course.

The young man goes to college at his most impressionable age. Will you at this time put him under the instruction of a godless man? Will you let the unbeliever put the first stamp on this man that is to be a servant of God? When the secular institution has done with the young minister, will the seminary want him at all? No! Our colleges must be "feeders" for the seminaries. This is the natural order: The Baptist college and then the Baptist seminary!

It is well to remember also that secular learning does not like a theological seminary any better than it likes a denominational college. It would abolish Christian education entirely. It would have a "divinity school" of its own, divorced from creed and from the Bible.

The secular institution would give the young preacher his college training, and then retain him for his divinity course. Then what? The Baptists are not ready yet to sell their birthright for a mess of poisoned pottage!

Why Education in Baptist Colleges?

Because when we own the colleges we can make them positively Christian. The word "Baptist" is dear to us, but not so dear as the word "Christian." We want our children to be Baptists, but Christians first. A Baptist college in name only will not please us. It must also be animated by the Spirit of Christ. The main reason for having our own colleges is that we may have Christian schools where we can educate our children. The friends of Christian education need now, perhaps more than ever before, to foster and guard their institutions. Many schools, founded by the gifts of pious people, are drifting away from Christ. And in many secular institutions, there is unconcealed and even violent opposition to our religion. Professors, supported by our taxes and the gifts of Christian people, do not hesitate to attack publicly, in classroom and lecture hall, some of the most sacred and vital truths of Christianity. How shall we counteract the influence of these enemies of the cross? We must have Christian schools, support them liberally, and send our children to them for their higher education!

Most of our children get their primary training in our public schools. These are not Christian, but they are not un-Christian. Our public school teachers, as a rule, are Christian men and women. They come out of our best homes, and are in sympathy with our pious wishes to bring up our children in the Lord. It is possible, perhaps not best, for them to give religious instruction. But they will not sow tares among our wheat. Besides, the children are at home under the religious training of parents and Sunday school teachers.

It is a matter of regret that most of our young people go from our public schools into the business of life. Yet many—and may the number grow!—desire a higher education. Nearly all of these must go away from home to attend college. The day of the boy's departure for college is an anxious one for the parents. This is natural. Yet parents should look at the bright side. The young bird must leave the nest some day, and must learn to fly with his own wings. And the boy must get out and make a place for himself in life. The college life is an excellent training for him—a good halfway place between home and the wide world. He will learn much of life, besides what he gets out of books. Only send him to a good Christian institution. Do not leave it to him entirely to choose his college. He may select one where many of the teachers are unbelievers, and where there is "fast" living and too much of the sporting spirit. Do not allow him to be instructed by a sneering agnostic. Do not send him to college where life is extravagant. You may be rich, but you would better not teach your boy to squander money. In a good, plain Christian college he will be exposed to very few temptations. Such a college is the next best place to home for an innocent, inexperienced boy.

Baptists should have colleges of their own and make them positively Christian. What does this mean?

The teachers should be pious Christians. No unbeliever should ever fill a chair in a Christian institution. He may be discreet, not a violent enemy of Christ, and yet he is unfit for the place, for he cannot exert a positive Christian influence. The man is more than the teacher.

But can we get pious teachers? Yes, for every department of learning, even for biology! There are many such teachers who have had the best training that the world affords. We can get them if we will, and we will if we understand our business. They prefer to teach in Christian schools. The "liberty" there offered them is the kind they desire. In un-Christian schools they are fettered. Their unbelieving colleagues may assail the Christian religion, and be upheld on the plea of "liberty of investigation," but if they say a word for Christ they are called "sectarian." It would be a joy to their hearts to work with pious associates in a college where the Spirit of Christ reigns.

Sometimes even professedly Christian teachers depart from the faith, and teach things that subvert the faith they once professed. If we control the school we can remove them. Of course, they will howl about "liberty"; all of them do when they are forced to go to their own place. But we should not mind that. We are conducting a Christian school—this is understood when we employ teachers—and we do not intend to pay men to pull down what we employed them to build up. They should have the manhood to withdraw. But if they should not, we should have the courage to ask them to. The trustees have a sacred trust, and they owe it to God and the brethren and the young people to keep that trust sacredly.

The college life should be made both moral and spiritual. In some institutions no attention is paid to the morals of the students. Those in charge contend that it is their business to teach, not to watch over the morals of their pupils. They ask questions in the classroom, but none outside! But the teachers in a Christian college realize that the parents have committed the morals of their sons to them, and that moral training is more important than intellectual. They know that it were better for a boy to remain at home and never get a college education than to go out of a college a moral wreck. So in the fear of God, they watch over their pupils, and by advice and warning and example try to guide them in the way of holiness.

Even more important than morals is the spiritual life in college, for the basis of morals is religion, faith in God, genuine piety. Christian teachers worship God, believe His Word, and are faithful in all their religious duties. Thus they create a spiritual atmosphere. In the classroom, on the campus, in all their dealings with the students, their spirituality is uppermost. Who can estimate the influence for God of these godly men on the impressionable minds of the young men who look up to them for instruction and guidance from day to day for four years? All the book learning on earth cannot equal it in power and blessing.

Is it possible for a college to have such a spiritual atmosphere? Why not? The teachers make the intellectual atmosphere; why not also the spiritual? Let us get rid of delusions. Brick and mortar and money do not make a college. The teachers make it. If they are really good pious men, they will create a spiritual atmosphere in the college, and all the students will have to breathe it. And it is not a hindrance to learning, but a positive help. It quickens the mind. It also restrains the students—it is disciplinary force of great power. Yes, indeed, it is possible to make the college life spiritual, and it is the solemn duty of those that govern a Christian institution to see that it is filled with the Spirit of Christ.

The college should be an evangelical agency—a missionary institution. Many young people enter college unsaved. We are not so foolish as to suppose that education will save them—they must be born again! And the saving of a soul is a greater work than the education of a mind. "He that converteth a sinner from the error of his way, shall save a soul from death!" Every Christian teacher believes this. But in some institutions conversion is ridiculed. President and professor go out of their way to speak and write against it as a silly and harmful superstition. This rage against the gospel cannot blind our minds to the supreme need of a soul. In our Christian colleges we must and will seek the conversion of every unsaved student.

Soul-winning is not generally recognized as a part of college work, but it should be. The young people are committed to us for the best preparation for their life work. What is better than faith in Christ? To learn of Him is to learn the most important lessons. The Christian teacher must look upon his pupil with a longing for his salvation—hoping and praying for his conversion. And if he passes out of college unsaved, his pious teacher can but sigh to see him going away with his diploma but without a title to a mansion on high. This sadness is intensified by the fact that this is a sort of last chance. The boy has gone through the home training and church influences before coming to college, and now he is going out into an active, engrossing business life. He is drifting away from the most powerful influences of divine grace. But there is hope. This careless, bright boy will soon be a man, and his thoughts may take a more sober turn. Often the wise words of his godly teachers will come back to him, and the pious influences of his college life may bear fruit in his salvation. Many times has this occurred.

In thus seeking the salvation of the student the teacher does not take advantage of him. He works in harmony with the wishes of the parents. They sent their boy to college with a prayer for his conversion, and they will rejoice over this more than over his graduation. And the boy himself will always feel grateful to his pious teachers whether he is converted through their efforts or not. But the highest justification of this evangelical work in the college is the approval of Jesus Christ. He expects it of an institution that was founded in His name!

The Bible should be taught in the college. It can be taught in a Christian college. The teachers believe in it. They put it in the curriculum, not for its literature and history, but for its ethical and religious teachings. None but pious people can teach the Bible properly. Neither can a pious teacher teach it effectively in an un-Christian institution. An unbelieving colleague can spoil all his work. A few sneers, and a little ridicule, and some high-sounding phrases would destroy the respect of the students for the sacred Book.

Some un-Christian schools realize that the exclusion of the Bible puts them at a disadvantage with some of the best people, and try in a feeble way to put it in the course of study. But the effort is a failure. The atmosphere is uncongenial to the Word of God. It must be taught and studied in a sympathetic way. They say it must be treated as "literature," as we teach any other book. But we all know that this is not so. Mother's letter is not like any other letter. God's Book is not like any other book. It is a Father's loving message to His erring children. Those that overlook this fact would better let it alone. Of course, these cold, unsympathetic critics have done some good in an indirect way—not many thanks to them. But we do not believe in their way, and we will not support them in it. If they want to do this kind of work they should set up an institution for the purpose and so advertise their business.

God's Book Is God's College

This is the proper place for the teaching of the Bible. Here it will be taught by the people that love it, for the glory of its Author, and for the good of His children. A Baptist college justifies its right to exist and claims the liberal support of God's people when it lovingly and faithfully instructs the young people in the divine Word.

And who can reckon the results of teaching the Bible to the young people of our land? Who can estimate the influence of our Christian colleges? Thousands of young people devote themselves ardently to the study of God's Word under able and pious teachers. They not only learn the letter of the Word, but also catch the spirit of it. As a matter of culture, the result must be great and blessed, but the influence on morals and religion will be tenfold greater and more blessed. These young people will soon go out in the world to fill important places in society. As they scatter abroad they will carry with them this precious knowledge, and put these holy principles into practice. In the home, in the church, in business, in the affairs of state, in the army, in the navy, at home and abroad, they will govern themselves according to the teachings of Christ, and will be His living epistles to all men!

The Bible has never had a fair chance. It has been pushed aside in many so-called Christian schools to make room for creed or catechism or superstition. In others it has been taught in a cold, critical way that has rendered its teachings impotent. Give it a chance! Let it speak directly to the young people in its own plain, simple, loving way. Let them imbibe it as God's Word for the quickening of their own souls, and the inspiration of their own lives. Then it will do its blessed work. A new era will dawn, a new race will spring up. Jesus Christ will be supreme.

Christian people are awakening to the importance of Christian education. Every year millions of money are given by pious people for this good work. But there is room for improvement. Our denominational colleges are the hope of Christian learning. The secular institutions will not exalt Jesus Christ.

God's people should rally around their colleges—send their children to them, and endow them munificently. No investment for Christ could be safer. In no other way can one do more good with his money.

CHAPTER EIGHT

Why Become a Baptist

DAVID M. RAMSEY

Eighteen years now have passed since the struggle closed. Up to this time there has seemed to be no reason for giving to the public this private and intensely personal piece of history which has never before breathed the air. Yet there is a psychological law which ever causes us to be interested in the earnest soul-conflicts of our fellow men. Even a heathen was applauded to the echo in Rome for the noble sentiment: "I am a man and nothing that affects man is foreign to me." Time enough has elapsed to temper the writer's feeling and also to remove from the mind of the reader that tinge of suspicion and touch of reserve with which we are wont to receive the statements of a too-recent convert from the ranks of another denomination. Moreover, I am persuaded that if the experience of our life be helpful to other lives, like the timber for a good vehicle, it must be well-seasoned. The specific reason for my writing on the subject of becoming a Baptist is that it embodies my personal experience, and hence the form is necessarily biographical and the substance experimental. There is nothing to do but to tell the story of this portion of my life. It is entirely justifiable to perform vivisection in the interest of truth.

When About Seventeen Years of Age . . .

I went from the home of my boyhood in Greenville County, South Carolina, to Storeville, in Anderson County, some forty miles distant, to enter a high school. The institution had as its principal a young Baptist minister capable and cultured, whose name I here write with a sense of abiding gratitude, the Reverend E. R. Carswell, Jr. This school was chosen because of the fact that of the several letters received, the one from Mr. Carswell was most pleasing to the lad who was permitted to make his own choice. Prior to this, I was converted under the preaching of the Reverend Ripley Jacobs, an eloquent young Presbyterian preacher, and I joined the Fairview Presbyterian church where my forefathers had long been members, and of which denomination my father is and has long been a ruling elder. My mother also was a member of this church. Ours was one of those orderly Presbyterian homes of a former day where the children were scrupulously fed on Sundays on half moon pies, loaf bread, and the Shorter Catechism. It was rather a dry day. I remember that my father once stopped me from whistling with the remark that the noise was too shrill for the holy Sabbath. Doubtless it was not superior music. It was a godly home for which I have ever been devoutly thankful.

Soon After I Entered the Carswell Institute . . .

the young Baptist preacher in a spirit of pleasantry asked his Presbyterian pupil for a good text for a sermon on infant baptism which he intended to preach the following Sunday, stipulating to use the very strongest one favoring this custom which might be produced. The terms were agreed to, and at once the search began in good earnest. The boy chuckled over the embarrassing predicament which the preacher and congregation would find themselves in the next Sunday.

But soon the subject became distressingly serious. One of the first passages turned to of course was, "But Jesus said suffer little children and forbid them not to come unto Me for of such is the kingdom of heaven." To my surprise there was not a word here about any kind of baptism. The Baptist minister could do all this for his own babe next Sunday at the close of his sermon, if he thinks there is nothing sacrilegious in a poor mortal man's imitating the Divine Redeemer in bestowing a blessing.

So one after another of the familiar passages were examined with similar results. The household baptisms mentioned in the New Testament failed me for they possessed no remotest hint that infants were present. On the contrary, I remember very distinctly that in every case studied in my crude way the startling fact came out prominently that there was proof that each one baptized had previously exercised faith for himself. The concordance was patiently consulted but no relief came. About Friday the preacher insisted on having his text. I think now that there was in his eye a twinkle of almost cruel pleasure over my discomfiture and awkwardness as I made my lame excuses of absence from books and counseling friends, lack of time, etc. With the assurance on my part that he should hear from me again on this subject, the preacher was left to select his own text according to his liking.

The Heart's First Burden

Now, who was the most unhappy youth in all that neighborhood? Why, that same lad who left his teacher's presence with a cheerful and careless manner, but whose heart had taken on its first real burden, not to be thrown off for weary years; and like all sorrow in this life, it possessed a strange power of isolation. He felt somewhat as men feel in an earthquake when that solid globe which they have ever called "terra firma" seems breaking from her ancient moorings and driving headlong into chaos. Every spare hour was spent in reading and investigation.

While I am penning these lines my hand is resting on the most precious treasure I possess. Money would not buy it, that is, it is not for sale, for a thousand precious memories cling to the inanimate thing almost transmuting it into a person. It is simply the little red-back Bible I purchased in the town of Anderson at the cost of twenty-five cents—a good sum for that purse. There were plenty of Bibles in the house, but this expensive outlay must be made that no one see the evidences of what my soul was passing through. Its pages are well-pencil-marked and on the fly leaves I find "circumcision" with many references telling the story of months of mental confusion. In another place is this significant heading, "Baptism, where mentioned," with chapter and verse given in a long list.

Seeking Advice

About this time I opened my heart to a very agreeable and intelligent Presbyterian gentleman whom I had come to know quite intimately. I stated my troubles, giving him the result of my recent studies. He told me that some years before he passed through a similar experience, and that his mind was set at rest on the subject by reading a booklet written by Dr. Stacy, of Newnan, Georgia. Taking my friend's advice, I wrote directly to the author, asking for his treatise which he kindly sent with promptness. To my mind the discussion was unsatisfactory as a piece of reasoning and hence failed to bring rest to my disturbed soul.

If my memory serves me correctly, the author's object was to prove that there was an Old Testament church merged into a New Testament church, and that baptism in the New simply takes the place of circumcision in the Old. The schoolboy was then a member of an active and excellent debating society, and was very fond of that kind of work. He saw plainly that there were too many weak points in the argument for it to get a favorable verdict were it made before that truly shrewd body composing the Eclectic Debating Society of Carswell Institute. I remember well that this was the test to which Dr. Stacy's reasoning was subjected in my mind. Two or three patent facts seemed fatal to his position. That Jesus Himself was baptized after His circumcision, that baptism was for both sexes while circumcision was for only one, that the whole theory was an assumption without one passage of Scripture in its support, and other similar facts caused the searcher after truth to part company with Dr. Stacy's argument.

But My Conclusion Appeared Arrogant

How often had we heard from that truly angelic spirit, our Aunt Mary, whose sweet, unselfish life had been spent in our home, that the scholars and educated preachers for the most part are found in our denomination. That proved the most convincing piece of logic up to date.

Now it was that the conscience was set at rest with the jugglery of a phrase—baptism is not essential. Why then be schismatic? It is nothing else but bigotry. It is not good form. I forgot to ask the question, essential to what? For Jesus, it was essential to fulfill all righteousness—essential to the salvation of the world. If it is not essential to our own salvation and yet necessary to obedience or to the discharge of duty, or the full expression of love, it is a large and blessed truth.

But some time subsequently I experienced a poetic awakening to the character of this blinding and seductive fallacy. A revival arose among the students and many were converted. Those who joined the Baptist church were to be baptized down at the ford on the Rocky River. I was there. It was a crisp autumn afternoon, the leaves were falling—a typical gray day of that melancholy season. A large gathering lined the banks of the river. Our young preacher read in a clear voice and kindly manner several passages from the Bible, setting forth baptism by immersion. It did seem very easy to find the appropriate Scripture! If it had been written for the occasion, it could not have suited better. It does not matter, I thought, for it is all settled anyhow, baptism is not essential.

And then, closing the book, the preacher said something like this: "Our Lord must have walked some forty miles across the desert country to come down to the Jordan to be baptized by John in the river. Jesus, calm and silent and unrecognized, had been working in the carpenter's shop in Nazareth, but now He leaves these duties to enter upon His vast labors as the world's Redeemer. First He must be baptized in the Jordan. Here stand His baptism on the threshold of His life work. It was a solemn hour and tender experience, for Jesus Himself said it was necessary for Him to be baptized to fulfill all righteousness. I know not all the deep meaning of that utterance. By example and precept He has taught us that it is our duty to be baptized, and I think if we love Him it should be pleasant to keep His commandments."

As the Minister Spoke . . .

he seemed to fix his eyes on me. At least the words like arrows fastened themselves in my bosom. Then he led the young Christians down into the water. I had heard that baptism by immersion somehow was unbecoming to ladies—indeed it was not quite refined, but yonder as they emerge from the water what a heavenly scene! And the most beautiful one of all that number never before seemed so divinely lovely as now. I remember how my heart smote me. "Thus it becometh us to fulfill all righteousness" kept ringing in my ears. With one stroke the booth which I had been hiding behind to escape duty was stricken down by the sword of the Spirit. Thus vanished forever my pleasant little conceit that New Testament baptism is nonessential. And the words went with me up from the river that Sunday afternoon: "If you love Me keep My commandments."

Through the rest of the school term conviction grew apace. A friend loaned me *Theodosia Ernest* which struck me at the time as one of the most wonderful books I had ever read. The limpid style, the fairness in debate, the river-like progress of thought on to the end, the simple but happy little plot with many a cunning and clever literary device for sustaining the interest of the reader, but above all the strong exegesis of the Scriptures, marshalling the Bible truths into a phalanx of irresistible argument went far toward capturing and disarming the young knight. Still, appearances of having all intact must be kept up until the conclusion of the whole matter was reached and stability of conviction was assured. Not even my most intimate friends, so far as I know, ever suspected any change of views. Ample opportunity was afforded for deliverance during the following two years which had to be given to making money to defray the expense of a college course. School teaching was chosen. What meditation during the long walks to and from school, what ingeniously conducted controversies with intelligent laymen and preachers of all denominations, slyly testing my opinions from the viewpoint of other men, on the subject ever uppermost in my mind!

One Incident . . .

occurred about this time which came near leading to an expression of my secret creed. While teaching school at Rabun Creek Church in Laurens County, contrary to my earnest wishes, I was elected superintendent of a Baptist Sunday school. The pastor was a loyal and consistent Baptist, possessing strong convictions undiluted with the water of expediency. He boldly told the church to their face that it was a great wrong to place a Presbyterian in charge of their Sunday school. Hard feelings arose in the church as the result. I tried in vain to pour oil on the troubled waters. Little did the dear conscientious brethren know what a harmless wolf they had let in among the Baptist lambs. The time was not full, however, for opening my heart, and so with my secret locked at present in my breast, I took up my task and moved on for another six months.

Then came the sorest trial of all that I had been called on to face up to this time. A strange and at first undefined feeling overtook me that I must become a preacher of the gospel. Hitherto, I had been expecting to enter the legal profession. At last the impression that preaching was to be my life work moved out into the realm of clearness and became a firm conviction of duty. It seemed to me that my life would be a failure if I went into any other calling, which I suppose was the state of soul which Paul was in when he said: "Woe is unto me if I preach not the gospel."

But where to preach was the puzzling question. To enter the Presbyterian ministry would be to preach, teach, and practice that which I did not believe on the subject of baptism, and in support of which I had not been able to find one passage of Scripture after years of searching. I could not escape the conclusion that for me at least such a course would be unmanly and sinful. On the other hand to join a Baptist church and enter the ministry, the difficulties seemed well nigh insurmountable. I knew but few influential members of that denomination, nor in the circumstances did I feel willing to ask favors. This poor soul had no Barnabas to introduce him to the brethren and vouch for his conversion. The money saved by teaching must be utterly inadequate to meet the expense of a seven years' course at college and seminary.

The Season of Tenderness

Well do I remember that this was a season of tenderness and prayer. For some reason that I have never been able to understand fully, there were ever with me thoughts of my sainted mother, who died when I was six years of age. There came up simple little incidents of childhood memories, such as my learning to read the fourteenth chapter of John's Gospel while sitting on her lap one Sunday afternoon. But oftenest there was before me the pathetic scene connected with my dear mother's death. I remembered, oh so distinctly, how she kissed us all goodbye, one by one, as we were lifted up to her bed, and then how she turned her fair radiant face and set her blue eyes on my father, who stood at the foot of the bed like a statue, but with feelings that lay too deep for tears. I shall never forget that when they said she was gone I went into the room alone and fell on my knees and tried to pray. It was a child's sorrow but deep. I did not know that my mother could die. I had always thought of her as immortal because I knew her only as love.

This experience is recorded in this connection simply because it is strictly true to the facts. A possible explanation of this peculiar experience which was ever with me in these days has come to my knowledge. It seems almost mystical, and yet it is such a striking coincidence that it must be related. A few years ago my aged aunt told me with much feeling that when my mother lost by death a singularly fine little boy, her firstborn, she said in her grief that she had named this child Samuel, and had given him to the Lord to be a preacher if it should be His will. But the Lord spake to little Samuel and the child went away to be with Him perpetually in the upper temple. Also the mother went a few years later, leaving one boy. Long afterwards, this son is called into the ministry. I wonder if heaven has not a minute plan being slowly carried out in it all. With more than maternal sweetness God seemed to be pointing out the way.

Then Finally . . .

the time came for summing up the facts and from all the data to draw the conclusion on this subject. Here is my little red-back Bible with its oft-marked pages. But what of it? The process of thought which followed may be briefly outlined. I find that I take this Bible as the source of information and the final authority for man, the sufficient rule of faith and practice. Tradition is not needed, nor is it safe or authoritative. Neither "the church" nor any man or collection of men is empowered to change these teachings of the inspired record, nor has anyone the power of private interpretation. That being the case, the one important point for me to settle is, what does this Book teach me to be my religious duty? I find that the great bulk of that which I have been taught from childhood I now most heartily and lovingly accept, but in several important doctrines, I am at variance with my early instructions.

The distinctive doctrines of the Baptist denomination seem quite near to New Testament models. These early churches had a simple and natural polity and were evidently self-governing without any higher ecclesiastical courts. The doctrine of restricted communion commends itself to my mind as the consistent and logical sequence from the teaching of believers' baptism. So after all baptism, it would seem, possesses the strategic element. Now clearly there is no scriptural authority for infant baptism, for the subject must be a believer in Jesus as his personal Savior.

As to the matter of what baptism is, I see wherever it is described at all it is performed by putting the candidate into the water. Not only so, but the reason for immersion is plainly given, showing that it must be a burial, symbolizing our death to sin and resurrection to a new life in Christ. Then to change to sprinkling or pouring is to destroy its very character and to lose all its beauty and instructiveness, and also to foil its important mission, in making the good confession before the world. Here is a most significant fact which amounts almost to a demonstration of the correctness of the truths held by the Baptist denomination, namely, if Pedobaptists wish to attack the distinctive doctrines of the Baptists, they must take Roman Catholic grounds for waging the warfare. On the other hand, if the Pedobaptists wish to combat the errors of Romanism for successful controversy, they must occupy Baptist grounds in the defense.

One Day in Early October

At last after four years the battle is over, the die is cast, the Rubicon crossed. One day early in October, 1880, the Reverend J. K. Mendenhall came down from Greenville at my invitation to Columbia Church in Greenville County to perform the baptism. The morning of the baptism came, and I had not yet apprised my father of the step I was about taking. The reason for the delay in informing him was his extreme illness. Indeed on this account the baptism had already been postponed for several days. When I made my mind known to my father, he replied quietly and kindly that this course was a sore disappointment to him, but he would offer no objection, leaving me to act according to the dictates of my own conscience. This gentle and affectionate spirit almost broke my purpose. It seemed harder to bear than opposition, especially in all the circumstances. At this time the tempter came with many an ingenious argument and wily plea, pursuing me to the confines of torture, that he might turn me aside from the clear path of duty.

Oftimes since that morning I have stood on that same spot where I poured out my soul in prayer for guidance and strength. It was a pivotal hour in my life. There came over me a sense of utter loneliness in the world. I know now that I was weak. It was one of those inclement days which seem to slip the wings of hope. But He who said, "Lo I am with you through all the days," fulfilled His rich and precious promise, and I went forward in strength not my own.

Every incident of the day is fresh in memory. Trite details have taken on an importance in my own mind out of all proportion to their intrinsic merit. Taking a satchel in front of me on a horse, I rode away to the church some seven miles distant. It fell upon a time when a protracted meeting was in progress. When Brother Mendenhall reached the church, he was invited to preach, and he gave an admirable discourse, full of consolation and encouragement, on the manliness of the true Christian. At the close of this tender sermon I was received into the membership of the church. I remember that a neighboring Baptist minister, the same who objected to having a Presbyterian superintendent for his Sunday school, was present, as I was told, to object to my baptism, having been incorrectly informed that I was seeking baptism by immersion with the intention of remaining a member of the Presbyterian church. But when he learned that the candidate was coming in the regular way, without any reservations, he offered no objections.

The Baptism

So it came to pass that about noon on that autumn day, near the place of my birth, in the presence of a vast assembly of my neighbors, together with many of the children whom I had taught in the day school, there on the banks of the purling little stream, we sang and prayed, and the preacher and I went down into the water as my Lord had done, and as He commanded me to do, and we came up straightway out of the water, and like another in that far off day, I went on my way rejoicing. Then I had peace of mind and great happiness.

CHAPTER NINE

Why Conventions of Baptist Churches

J. B. GAMBRELL

The New Testament ecclesiastical unit is a local church, and there is no other. Each church is independent of every other, and to each is committed the oracles of God to be preserved, taught, and executed. Each church is subject alone to its Head, the Lord Jesus Christ.

All ecclesiastical power or authority is vested in each separate church, which is an executive of the will of Christ. Church power is all delegated by Christ, and cannot be redelegated. The expression "church sovereignty" is not strictly correct. Christ is the only sovereign, and His churches are His executives, acting under His law and guided by His representative on earth, the Holy Spirit. Even the word "independent" applied to churches must be used within narrow limits. The churches are wholly dependent on their Head and subject to His law, but independent of each other and of all other bodies whatsoever. To each separate church the whole commission is given, and it is given to no other kind of body. Nor can churches transfer it to another body.

These propositions have common consent among the advocates of New Testament ecclesiology. But everywhere among the same people are other organizations variously called societies, associations, or conventions. Into the nature, functions, and purposes of these, we do well to look. With respect to general organizations, their nature, and the relation of the local bodies to them, there are two general theories extant. To one or the other all Christendom holds.

The First Theory

By one theory, the local bodies merge into the general body, become a part of it, and are subject to it. Whatever authority or power belongs in the local organization is transferred with varying degrees of completeness to the large organization. This is the Romish theory. All hierarchical bodies hold it. So, also, in a more modified form, all Presbyterial bodies. Hence the expressions, "The Holy Catholic Church"; "The English Church"; "The Methodist Church South," "North"; "The Southern Presbyterian Church"; etc. In all these bodies the local congregations have been legally merged.

There is no such phraseology in the New Testament. We read of the "Churches of Galatia," "all the churches," "the church at Corinth," "Ephesus," "Philippi," etc., but never of one church taking in the local congregations of a province or of the world. On this apostasy from the New Testament ideal of a church Rome and all hierarchical and Presbyterial denominations are built. The restoration of the true conception of a church would destroy them all in a day.

The Second Theory

The second view is that held by Congregationalists and Baptists. According to this, the church never merges into, nor becomes a part of, a general body. It is, indeed, common to hear statements to the effect that a certain church belongs to a certain association or convention; the meaning being that it is one of a group of churches which affiliate with and work through the body named. As to the body itself—that which meets from time to time for the consideration of questions of common interest—churches do not and cannot belong to it. They could only do so by meeting all together, or by delegating and transferring their functions and powers through chosen men into general bodies. Under the first conception, the churches would merge into a great mass meeting and lose their autonomy. Under the second, as under the first, the churches would violate their divine charter and cease to be New Testament churches.

The true conception of a general body is that it is for counsel, with no ecclesiastical functions, and, therefore, having no authority over the churches. No particular kind of organization is ordained for general gatherings, though the Scriptures warrant both counsel and cooperation between New Testament churches. General bodies are variously formed according to the wishes and needs of those forming them. They severally exist with their own constitutions. Connection with them is purely voluntary. Some of them admit messengers from churches only. Some adopt the numerical basis. Others adopt a financial basis. Others still, a mixed basis. The whole matter of organization is with those forming the constitution.

These General Bodies

It is of the utmost importance to keep it clear that these general bodies, however great or worthy, can add nothing to the churches. The least church in the land is complete by itself. If it cooperates, it is simply a church. If it does not cooperate, it is not any the less a church. A convention adds nothing to a church. Whatever privileges any church may enjoy in cooperation spring from the constitution of the convention, and not out of the constitution of the church. Privileges of membership may be, and constantly are, enlarged or contracted according to the judgment of those forming these general bodies.

Arguments from the nature of churches in support of representation, according to numbers and from churches only, all arise from a misconception of the true idea of conventions. They are not and cannot be representative bodies in the common acceptation of the term "representative." The churches cannot invest messengers with any of the rights, powers, authority, or responsibilities of the churches themselves.

Why Baptist Conventions?

The foregoing being true, why Baptist conventions? If the churches cannot transfer to a general body any of their functions or burdens of responsibility; if every ecclesiastical quality must remain at home, even in the weakest of churches, why be at pains and expense to hold conventions?

Conventions stand, like Sunday school, newspapers, printing houses, and much else, in the order of means, and not in the realm of doctrine and divine order. For lack of a proper discrimination between what stands in the order of means and what stands in the order of doctrine, many minds have been confused. Singing and making melody in the heart to God is doctrine, never to be changed by church choirs or what not. Hymn books and organs are means to be used or not as worshipers choose.

Church independence, like the freedom of the redeemed soul, is a great blessing, full of gracious possibilities. But it may be turned to a very poor account if there be not sound discretion. It needs to be well considered. Independence is not isolation. Free men and free churches need not adopt a hermit life. Independence ought to and will stand for all that common sense, led by the Spirit, makes possible, if we be worthy of it. The New Testament doctrine of church and individual liberty opens the way for all cooperation that gracious hearts and wise heads can think or plan. In the apostolic age blood-bought liberty turned, under the lead of the Spirit and by the persuasion of a common purpose, to cooperation. Antioch and Jerusalem cooperated in counsel and act to uphold sound doctrine. Many churches cooperated in spreading the gospel, as Paul's letters show.

The Purpose of a Convention

The purpose of a convention is to promote cooperation in matters of common concern. How is this accomplished? Let us consider the following: A convention should be, and usually is, composed of that element among us most interested in the things for which the body was organized. For this reason, a financial basis is wise and right. Those who see the farthest, feel the most, and give as they feel will make the best leadership in thought and plan. While the churches cannot delegate anything, nor in any wise project their powers beyond their limits, still, if they choose, they can name brethren to attend a convention.

These "messengers of the churches," male and female, representing the working and most interested part of the various church memberships will bring with them, not the authority of the churches, but the feelings and wishes of the bodies sending them. Assembled in numbers from over a given field, convenient for cooperation, the general body will represent a consensus of opinion and feeling, and out of that consensus will come plans to submit to the churches for their adoption and use if they so wish. These messengers are the nexus through whom the wishes of the churches are conveyed to the convention, and the common feelings and wishes of the brotherhood, conveyed back to the several churches. The effect is unity in plans, great spiritual stimulation, and, as a result, practical cooperation, and increased usefulness in doing the work committed to the several churches.

And this is why we have conventions: to unify thought by disseminating information, to perfect plans, to promote active cooperation by opening channels through which the churches may unite their efforts in gospel work. All this is done without the least authority from the churches to the conventions, or back from the convention to the churches. It proceeds on the great New Testament principle of voluntary service. If any dream that this is a weak arrangement, the answer is easy. It is as strong as the piety and common sense of redeemed people, and nothing in religion can be stronger. Whatever is more than this is of men and is weakness. No service to God is good or acceptable that does not proceed on the voluntary principle, guided by an intelligent piety.

It is proper to note and emphasize the fact that conventions in reality do nothing which the churches are organized to do. They do not ordain men to preach. The churches do that. They do not authorize anyone to preach, either directly or indirectly. All authority to preach comes from God and is recognized and sanctioned in ordination by the churches. Boards, which are creatures of conventions, agree to pay men to preach at certain places on certain terms. But the boards do not actually do mission work. They are channels through which the churches do the work, just as the brethren—"messengers of the churches"— we read of in Paul's second letter to the Corinthians were the channels through which the churches fed the poor saints at Jerusalem.

Boards are channels, not fountains. They are means, not forces. The churches use them to convey their contributions as men turn a thousand streams into one channel to carry their united volume of water to arid plains that they may be watered and become fruitful fields. To elicit, combine, and direct the energies of willing workers for the carrying out of the will of Christ is the function of a convention, and this it does, not by authority, but by persuasion and the influence of intelligent piety.

The practical use of conventions is demonstrated in the conservation of forces. By a wise organization of forces, more people are reached, more money elicited, and by an intelligent direction, it accomplishes more good. A single great organization, as the Southern Baptist Convention, pursuing several lines of work, will not only conserve the forces that are to cooperate to the accomplishment of one line of work, but by a sympathetic correlation of forces, help every line of work. For instance, the Home Mission Board, with all of its influence, mightily stimulates the spirit of missions and opens up fountains of missionary supply for the Foreign Mission Board. While it is doing this, the Foreign Mission Board exerts a powerful influence on the Home Mission work. The Sunday School Board, disseminating intelligence, becomes a great factor in denominational life by helping both of the Boards.

Intelligence in Christian work, and organization for economy, and for the proper conservation of forces, through great denominational councils, becomes a denominational duty. The Scriptures abhor waste, and everywhere teach the lesson of economy. Sporadic, divergent, and often antagonistic movements always tend to waste. Unified, sympathetic movements, running, perhaps, on different lines but in harmony, always tend to economy and the highest efficiency.

CHAPTER TEN

Why Use Money for the Cause of Christ

C. E. TAYLOR

Before trying to answer any question, it is always desirable to have a clear notion as to the meaning of its several terms. Sometimes it will happen that as soon as these terms are understood in their full content and significance, a query finds itself half answered. Perhaps this may be the case with the question before us.

What then is meant by "use," "money," and "the cause of Christ"?

The Word "Use"

The word "use" evidently means in this question "to employ as an instrument." To use money is not to avail ourselves of it as an end, but as a means to an end.

The Word "Money"

"Money," whether regarded as a standard of value or as a medium of exchange, is always a representative of wealth. And the most essential ideas suggested by the term "wealth" are, first, that it is adapted to gratify human wants, directly or indirectly, and, second, that it is always the product of labor. Even the simplest act of appropriation of the bounty of God in nature requires the exertion of mind and muscle. Now, all exertion, from a physiological point of view, involves the loss of blood. Every movement of the body or of any of its parts destroys muscular tissue. In rebuilding this, fresh blood is necessarily consumed. The same is true, though to a much greater extent, in mental work, for which the brain is the organ. No thought, sensation, desire, or volition is possible without the loss of blood in repairing the waste of nerve tissue. The brain is only about one-fortieth of the weight of the whole body. But it uses up about one-fifth of all the blood that the whole body uses.

The blood is the life. That which is used up in work, mental or muscular, is life-blood. Hence it is true that one's life passes into the products of his labor.

Let us repeat and emphasize this fundamental and important conception of money. Life-blood goes into one's labor. Labor is transmuted into products which have utility for the gratification of human wants and thus creates wealth. Of this wealth, money is a representative. Hence, into all the money that we have honestly earned by any kind of work, a part of our life has passed.

"Christ's Cause"

The next term to be analyzed is "Christ's cause." We may truly say, I think, that every enterprise which has for its object the spiritual or temporal well-being of men is Christ's cause. Every hospital for the relief of suffering and the prolonging of life, every library for the dissemination of knowledge, every art gallery for satisfying and increasing the love of the beautiful—all these and many others like them are institutions which have the endorsement and sympathy of the divine Master, and in a wide but true sense may be said to be embraced in the scope of His cause.

All these, however, are secondary. They are only the results of something which is more radical and vital. They are the natural outcome of the growth of the kingdom of God in the world. For when we pray, "Thy kingdom come," we are implicitly asking for improvement in government, amelioration of social order, increase of knowledge, and multiplication of charitable institutions.

To aid actively, therefore, in the building up of Christ's kingdom in the world will be the best and most direct way to aid His cause. The preaching of the gospel everywhere by men called of God to this work is the divinely appointed method for building up the kingdom. Subsidiary to this, but closely related to it, are Sunday schools, Christian education, and Christian literature of all kinds.

All who in Christ's name and for Christ's sake are preaching, teaching, organizing, writing, or publishing are helpers toward the coming of the kingdom. The same is true of all those who, by giving, help others to do these things.

To promote Christ's cause is, then, first of all to labor for the conversion and consecration of men and women. Success in this means, of course, the advance of Christ's cause also in the wider sense; for religion, once in the heart, works outward. Each individual, when soundly converted, becomes a constructive force in society. The growth and purity of the churches is the best guarantee of municipal order and of the establishment and support of all kinds of charitable and educational institutions.

Our question, then, resolves itself into this form: Why should a Christian employ as an instrument for advancing the kingdom of God the wealth into which a part of his life has been transmuted?

Many answers, varying according to the point of view occupied, suggest themselves: Of these answers, the following are submitted:

First

Because in this way the highest ends of a human life are fulfilled. To cooperate in building up the kingdom of God is to enjoy the exalted privilege of being a coworker with God.

The development of this kingdom is the central fact in human history. Compared with it, the victorious careers of conquerors and the most far-reaching achievements of statesmen shrink into insignificance. The constitution and laws of this kingdom of redemption were made by infinite wisdom at the behest of infinite love. That this constitution is to be established and that these laws are to be enforced is as certain as that natural law is now asserting its sway. This culmination may be a "far off event," but for centuries it has been evident that the one constant purpose which runs through the ages is a divine purpose and that it will be fulfilled only when the kingdom of God shall be coextensive with the whole world. In proportion as any man, by giving as well as by laboring, shall transmute his life into an active force for extending the kingdom of redemption, he is making the most possible out of that life. The life that passes into money, when devoted to other things, perishes; when it is built into the kingdom of righteousness, it will endure forever.

Second

Because it results in the development of Christian character. The very thought that one is a coworker with God in the highest and noblest endeavor possible for a human being will lift a man up out of himself and straighten him up toward the dignity of the highest manhood. It will call into exercise all the best powers of his soul and develop each into fullness of power.

God is not dependent on the churches for the means with which to extend His kingdom or feed His poor. He knows where numberless diamonds sparkle unseen by human eye, where thousands of tons of gold are hidden in the earth, undiscovered as yet by human avarice. He could, if this were His plan, send an angel to whisper in the ears of mission secretaries and college treasurers the hiding places of these treasures. No, it is not because of any dependence on us that God calls for our labor and gifts. He could have achieved His purpose without our aid. But He knew that it is more blessed to give than to receive, that reaction is as important as the action, and therefore He calls upon us to give and to labor. Otherwise there would be no opportunity for cultivating and developing the benevolent affections. Evangelization and sanctification are to be reciprocal.

Beneficence is one of a sisterhood of graces. When Paul urged the Christians in Corinth to "abound in this grace also," he put beneficence in the same family with faith and love and diligence. All these graces are products of the work of the Spirit in regeneration and sanctification. The product of the new birth is a new man—not a mutilated or partial man, but one complete in every part, though there may be imperfect development. To speak of a Christian without beneficence is as absurd as to speak of a Christian without faith. God has made no such oversight as to convert a man and yet leave him under the control of covetousness. Of one who has not learned to give, the Scripture asks, "How dwelleth the love of God in him?"

Third

Whether we take this inspired expression to mean Christ's love for us or our love for Him, we find in it a reason and a motive for giving. Paul referred to "the grace of God bestowed on the churches of Macedonia" which was manifested in "the riches of their liberality" as an example for the church at Corinth. He appealed to this church to give liberally "to prove the sincerity of your love" for Christ, and then reminds them of Christ's love for them as another motive; "though He was rich, yet for your sakes He became poor, that ye through His poverty might become rich."

Love kills selfishness and begets beneficence. As Christ's love for us constrained Him through sacrifice of Himself to bring us into His kingdom, so our love for Him constrains us, through sacrifice of ourselves, or of that into which our lives have passed, to lead others into His kingdom.

Fourth

Because giving is demanded by our relations to our fellow men.

Paul recognized the obligation when he said that he was a debtor both to the Greeks and to the barbarians—to all men, civilized and uncivilized. "All the law," said he, "is fulfilled in one word, even in this, thou shalt love thy neighbor as thyself." And Christ has answered the suggested question, "Who then is my neighbor?"

There is human brotherhood because there is divine fatherhood. We are to do good unto all men as we have opportunity. And there comes to us a widening conception of the "opportunity" when we remember that through the transmutation of ourselves into money, which is a universal representative of wealth and labor, we can do good to thousands now living and yet unborn, in all lands. We have no right to limit our efforts and gifts to those in our own community whom we can reach directly. Duty demands that indirectly, also, we shall give ourselves to those whom we have never seen and never can see.

Fifth

Because giving is commanded by Christ.

Numerous are the spiritual admonitions in regard to giving; numerous are the promises to the liberal. The commands may all be summed up in the brief order of Him whom we call our Master and King. "Freely ye have received, freely give."

If there were no other answer to the "why" under consideration, this one would be sufficient. The Lord, dealing with us as intelligent moral beings, reveals to us or enables us to discern for ourselves many reasons for the discharge of our duties. But if, in any case, we can discover no ground for an obligation save that it is the will of Christ, this is sufficient.

Especially should Baptists put strong emphasis upon this last reason. In all matters pertaining to church polity, we insist upon strict obedience to Christ's commands and upon compliance with apostolic injunction and example. We should insist upon an obedience no less prompt and exact to our Lord's command to give freely.

Christ bids us go into all the world and preach His gospel. We obey through the money which we freely give. Our life passes into the money. The money buys that which passes into the life of far distant workers. Through this medium our life-blood passes into their arteries. He that giveth and he that goeth are one and they shall rejoice together.

PART II

Selections from
The School of the Church,
by J. M. Frost

CHAPTER ELEVEN

The Threefold Church Relation

Its Relation to the Church

The Sunday school of today is a school—a gathering for instruction. It has all the elements of a school, with some elements which make it distinct in character, unique in purpose, method, and curriculum. It is in the church, of the church, and for the church—a church school in every true and commanding sense. It has a threefold relation to the church, being a church institution, and, when in operation, a church service and agency. It is a mighty instrument for bringing things to pass in the kingdom of God, but gets its life, power, and directing energy in the church, in the very structure and efficiency of which it forms an organic part.

The question of the Sunday school's relation to the church was a subject of much discussion forty years ago. It held chief place on the programs of Conventions, and provoked oftentimes earnest contention and even conflict, but always without satisfactory settlement. That question, though not of easy categorical answer, has been settled, not however by discussion, but through wonderful development of spiritual forces and by what may be called the natural adjustment of spiritual agencies making for the building of the kingdom. As an institution, the Sunday school has the fostering care of the church, and when assembled is the teaching agency of the church, but so seasoned by prayer and song and lofty spirit as to make it a service of worship in the church of God. And so it has come to a conspicuous and commanding place, and its influence for good girdles the world.

The History of Its Growth

The Sunday school as an institution has come through the growth of years, more than a century now, and its history may be traced through the lives of illustrious men, who wrought each his part and passed it on to those who came after. It has a remarkable record, having come to its place by slow degrees, and oftentimes encountering grave difficulties and even severe oppositions. And yet in this respect it has fared perhaps as well as the weekday school. The present object, however, is not to write its history, for that would require a volume within itself, but simply to emphasize its record from what it was to what it is, and how from the smallest beginning, like the mountain stream that grows into the river, it has become one of the mightiest institutions in the world. It won its way and came to its triumph because of what it could do, as a propaganda of New Testament principles, and in the way of saving the young. It made the church more efficient in its mission among men for the honor of Christ as its Head and King, and for His glory as the Savior of sinners.

Robert Raikes and William Fox

The Sunday school was not of the church at first, but had its rise apart and in the interest of reform and philanthropy. The school of Robert Raikes of the Church of England, besides getting its name from the day of its meeting, had no connection with the church except perhaps in the character of the noble man with his largeness of heart as the product of the church. The church produced Raikes and Raikes produced his school, which opened in a private home at Gloucester, July, 1780, with a gathering of boys, for instruction in reading, writing, arithmetic, and spelling.

It was a Sunday school only because that was the day of its meeting, and Mr. Raikes himself with large benevolent purposes regarded the work as "attempts at civilization." But there he found his renown, for his school is thought to have been the foundation of the public school system first in England and then in the United States. Beginning with this class of boys, and with limited purpose, he yet built for coming centuries. It was but a beginning, and yet its future went beyond calculation as to what it should do in the history of the world.

Also simultaneously with the Raikes movement came the independent movement of William Fox, a layman in a Baptist church. He was born in the same county as Robert Raikes, the same year (1736) and the same day of the month—Fox, February 14th and Raikes, September 14th. As a young man Fox began business in London, first as retail merchant, then wholesale dealer, and became wealthy. He purchased his old home estate at Clapton, where he was born, and there started his first school, also in a private house. This school had its meeting on weekdays, but with the Bible as its textbook, and paid its teachers for their service. This was the beginning of the Bible school which would become the Sunday school.

In correspondence and conference with Raikes, William Fox got the idea of Sunday as the day of meeting. He brought the Bible into the Sunday school, put the Sunday school in charge of the Bible as its textbook, and made the study of the Scriptures its chief purpose. Later looking to the enlargement of the work, Fox offered a resolution in a meeting of the church of which he was a member, May, 1785, "that the meeting call upon the various denominations of England to unite in the organization of a society for the promotion of Bible study among the children of England." The resolution was adopted, the call was made, the society was organized September 7, 1785, and became "The Society for the Support and Encouragement of Sunday Schools."

The name was afterward changed to "The Society for Promoting Sunday School Throughout the British Dominion." But that date and meeting marked the real beginning of the modern Sunday school movement as an organized effort for the study of God's Word. Two years later (1787) Fox closed up his business, and devoted himself to advancing the Sunday school cause of Great Britain, and was for forty years England's most prominent Sunday school man. In a little while William Brodie Gurney, who in his boyhood days was frequently in the home of William Fox, appeared on the scene. He was a younger man than Fox, but became companion and associate with him in his new movement, and gave his services as teacher without pay, and so started the volunteer system of Sunday school teaching.

Fox fixed the baseline along which the whole movement should go through the succeeding years. From his time on, the work grew rapidly, making not only its own history but also a place for itself among other great movements in history, which have since blessed and gladdened the world. It would be interesting to trace some of these, and show the relation of this mighty growing power to other great enterprises in their rise and onward progress. Always helping and never hindering, the Sunday school has proved a blessing everywhere, whether in making individual character, or as a dynamic force in the churches, or exerting its influence in the educational life of the nations. Over against this humble beginning we simply place the present imperial character of this institution, with its gigantic enterprise and investments for the kingdom of God as seen in the churches today.

From William Fox of London
to Benjamin F. Jacobs of Chicago

They were separated by almost a century, and yet over the chasm of years they joined hands in oneness of spirit and purpose—Fox in his movement for promoting Bible study in the Sunday school, and Jacobs in his Uniform Lesson System for making the Sunday school what it is, and for unifying the Christian world in the study and teaching of the Scriptures. The Sunday school antedates and made possible the International Sunday School Association, and in turn the Association has done wonders in advancing the Sunday school cause and for development in the Sunday school of all the elements of real power and greatness.

The Association draws its life from the several denominations, and then brings to them large returns in the way of inspiration, and in setting before them high ideals for the betterment of the Sunday school cause in their own churches. Moreover, to meet the demands of the Sunday school, there are immense business interests and investments which easily count into the millions. Large moneyed powers, therefore, are set for its advancement.

And measured even by commercial standards, the Sunday school as an enterprise in church life is gigantic and of almost startling proportions. Out of all these phases of its activities, energies, and relations comes its almost boundless power to help and bless, to uplift and enlarge, to save and train for Christ in the service of His kingdom. Throughout all the years, and with a growth beyond compare, with shifting and changing methods, the Sunday school holds steadfastly to its original and cardinal idea of a school in the church for teaching the Word of God.

Its Center of Energy in the Local Church

The Sunday school is a local affair, has its definite center of activity, and does its work within its own sphere. Even what it does in the widest sweep of its activities, it does as having the center of its energies in the local church. This is true notwithstanding the Sunday school itself is sometimes the planting of some mission station from which a church eventually comes. This indeed has often been the course of sowing and reaping. Behind every such planting there is the influence of the church again directly or indirectly—one planting, another watering, and God giving the increase. The local Sunday school emphasizes the local church as the center of its agency, enriches the life of the church, and augments its efficiency.

The word "church" designates a local organization, called sometimes the individual, particular, or single church, to distinguish it from the larger conception and more general idea. This makes more definite and holds more strictly to what is here intended in our thought of the Sunday school as a church school. Christ's church as He set it for the expression and making of His kingdom was first one, then more than one, then a vast multitude, multiplying throughout the countries and centuries—but holding always its local idea and mission, as in the church at Ephesus or the church of God at Corinth. Then as now Christ first saved men individually, then grouped them into churches.

Men are regenerated by units, renewed by the Spirit of God one at a time, then set in churches for Christian culture and service. So the church has a spiritual membership, is entrusted with keeping the ordinances of the Lord's house as He commanded, and is commissioned to propagate His gospel to the uttermost parts of the earth. Christendom does not appear as a church, not having local habitation or organic life. Christians, as we think of them, the world over and in the aggregate, are not a church, but a glorious people, a mighty host saved by the grace of God, and gathered in churches almost without number, as may come from conditions and circumstances.

These churches are local centers of Christian energy and activity. This is no disparagement of the individual member in the fullness of all he may do for Christ. It rather makes him the greater through the oneness of the many and in the force of aggregate power. This is the fellowship of life and service, of doctrinal character and power, a sitting together in heavenly places in Christ Jesus.

A Chosen Agency in the Furtherance of Its Work

The Sunday school in the church is a manifestation of church life, an outgo of energy, a method of activity, with definiteness of purpose and aim. It is neither "the nursery of the church," nor a "workshop," but here the church, through its school as one of its chosen instruments, is itself at work in the spirit which it has caught from heaven, and for the fulfillment of the mission which it receives from the heavenly King. Everything the church holds dear, every great interest and enterprise in which the church is engaged, everything which the church needs, whether for making it strong and mighty within, or powerful and projective in its influence upon the community—all is fostered and magnified in this school of the church, first made possible and then brought to pass.

The school becomes as an agency what the church makes it; it is capable of almost indefinite expansion in church efficiency as a channel for the output of its energy and life. While holding steadfastly to the one basal purpose of teaching the Scriptures, the Sunday school has yet greatly widened in its aim. As a force for study and teaching the Word of God; as a force for evangelizing and bringing lost sinners to the Savior; as a force for instruction and education in the mightiest things claiming the attention of men; as a force for mission operation in the world-wide sense; as a force for making Christian character in men and women; and for opening the door of usefulness on a large scale—in all these things so essential in the life and mission of the church, the Sunday school holds rank among its very first and chosen agencies.

It is at once field and force, giving opportunity to do and power to do, for building the kingdom of God. The Sunday school was not this at the first, but through the growth of years has come to this rank in modern church life, and challenges the admiration and cooperative support of all who themselves would do large things for God in the world, and who desire to see the church come to the full in turning many to righteousness, in shining as the stars, in making the name of Christ great among the nations of the earth.

Where the Altar Stands for Worship

Furthermore, the Sunday school in session, while still maintaining its function of teaching and its service of activity, is also a service for the worship of God. This indeed should be the chief glory of the Sunday school. The worship of God in the beauty of holiness should distinguish its meeting as a sacred meeting, and its service as a holy service. This should be the all-pervasive and holding power with the school as a whole in the opening and closing moments, also throughout all its grades and in every class whether of beginners or adults.

This is the most momentous phase of the service, demanded by all urgent and lofty considerations. It rests with teachers and officers as to whether this worshipful spirit shall be present or absent. This will be the mark of whether the school is "sounding brass or tinkling cymbal," or a living power in fulfillment of its mission and purpose. It is not easy to maintain this spirit of devotion and worship in the stir and drive of the school; it will require thoughtfulness and previous consideration, with earnestness of purpose to hold oneself to this supreme and most commanding attitude of mind and heart.

I am not pleading for a goodness that is "goody-goody," but for worship in spirit and in truth, for a godliness that is robust and cheery, for a godliness in form, but also in such power as makes heaven what it is. Let there be no thought for a moment that the worship of God has anything of gloom or shadow. Rather with soberness and deepness of spiritual flow, it will augment the buoyancy and joy of the service. It will bring in the sunshine and give dignity of character to all that is done, whether in singing, or praying, or talking, or teaching. In the presence of such worship, and under the spell of its power, unobtrusive but felt throughout the school, even the minor matters feel its touch and marshal up with the things which are great.

Of course God in the majesty and glory of His being is not circumscribed by time or place as to where we may worship

Him. God is no respecter of persons, and there is access to the throne whenever and wherever the soul cries out after Him. And yet it is manifest from His Word, from all history of dealing with men, and from the experience of His people, that it is worth while to have a set time and place for meeting Him in worship. And there is no better place than His sanctuary, and no better time than in His service.

The training influence of worship is immense, of the highest character and helpful in every way. It fosters the sense of reverence as the basal element of character, and makes for strength in doing work for God. This high service cannot be commanded; it comes not from dictation nor from simple requirements. The ringing of a thousand bells cannot ring it in. It comes as the daylight comes, as the atmosphere comes, as the sweet aroma of devout hearts, as the indescribable outgo of spiritual imbued with the Spirit of God. Blessed, many times blessed, are those who without ado can yet make God's presence felt in the Sunday school as a real power, and can add to the beauty and richness of its service in the worship of Him who is all glorious in praise. It puts the Sunday school in kinship with the service which the angels render, glorifies it, augments its power to compass the ends for which it meets.

Viewed as It Now Is

No words can portray the Sunday school in its present commanding character, or its unmeasured power for God, as seen in its threefold relation to the church as institution, agency, and service. This chapter may come to a fitting close in giving the estimate of another—Dr. William E. Hatcher, of Virginia, in his book *The Pastor and the Sunday School*, when speaking out of the fullness of his heart and from large experience in practical work as a pastor:

> These simple reflections lead us up to the central thought of this lecture—the imperial rank of the Sunday school in the community of Christian enterprises. . . . In many respects the Sunday school is a modest institution. It is a vast improvement on the past, and is one of the phenomenal products of Christianity, worthy of universal recognition

as the most flexible, far-reaching institution ever yet devised for the conversion of this world. . . . It came into existence without flourish of trumpets, gained admission into the Christian heart of the world, and has received a welcome from every creed and sect. It wears about it the loftiest dignities, and yet comes with a smile for every child and a message of peace for every inquirer after the way of life.

It is not an easy task to estimate the value of the Sunday school. It is a school with a single text book, and that the Word of God, and this invests it with an interest all of its own. It has calmly chosen the entire human family as its constituency, and is enrolling its students by the millions. I stand uncovered before the achievements of the Sunday school. What mammoth organizations it has called into existence to do its bidding and minister to its wants. It has created a literature of its own, and is fast learning how to appropriate to itself all true literature. It has kinship for all noble things, and draws from every quarter material for its own advancement. Itself a peerless educational power, it infuses its broadening educational spirit into all other things.

What royal friends and supporters it has—ministers, scholars, eminent teachers from colleges and universities, men of every noble profession, men of affairs, men of wealth and power in the large walks of trade and finance, and better yet, women chosen of God and in living fellowship with his Son, Jesus Christ, missions of them, whose perpetual joy is the study of the word which God has spoken unto us.

"no statistician will ever be able to count up its contributions to the kingdom of heaven. . . . Think of the countless thousands which year by year are conducted to the gates of the Celestial Kingdom and introduced into the master's service by this benign Christian force. Think of the armies upon armies of the young who have gone to heaven shouting the Redeemer's praises as they went. They were the fruit of the Sunday school, and yet the schools, like the orchards of God, are bearing twelve manner of fruit every month.

Such is the commanding place of this school in its threefold character. It is a church institution, living, powerful, and growing, an agency of the church mighty in doing things for the kingdom, a church service of teaching and worship exalted and preeminent in place and purpose. The mission and glory of the church becomes the mission and glory of its school.

CHAPTER TWELVE

The Teacher as God's Interpreter

The Process of Teaching

We come now to the teacher's task of teaching. In the process there are three elements—the teacher, the pupil, and something to teach. The teacher may teach books or boys—if boys, then he must have something to teach; if books, then he must have some one to listen and learn. The teacher has two related questions—what to do with his pupil, and what with his subject. One question relates to class formation and management, the other to the process of teaching. To match the one to the other in a way to be effective and have the scholar learn, the teaching must be adapted to the pupil, and the teacher must all the while keep in view his purpose and aim.

The synonyms of teaching are significant: "To give instruction, inform, inculcate, tell, guide, counsel, admonish." In every case there is teacher, subject, and scholar, but what is the teaching process?

In the last analysis the teacher is interpreter, and teaching is interpretation. This is true of all teaching, concerning all subjects and in every school. The process is begun in simple form with teaching the alphabet in the secular school or the illustrative work of the kindergarten; it is followed on through the higher grades, through college and university, and on beyond the schools with all subjects, and in every department of learning where teaching is done. The teacher throughout interprets, connects heart with heart, spirit with spirit in the process of thinking, and in the deeper process of feeling, transfers thought from mind to mind, while the teacher teaches and the scholar learns.

Something like this is the process, wherever teaching is done, and points out the teacher's task, whatever be his subject of his school. The teacher stands before his class to say concerning any subject, *which being interpreted means.* This applies with special emphasis in the Sunday school, and requires mastership in teaching for this church service where the Word of God is the subject for study and interpretation. The Sunday school teacher is God's interpreter among men, makes Him known out of His Word, points out His will and way, in high sense speaks for Him. There must be earnest purpose and aim to interpret aright the mighty themes which engage his attention—to tell what they mean as the doctrines of God, and apply them to those who hear. The teacher is a bearer of God's thought in God's Word.

Christ Our Model Interpreter

He was the incomparable teacher, because He was the world's greatest interpreter. He really taught; His teaching was teaching, the lodgment in heart and mind of the mighty things which He communicated to men. We need a new vision of Him as teacher. Of course He was more than teacher—God manifest in the flesh, the Savior of sinners by His death on the cross. But He was also teacher, and these higher qualities gave emphasis to His teaching and exalted His office and function as teacher. No man ever taught as He taught, simply because no man interpreted as He interpreted. With His Word He touched human hearts, and they lay open to the sunlight; He touched the mysteries of the kingdom of God, and they became simple, beautiful, fragrant, like flowers of the garden.

He taught His disciples, taught the multitudes, taught them out of the Scriptures, taught them the things of the kingdom. Under His touch old things were set in new relations, and took on new meaning, while new things came at His call to enlarge the world's vision and make glad the hearts of men. In His parables nature and custom and commonest affairs did His bidding to convey the mightiest truth to the people, so as to have the people understand His meaning. In growing trees He made His disciples see His kingdom expanding and coming to fullness. In the golden harvest fields He made them see the world's need and hear the call for more laborers.

His ever-recurring Word, "the kingdom of heaven is like unto," was the signal for coming wonders, and His resemblances are fresh and powerful unto this day. Our Lord made nature vocal in explaining the mysteries of the kingdom. With His touch of interpretation, the falling sparrow took on new meaning and made luminous the great doctrine of divine care and providence. The lily of the valley, too, heard His Word, and opened the morning sun with fresh notes to declare the glory of His kingdom and the greater glory of the King.

The Interpretation of Transcendent Themes

We need to renew our study of Christ as teacher, the model interpreter, not only as to method, but also as to substance and purpose of His teaching. We must have His vision and viewpoint, see things as He saw them in their proper relation, and maintain His point of emphasis and His vital Word of authority. We need to follow Him in teaching as well as to obey Him in keeping His commandments. Even though we look on Him as incomparable and unapproachable, we can yet follow after Him in method and substance of teaching. Having His Word for our

Word, His eyes for our eyes, we may see as He saw and interpret as He interpreted—speak His Word after Him, and the word which He bids us speak.

The subjects which engaged our Savior's attention were of infinite moment to men in every age of the world's history, and concern them both for the life that now is and the life which reaches beyond the stars. In His person, life, and teaching, He interpreted God and God's Word; interpreted Satan as a dark shadow on His path, a person with purpose and ever-driving effort to thwart the things of the kingdom, and as set for the ruin of the souls of men; interpreted sin with its deadly effect in human hearts, with its blighting and ruinous power wherever it touches; interpreted men to themselves, in their relation to each other, in their high relation to God, how they should conduct themselves in this life, and what they should do for His kingdom; interpreted human destiny as wrought out here, but finding its fruitage hereafter, when the King shall come in His glory with the holy angels to judge the world, and men shall be separated, some to everlasting life and some to everlasting punishment.

He brought life and immortality to light in the gospel, and by His resurrection from the dead opened a highway through the grave and demonstrated that He was the Son of God with power. His Word is the authoritative Word on these great subjects, and all related subjects. Our Lord had His audience now with many, and again with only one; sometimes with His select few, and again with the multitude, who gathered to hear His message or for the loaves and fishes. He taught them all, whether one or many, the things concerning the kingdom, and adapted His teaching to His hearer and with heart-searching fitness—probing deep or touching with a gentleness and tenderness which would not break the bruised reed or quench the smoking flax.

He opened the Book, "found the place where it was written," and taught the people as one having authority. Their eyes were fastened on Him, their hearts were moved under the power of His teaching, and they wondered at the gracious words which proceeded out of His mouth.

The Sunday School Teacher's Audience

What to do with his subject is the teacher's most urgent question, but that cannot be determined apart from the pupil or scholar, whether many or few, and what to do with an audience or class is itself a momentous issue. The same subjects which engaged our Lord's ministry, which then awakened and made glad the hearts of the people, are today the subjects of Sunday school teaching. Here, even as the Master did, the teacher opens the Book, made larger now by the New Testament, and finds the place where it is written. Out of the Book he gets his authoritative Word, speaks for the King, gives out his authoritative message of grace and truth. The teacher should magnify his class in heart and mind as his audience, worthy of commanding consideration, regardless of how many or what age. He comes to his class even as his Lord came to the people, bearing treasures from the storehouse of the King, laden and rich with the good things of the kingdom.

We use the words "pupil" and "scholar" in a somewhat elastic way as applied to those attending Sunday school. This is unavoidable perhaps, and yet unfortunate, lest we fail to accord this service its rightful dignity and character as a school, and then fail again to rightly recognize its class work as a teaching process. But there is advantage in the wide range of condition with those who attend; it makes the field more diversified, and ever white unto the harvest, enlarges the opportunity, and gives possibilities which no man can measure. The attendance is of all ages, from the very young child to men and women far advanced in years, of all degrees of training and lack of training, of all conditions in social life, family life, and other methods of classifying and grading.

These present almost infinite variety, but also infinite possibility for God and for the good of mankind—much like the multitudes, we may imagine, which greeted the great Teacher on the mountain side, the lake shore, or the crowded street. They are gathered here in this teaching service of the church of Christ, with Him as its center and inspiration, with its teachers to stand in His stead and teach out of His doctrine as His interpreters among men.

Assembled in Classes for Instruction

"Pupil" has reference to setting them in classes for direction and management; "scholar" refers to learning on their part and teaching on the teacher's part. There must, of course, be wise distribution of scholars and teachers, with graded lessons, and especially graded teaching—grading the classes by age for the most part, but possibly sometimes by other considerations, separate classes and separate classrooms, with everything done to the best advantage and for the most effective service. Notwithstanding this distribution of scholars into classes, the school preserves its strong and beautiful oneness. It is the amalgamation of many into one, made homogeneous somewhat, combined into one uniform whole, with one purpose and largely in one spirit, while the separate class as the teacher's audience opens the way for the teacher and gives emphasis for the teaching service.

This one class is the teacher's concern, the burden of his heart, but also his joy and crown of rejoicing. The conditions call for the best teachers, and these teachers at their best. There must be devoutness of spirit and faithfulness in teaching. "The humblest worker in the mill can do an absolutely ideal work if he is doing it in the right spirit. This whole social fabric of ours is only a gigantic mill, and the eternal value of our work does not depend upon the question of whether the wheel we have to turn is a small one or a large one." These noble words from Professor Munsterberg, so true and beautiful for every position and relation of life, have distinct significance for the Sunday school teacher with his one class gathered in the church service to study and teach the Word of God.

How often and sadly we do miss it, in our judgment as to what is small and what large. In this school throughout, the present borders on the future, the temporal on the eternal, the mightiest educational processes are at work. The teacher who sees nothing great in his class, nothing momentous in this teaching hour, or has inadequate sense of responsibility in handling the Word of

136

God is like the preacher who fails in personal respect for his audience and undervalues its meaning. He dishonors his message as coming from the King, and falls short in his ministry of the high calling of God. The greatness of the Sunday school class is measured not by the number or age of its members, but by their spiritual need, by the greatness of the teacher's message, by the immeasurable greatness of his possible achievements. This exalted but just conception of the teacher's function greatly magnifies his office, and should be his inspiration and joy.

To Interpret God and His Word

This is the process and first aim in Sunday school instruction, and is needed alike by all scholars, whether adult or children of very tender years. The large classes of men, being formed in Sunday schools throughout the country, and becoming more frequent and commanding, greatly emphasize the importance of Sunday school work and augment its efficiency for making better church life and better service in the kingdom of God. But we must not allow ourselves to undervalue the smaller class or the work of teaching those who are younger—even the youngest and most unpromising. It is wonderful to teach anyone in the thought of God, child or grownup person. Their spiritual need is much the same, and must be met in much the same way through the Scriptures as the instrument of teaching, with the teacher being interpreter of God's thought and Word and will.

Our Savior was moved with compassion when He saw the multitude, not merely the number, but the need of those who thronged Him. He saw their hunger, but also their deeper need. They were as sheep without shepherd, lost, and without a Savior. This condition of the class, this heart need of the scholars, of whatever age, and whether many or few, is what holds the teacher to his task, and stirs in him the spirit and mission of his Master. He is moving in the sphere of eternal value, is at the very point where heaven and earth cooperate in a way to make joy among the angels of God.

The teaching hour is a momentous hour. Mighty issues hang in the balance and await the turning of the scale. The teacher thinks God's thought after Him, speaks His Word as He would have it spoken, and in the meaning which He intends, interprets God and His Word that others may know Him. The question who is God, and what of Him, is incomparably the greatest question which can engage the human mind, a question the right answer to which is paramount to all else, a question, too, in reach of the child and the unschooled, while taxing to the utmost the profoundest thinkers.

Bunyan's "Mr. Wrong Thoughts About God" was a real character, whose successors even now are abroad in the land, working havoc in nearly every department of learning. A recent writer charges even the great theologians with "misrepresenting God." But the man who can set aside the world's great theologians with a wave of the hand is liable himself to be wide of the mark, and little suited to lead others aright in their thinking.

Manifestly we are dependent on the Scriptures both in forming our own views of God and in teaching others to know Him. We need to follow the thought, and even use the language, of those who spoke for Him when moved by the Holy Spirit in the day of special inspiration. To tell who God is, what God thinks, what God says, and what are His purposes—to venture into this kingdom of high interpretation, is enough to make an angel hesitate, and yet is exactly the sphere and mission of the Sunday school teacher. To think right thoughts about God, and to rightly represent God's thoughts, is of infinite concern. It gives base line and bearing for correct thought on religion and all religious matters; is the undergirding of all Sunday school instruction, the bolting through and through of all doctrinal character and life, of all holy living and godly endeavor.

Examples of How to Interpret

It is not possible to define God. The Bible nowhere undertakes either definition or proof of His existence. It tells glorious things of Him, however, things which speak for themselves as the sun in the splendor of noon, of His being and person, of His infinite attributes and inexpressible greatness. Those who know most of Him feel most profoundly that there is "none like unto

Him, glorious in holiness, fearful in praises, doing wonders." The heaven of heavens cannot contain Him, and the whole earth is full of His glory. Yet with condescension pass finding out He bends the heavens and comes down, is mindful of men in these wondrous words of His own speaking: "Them that honor Me I will honor; they that despise Me shall be lightly esteemed."

In the Book of God we may walk with Him and think His thoughts after Him. In its pages, heaven-lit with the glory of His presence, we have examples of interpretation and lofty terms in which we can think and express our thoughts concerning Him. This is our standard of interpretation, and must command the heart and conscience in teaching. It is lofty thinking, and the noblest mold in which to cast our thoughts. The writers in the Old and New Testament alike spoke with unerring authority while our Lord was Himself His own authority in making revelation of the Father.

These interpret God so that others may know Him in relation to their sin, show Him at once the God of wrath with consuming fire for those who repent not and believe not, but also the God of infinite love with saving grace to such as seek His pardoning mercy in the blood which was shed for sin. They came by the way of the cross in their interpretation, and we must follow as they lead. This twofold view of God is of infinite moment to us, if we would know Him aright ourselves and interpret Him aright for others. Anything short of that is short of the truth, a discredit to the teacher, a dishonor to God, and endangers the very soul of those whom we teach, regardless of their age or other conditions. We are thinking after the King, and need to walk in the King's highway.

The Teacher's Prayer as Interpreter

Prayer in its highest form is communion, fellowship, worship of God. While the teacher tells his class of God, he also tells God about his class. The more deeply the magnitude of his work takes hold on the teacher's heart, the more he feels the need of divine help, both in the interpretation of His Word and in opening the hearts of the scholars to hear. He needs to come face to face with God before he comes face to face with his audience. He needs to pray as Moses prayed: "I beseech Thee, show me Thy glory. Send us not up hence unless Thy presence go with us." How we do need the heavenly assurance, "My presence shall go with thee."

The teacher must keep God in mind as God, and with his class must worship Him in the beauty of holiness. This is basal to all else and starts where the Bible starts. Godhood comes before Fatherhood; universal Godhood before universal Fatherhood. His being God—the I Am that I Am—gives meaning and strength to every other phase of His character and work. It is this tremendous fact that awakens the sense of reverence, worship, and awe. It is sublime and joyous to interpret God to others, whether adult or child, and of infinite moment to interpret aright that they may know aright.

A little child fresh from the Sunday school class was asked by a professed infidel this mightiest of all questions: "But how do you know there is a God?" She answered in the ardor of childhood: "Why, my teacher knows God—she just knows Him." That teacher surely walked in the ways of God, had been on the mount, and came to the class with a shining face. The child took knowledge of her, that she had been with God and learned of Him. "I beseech Thee, show me Thy glory. Send us not up hence, except Thy presence go with us."

PART III

Miscellaneous Writings
of J. M. Frost

CHAPTER THIRTEEN

How the Board Came to Be

The Sunday School Board at Nashville was established by the Southern Baptist Convention in the session of 1891 at Birmingham, Alabama. It was the final issue of a discussion which ran through several years, was conducted with tremendous energy, and stirred our people profoundly throughout the South. It was the settlement of one of the most vital and momentous questions ever raised in the Convention, and determined the far-reaching policy, that the Baptists of the South would act for themselves, and not depend on others to make their literature or conduct their publication interests or foster their Sunday school work.

The Agitation

The agitation arose first over the question whether the Convention should publish a series of Sunday school helps, and then the issue became more definite and concrete whether the Convention should have a separate and coordinate Board to take care of these several interests. The discussion went through several annual meetings of the Convention with stirring times intervening: Augusta, 1885; Montgomery, 1886; Louisville, 1887; Richmond, 1888; Memphis, 1889; Ft. Worth, 1890; and Birmingham, 1891. These dates tell simply the chronological order of events as the matter went forward. The successive meetings grew, even became crowded in attendance, while the interest became deeper and more intense, and each time the result issued in the same direction as if guided by an unseen hand toward a final goal.

Former Sunday School Board

We must, however, go further up the stream to find the source. There had been a former Sunday School Board of the Convention. It was created in 1863 at Augusta, and located first at Greenville, South Carolina. It was later removed to Memphis, and then discontinued by the Convention in the session 1873, at Mobile—marking among our people a decade of almost tragic effort, of noble achievement, and of memorable history. This early movement was led by Basil Manly, Jr., and John A. Broadus, who had charge of the Board as President and Corresponding Secretary. They were at the time professors in the Southern Baptist Theological Seminary, then located at Greenville, South Carolina, and were making an effort for the betterment of the Sunday school condition, while at the same time laying foundations for our great school of the prophets now located at Louisville, Kentucky.

Under the management of those men and their associates, that former Board founded a Sunday school paper, which was called *Kind Words*, indicative of its spirit and purpose as issued among somewhat conflicting conditions. The paper, of course, went with the Board to Memphis, and when the Board was discontinued, the paper was entrusted by the Convention to its Home Mission Board, located then in Marion, Alabama, now in Atlanta.

Kind Words abides to this day, having been published successively at Greenville, Memphis, Marion, Macon, Atlanta, and now Nashville. Through all this half century of somewhat checkered history the paper has never missed an issue, and has grown from a small monthly as a child's paper to a goodly-sized eight-page weekly, very popular with all classes. Dr. Samuel Boykin became its editor at Memphis, and continued with it through all the years until his death at Nashville in 1899.

This paper may be traced like a golden thread through the annals of the Southern Baptist Convention, and is the connecting link between the past and present, between our prosperity of today and the severe struggle of our fathers in those faraway years. It is in great sense the basis of all we have today in Sunday school life and literature. And Samuel Boykin, who, more than any one man, kept it alive, deserves a place of high rank in the world's cabinet of Sunday school heroes.

Four Years of Conflict and Progress

The removal of the Home Mission Board from Marion to Atlanta, 1882–83, with Dr. I. T. Tichenor as the new Corresponding Secretary, opened a new day in the South for Home Missions. It gave to the Home Mission Board a new career of usefulness and great enlargement. Dr. Tichenor coming to his new position walked in fellowship with Dr. Samuel Boykin, then also recently removed to Atlanta, as editor of *Kind Words*. They were possibly related by marriage, and were certainly of kindred spirit. The editor strengthened the stakes, the Secretary lengthened the cords; one held the base while the other swept the field. No one surpassed the new Secretary as dreamer of dreams and seer of visions in denominational needs and power of conquest, and not many equaled him in making others, through his eloquence on the platform, see what he saw and believe what he believed.

Under his leadership the Southern Baptist Convention was first brought to consider the proposition at Augusta, 1885, and then a year later at Montgomery, to authorize the Home Board to publish a series of Sunday school helps—provided no indebtedness should be incurred. The plans were laid and carried out with great forethought and ability. The committee which made this report to the Convention consisted of E. W. Warren, Georgia, chairman; W. C. Cleveland, Alabama; A. T. Spalding, Texas; H. H. Harris, Virginia; D. A. Wilson, Mexico; M. D. Early, Arkansas; A. P. Scofield, Louisiana; H. M. Wharton, Maryland; and J. W. Bozeman, Mississippi.

Acting under the instruction and led on by their Secretary, the Home Mission Board issued the "Kind Words Series of Sunday School Periodicals" under a five-year contract with printers in Atlanta on a royalty basis. The series consisted of *Kind Words*, *The Child's Gem*, *Kind Words Teacher* (a monthly magazine), and three quarterlies. We shall have more to say of these periodicals further on in our story. They are introduced now simply as a new enterprise in the Convention's life, and the immediate occasion of perhaps the most trying disturbance in the experience of our people. Dr. Tichenor believed in the movement profoundly, even unto conviction, and walked the heights in his vision of what these periodicals were worth for the onward movement of our cause.

I recall an incident concerning him. We had attended a State Mission Board meeting in Selma, Alabama, where I was then pastor. Though after midnight, we stood at the gate of his friend Captain Hugh Haralson, with whom he was stopping, and talked for two hours—rather he talked and I listened. I was sympathetic, but unable to follow his sweep of thought in outlining the future, showing what the Baptists of the South might accomplish, and the imperative need that a people make their own literature.

Met with Opposition

However, the new movement met with prompt, vigorous, and increasing opposition. Honored men among us thought it unnecessary, unwise, and from the first doomed to failure. There had been other efforts in former years which had failed, and these failures made our people afraid. Furthermore, the American Baptist Publication Society of Philadelphia, with immense assets and resources, was in the field, and had many earnest friends in the South. It was offering creditable periodicals and employing many Southern writers. It had large patronage among our churches, and gathered large harvests in return from its business. It did no little benevolent work among our people, and had come to hold a high and strong place with many. From this vantage ground which can hardly be stated too strongly, the Society through its friends, and by all the forces at its command, withstood the Home Board movement, even claimed to have preempted the field and challenged the right of the Convention to publish Sunday school periodicals.

The opposition became more and more severe as time passed, becoming at times almost a war on the Home Mission Board in every department of its work. But over against it all, with heroism and generalship equal to the task, Dr. Tichenor and his splendid array of able associates and supporters held on their way with slow but steady advance. They carried the issue successively and successfully through sessions of the Convention at Louisville, Richmond, and at Memphis, the severest of them all.

So the Baptists of the South moved out into another Convention year after the session at Memphis, 1889, profoundly stirred from Maryland to Texas. The momentous issue was still pending, and had almost become a threatening crisis in the affairs of our people. Those days of storm and stress in our denominational life can hardly be appreciated except by those who passed through them. And it is quite manifest now, looking back after a quarter of a century, that no one on either side of the conflict understood at the time the full meaning of that gigantic movement. There was, of course, all along much on the side concerning persons and incidents, which may easily be recalled by one or more persons, but which cannot be told here. A great people were in the throes of "growing pains," were coming to their own in heritage and responsibility. God was leading them a way they had not gone hitherto, and bringing them to the kingdom for larger service in the hour of need and opportunity.

A New Question in the Issue

This narrative is following annual sessions of the Southern Baptist Convention, and in point of time has come into January, 1890. The question concerning the "Kind Words Series" was somewhat enlarged, and a new question was brought into the discussion, the question of the Convention creating a new Board to have charge specifically of these publications and to look otherwise after the interests of the Sunday school cause in our churches.

This new question brought me into the very heart of the conflict that was on. Indeed, the question of a new Board was of my making, and made the issue more sharp and concrete. Hitherto I had taken no public part in the discussion, though deeply concerned. I had taken little active part even in the sessions of the Convention, though always present and earnest in my study of its affairs. I was sympathetic with the Publication Society, and appreciated its work, but not as against this new movement of Southern Baptists. The Society had published my tract, and at this very time had one of my books going through the press. I had served on the program of its anniversary, and had defended its interests on more than one occasion. But when its request came for me to stand with the Society as against the Convention, my duty was plain, and the question had only one side from my point of view.

I could not consent to put myself into this narrative as is here being done, except for the many requests to write out the genesis of the Sunday School Board as I chance to be related to it. It is a task at once difficult and delicate, but the narrative shall move on in simple, straightforward fashion, and be left for the future historian, or as Dr. C. S. Gardner said in making his request, "For the student of the rise and progress of institutions." I make no effort to interpret others, but my experiences of those days were as intense as fire burning in my soul, and became part of my very being.

"God Touched Me and I Thought It"

Remembering an adverse word said at the time, I venture the remark that my first thought of the new Board had no outside connection with any person or place so far as I can recall now or knew at the time. I crave the privilege of saying in the simplest way, God touched me and I thought it. The sense of that experience deepened into conviction, and became an impelling power. My first article proposing the new Board was published the latter part of February, 1890, in the *Religious Herald* at Richmond, one of the leading papers among Southern Baptists. It had been adverse to the Home Board movement, and became adverse also to my proposition for a new Board. Though not recalling the date of the paper, the article itself, as I now recall, was signed February 10, 1890, my forty-first birthday. It looked forward and contemplated presenting the proposition to the Convention at Fort Worth the following May.

Going back of the article, it came about somehow as follows: Since the Convention at Memphis the preceding year I had gone from Selma to Richmond as pastor of the Leigh Street Baptist Church, and was living in the parsonage on Libby Hill, at No. 5 Twenty-ninth Street. One night the latter part of January, I was awakened from sleep with the thought of a new Board in full possession, and stirring my soul in such way as I make no effort here to describe, and for which I make no unusual claim. It worked itself out in a set of resolutions which I determined while lying there to present to the Fort Worth Convention. They were written out in the early morning light, and were shown first that very morning, when en route to my study, to Dr. T. B. Bell, now of the *Christian Index*, but then with the Foreign Mission Board, and a member of the Leigh Street Church. He at once gave his earnest approval, and said the resolutions would be "a clarion call to the Baptists of the South." He knew more of the affair in its relation to me as the time went on than any other person, was always earnest in support, a constant guide, inspiration, and joy as the conflict thickened.

The resolutions proposed a Board of Publication to have charge of the Sunday school periodicals and other related matters. The article set out more fully its purpose and advantage. I sent advanced proof sheets from the *Religious Herald*, through the courtesy of Dr. R. H. Pitt, then the junior editor, with a personal letter to all the denominational papers in the South, also to Dr. Benjamin Griffith, of the American Baptist Publication Society. My personal relationship to him justified this.

Although intended in spirit and purpose as a compromise measure, the article brought on the most vigorous discussion which we had yet had. The first word of commendation came from J. B. Montgomery, deacon of the Second Baptist Church, Richmond, and the second from Dr. I. T. Tichenor earnestly commending the proposition. Many of the ablest men in the denomination withstood it, some of them my warmest personal friends. The Baptist papers of the South, while saying kindly things, set themselves in opposition. I recall now only two exceptions, namely, *The Baptist and Reflector*, with Dr. E. E. Folk as editor, and *The Western Recorder*, with Dr. T. T. Eaton as editor. So the lineup was made and the discussion increased in vigor as the weeks passed.

And notwithstanding practically all the Baptist papers of the South were keeping a constant fire on my proposition for a new Board, I confined my discussion for the most part to the columns of the *Religious Herald*, where my first article had appeared; was careful not to have my replies too frequent, and yet have them survey the whole field and take account of what was being said in other papers. It was a trying ordeal, and I twinge a bit even now as it is all recalled. And yet there was no bitterness in the discussion, hardly anything even unkind or cutting. I maintained high regard for those opposing, wondered at my contravening their judgment and leadership, but was driven on with a conviction that could not yield. I wondered then, and wonder even to this day, as it comes back in memory.

At the time of writing my first article I did not know there had been the former Sunday School Board which has already been mentioned in this story. Immediately, however, Dr. John William

Jones, a noble and heroic spirit, at that time serving effectively in connection with the Home Mission Board, sent me *The Home Field*, containing a full account of that former Board, and giving his approval of my proposition. I saw at once that without knowing it I had in my proposition only gathered up the broken threads of history as if knitting them together again. Manifestly the unseen hand that touched the heart and mind in the night time was weaving the life plan for Southern Baptists.

Set Forward at Fort Worth, 1890

Things were shaping and lines being drawn for the issue in the approaching sessions of the Southern Baptist Convention. In April the Baptists of Georgia, in their annual meeting, the only State convention holding session in the spring, after a discussion, able, earnest, and prolonged, had voted for the new Board and sent a memorial to Fort Worth in its behalf. But our people in that great state were not of one mind on the subject, both sides having able and earnest supporters. Throughout the whole South, from Maryland to Texas, the Baptists were stirred with the issue, surging almost as the sea surges. I recall meeting Dr. James A. Kirtley, one of Kentucky's strongest and best men, at the depot in Louisville, both being en route to Fort Worth. His greeting was friendly and familiar, saying he had decided not to go, but his wife had urged him, saying, "Brother Jimmie Frost may need you." His kindly word was reassuring, but also intensified the feeling of uncertainty as to what the final issue might be—certain and courageous as to my own convictions, but wondering as to the outcome, not knowing what the people would say.

At Fort Worth in May, as intended, the resolutions as first published were presented to the Convention, and on my motion were referred without debate to a committee consisting of one from each state as follows: J. M. Frost, Virginia, Chairman; Joe Shackelford, Alabama; W. E. Atkinson, Arkansas; N. A. Bailey, Florida; J. H. Kilpatrick, Georgia; E. C. Dargan, South Carolina; C. Durham, North Carolina; Joshua Levering, Maryland;

F. H. Kerfoot, Kentucky; J. L. Lawless, Missouri; J. B. Gambrell, Mississippi; W. S. Penick, Louisiana; B. H. Carroll, Texas.

The best the committee could do after much effort was to present a majority report, which was adopted, with two members presenting a minority report. But even this majority report was in the nature of a compromise. It named a Sunday School Committee in place of a Board of Publication, to be located in Louisville, with an outline of duties specified.

This, however, was making headway toward the final goal, and set forward the new movement in some measure. The most marked feature perhaps of the occasion was the wonderful address by Dr. J. B. Hawthorne, one of the most eloquent and powerful ever heard before the Convention, in support of the report, even going beyond the report with a larger view and advocating still the new Board. Manifestly the work was not yet finished, and the end had not yet come.

Settled at Birmingham, 1891

Then followed another year of anxious waiting, discussion, earnest effort on both sides, for and against the new movement. At the Convention in Birmingham a year later the Sunday School Committee from Louisville on the first day submitted its annual report. There had been little for it to do under the circumstances. The contract for printing the periodicals had not expired, so the Committee held its place, and now recommended to the Convention the appointment of a Sunday School Board. On my motion the report was referred to a committee and made a special order for Monday morning. The Committee consisted of one from each state as follows: J. M. Frost, Virginia, Chairman; H. S. D. Mallory, Alabama; A. J. Holt, Arkansas; S. M. Province, Florida; F. C. McConnell, Georgia; W. S. Ryland, Kentucky; B. W. Bussy, Georgia; Joshua Levering, Maryland; J. B. Gambrell, Mississippi; R. W. Rothwell, Missouri; L. L. Polk, North Carolina; J. M. Mundy, South Carolina; W. C. Grace, Tennessee; B. H. Carroll, Texas.

The first meeting of the Committee was marked by a wonderful manifestation of God's Spirit with a season of prayer which greatly moved our hearts. Dr. J. B. Gambrell and I were appointed a subcommittee to formulate a report.

It was a serious task. We represented opposing sides of the issue, but realizing the mighty moment into which the denomination had come, and what would be the far reach of our action in the settlement of the impending question, we set ourselves to the task with the best that was in us. We both cherish in sacred memory the experiences of those days in working to that end. I make no effort to set on record a recount of what went on between us, though it is fresh in memory after all these years. After much conferring together, and at the close of a conference which lasted practically all day, he proposed to let me write the report and even name the location of the Board, provided he could write the closing paragraph. When the report was written and he added his words, they were accepted, provided he would let me add one sentence.

He consented, and the task was done so far as the subcommittee was concerned. It was the outcome of an effort by two men, believing in each other, differing widely at the start, and in the end thinking themselves together. That report stands in the minutes of the Convention, just as it was finished that day in our "upper room" in the Florence Hotel, without any shadow of doubt but what an unseen Presence was molding the two into one.

The Chosen Site: Nashville

The report created a Sunday School Board coordinate with the other two boards of the Convention, practically followed the lines of my original resolutions of nearly two years before, and named Nashville as the place of its location. It was unanimously adopted by the larger committee after some discussion, and later to the surprise of everyone was adopted in the Convention without discussion. That was a momentous outcome, and came about as follows, so far as such an occasion can be described on paper:

At the hour of the special order on Monday morning the great hall was crowded to the limit. I reached the hall with the report fresh from the committee, and was unable to enter the building, but was literally lifted in through a window and made my way to the platform as the report was already being called for. The excitement and expectation were intense. The rumor had gone out of a "battle between the giants," like the Battle of Waterloo, but with no one certain as to the outcome. I had scarcely finished reading, with the audience hushed to stillness, and before I could address the president, Dr. John A. Broadus was on the platform and in command of the occasion. And in less time than I can write it, he had brought the Convention to a vote. No one knew how, but all saw it done and acquiesced in the decision.

He did what few men may do once, but perhaps no man would try a second time. He did not move the "previous question," for that would have failed, but he accomplished the same result through the sheer power of his influence, and brought the Convention to vote without debate. I made no effort to reproduce what he said. He made no speech, besought that others would not speak—put a lid on the volcano, and waited to see what would happen—a sublime moment of heroism and faith. It was masterful in the noblest sense. Some thought his action part of a scheme, but not so. He no doubt had his purpose and plan well in mind, but if he ever told anyone, the secret has never become known to me.

So the report was adopted with thirteen dissenting voices. The end had come. The Sunday School Board had been established, with all that it meant for those years of struggle and for the succeeding years into whose joy we have come.

I crave the privilege of mentioning one other incident for the sake of history. Immediately following the adoption of the report, Dr. Gambrell presented a paper signed by himself and Joshua Levering, without my knowledge, nominating me as Corresponding Secretary of the new Board. It not only surprised but fairly startled me. I begged that it should not come to a vote, and protested that I could not consider it for a moment. They were kindly, acceded to my earnest plea, and the Convention instructed the new Board to elect its own Secretary.

CHAPTER FOURTEEN

Need for Doctrinal Emphasis in Teaching

This is a word for the leaders with both the Sunday school and the B.Y.P.U.; a vital word that calls for earnest attention. It means evangelizing plus didactizing as Christ gave us word and example. It means care for one's self in spiritual life and doctrinal character as urged by the great apostle—care for one's self that he may save himself and others.

The Sunday School Board, in its report to the Convention at St. Louis last May, expressed this great need as follows:

Lack of Doctrinal Conviction

Christian character and life of today, in almost startling degree, lack the doctrinal earnestness of Jesus. We may be suffering, as some say, because of reaction from the polemic of other days. We have the spiritual, the ethical, the social, and yet are sadly wanting in doctrinal conviction and conscience. We would not advocate returning to the method of other days, and yet the polemic was not an unmixed evil, as its absence is far from being wholly good. All polemics are not of a kind. It was Luther's polemic with which Europe was shaken to the center, and the Reformation of the sixteenth century wrought its way. It was Calvin's polemic that laid the foundations for superstructure of noble Christian belief and life through succeeding generations and centuries. In the days of Alexander Campbell it was the polemic of heroic men like A. P. Williams of Missouri, J. P. Jeter of Virginia, and hundreds of others throughout the Baptist ranks that saved the day for spiritual interpretation of the New Testament in general and of the ordinances in particular. In very truth, our fathers by their polemic laid the foundations on which we are building, and for the growth and glory of Baptist affairs through the South.

Didactic in Purpose

Christianity, as a system of truth and teaching, is essentially and preeminently doctrinal. While historical in its basis, it is yet doctrinal in meaning. Even its history—for example, the birth of Jesus, His death on the cross, His resurrection, primarily physical facts—is yet of doctrinal significance and might in making Christian character and doctrinal conscience. Its fundamental principles may not be put in didactic form or creedal statement, yet there must be didactic instruction. This is precisely what our Lord intended when He spoke of touching the observance of His commandments. He was setting the schedule and program for coming ages by means of which His doctrines were to live, win their way, and bless mankind.

We need to give emphasis to creedal character and doctrinal conviction as having practical virtue and value in everyday Christian living. A lack of this is our deficiency and weakness, leaves the present-day Christian subject to every kind of doctrine of whatever fad or fancy, if only it be labeled religious or Christian or church. We have in our Lord a commanding example of doctrinal spirit and character, of doctrinal life and earnestness in teaching. A faithful walk in His ways at this point would break up our methods and revolutionize our time, would substitute soundness for softness, strength for weakness, and mark a new day in the kingdom of teaching.

The Kingdom, the Church, the Book

Christ founded a kingdom with a church, using preaching and teaching as the outward means—evangelizing and didactizing. He committed the same forces to the apostles, and through them to us. And we have this today as our heritage from them—the kingdom, the church, and the Book. This may be taken as the expression of New Testament life and literature, as marking the life of all Christian purpose and endeavor.

Preach, teach, make disciples—train in Christian truth, evangelize—didactize. What God hath joined together let not man put asunder. Herein shall His kingdom come and His will be done on earth as in heaven. Herein is the line of Christ's triumph in saving the lost and winning the world so far as the outward means go. Herein shall we do most to serve His purpose, most also for His triumph among men, most also for the kingdom, the church, and the Book. Evangelize and didactize is the combination for which we stand, and in which the Sunday School Board is marshalling and directing all its forces, for the coming glory of the King.

CHAPTER FIFTEEN
What a Church Stands For

The aim of this chapter is to give an exalted view of what is usually called the local or individual church of Christ. The distinctiveness of its character, the uniqueness of its mission, its wonderful history in the world from century to century—these things give the church of Christ exceptional and royal standing. It carries within itself its own badge of honor. Its life, like the life of the individual Christian and through its aggregate membership, must justify its high claim before the world. Its doctrine and work among men are its credentials from the King.

Membership in the church is full of meaning. It is of exceptional honor, and calls for the noblest life. What Christ thinks of the individual Christian, what Christ thinks also of the individual church, like the church at Ephesus, for example, is of much moment, and serves as a standard for measurement and rating. Paul, with a great heart, said, "Christ loved me and gave Himself for me," and also to the Ephesians, "Christ loved the church, and gave Himself for the church."

The inspired writers everywhere speak of the individual churches in a most commanding way. We do well to follow their example, thinking their thoughts and using their words. The New Testament is the only resource for instruction in our study of church life. Throughout its pages great emphasis is given the individual Christian, and great emphasis also marks the individual church with its aggregate of individual members wrought into organic oneness. Individuality, whether of church or member, is never lost sight of, or merged into the mass; but is rather honored and magnified. The churches never become "The Church." The individual is God's unit. The church is His aggregation of individuals saved by His grace. But God has no aggregation of churches, except He will gather all into one at the final consummation.

Paul wrote one of his greatest letters to the church at Ephesus—a church founded by his preaching, and fostered through his ministration. It ranked high among the very best of the whole list of churches in the New Testament record. He had seen it come into its place of mighty power in that famous city, had seen it slowly but surely undermining and even supplanting the great Temple of Diana, had suffered and wept and rejoiced in his labors there as he saw this church becoming more and more an illustrious example of what the gospel of Christ could do. This church, like some others, indeed, was in his heart to the day of his death. His letter to the church is a love letter, rich and strong in thought, lofty and commanding in expression.

Take the following passage for example. It stirs our hearts even now after all these years, and is a letter for all times and any people who love his Lord. It is entered here not for a text, but for a kind of general setting of what is to follow as to spirit and purpose.

An Apostolic Estimate

Wherefore I also, after I heard of your faith in the Lord Jesus, and love unto all the saints, cease not to give thanks for you, making mention of you in my prayers; that the God of our Lord Jesus Christ, the Father of glory, may give unto you the spirit of wisdom and revelation in the knowledge of Him; the eyes of your understanding being enlightened, that ye may know what is the hope of His calling, and what the riches of the glory of His inheritance in the saints; and what is the exceeding greatness of His power to usward who believe, according to the working of His mighty power;

Which He wrought in Christ, when He raised Him from the dead, and set Him at His own right hand in the heavenly places, far above all principality, and power, and might, and dominion, and every name that is named, not only in this world, but also in that which is to come; and hath put all things under His feet, and gave Him to be the head over all things to the church, which is His body, the fullness of Him that filleth all in all.

But God who is rich in mercy, for His great love wherewith He loved us, even when we were dead in sins, hath quickened us together with Christ, and hath raised us up together, and made us sit together in heavenly places in Christ Jesus; that in the ages to come He might show the exceeding riches of His grace, in His kindness toward us through Christ Jesus; for we are His workmanship, created in Christ Jesus unto good works which God hath before ordained that we should walk in them.

Christ is the head of the church; and He is the Savior of the body; . . . the church is subject unto Christ; . . . Christ also loved the church and gave Himself for it; . . . that He might present it to Himself a glorious church, not having spot, or wrinkle, or any such thing, but that it should be holy and without blemish.

Now unto Him that is able to do exceeding abundantly above all that we ask or think, according to the power that worketh in us; unto Him be glory in the church by Christ Jesus throughout all ages.

Paul's Masterful Words

These lofty utterances were written under the sway of God's Spirit, and are Paul's masterful grouping of simple and yet wonderful words. There are groups within groups, like constellation within constellation, which shine with celestial splendor. Take these three for example: God, the Father of glory; the Lord Jesus Christ whom He raised from the dead; the church, which is His body, the fullness of Him and the glory of Him.

In the apostle's mind and heart, and he did not hesitate to say so when pouring out his soul to the elders at Miletus, the church at Ephesus was "the church of God, which He hath purchased with His own blood." Or when writing to Timothy, the church at Ephesus was "the house of God, the church of the living God, the pillar and ground of the truth." This was indeed high rating and ranking for the church at Ephesus, but holds good also for the other churches of the New Testament, or one of our country churches hid away in the mountain fastness. It holds good, too, as a standard for the church of Christ today in whatever community it may be located. There stands the church of Christ, whether then or now, whether Ephesus or Nashville, still the church of God which He purchased with His own blood, the house of God, the church of the living God, the pillar and ground of the truth.

The Church and the Church Home

For the present, at least, we need not discriminate too closely even between the church building and the church body, between the house of worship and those who gather there, between the members in their organic life and their church home. Indeed, the house in the eyes of the world easily partakes of the name and purpose, of even the uses to which it is put and their significance, and is the ever-present symbol of the people who gather there to worship within its walls. The log cabin in which Lincoln was born shines in the splendor of his life and achievements, in the eyes of the nation. The church home may emphasize in powerful and glorious fashion what the church people stand for.

At the dedication of the temple, "The glory of the Lord filled the house of the Lord." And the church home, whether ordinary or imposing in structure, easily becomes identified with the church itself and gives testimony and emphasis to all which it represents. Their house of worship is the house of the Lord. I wish this high view, which surely is not overdrawn, could make us think more highly of the place where we assemble for worship and in which we have our church home. That is where God in signal way has written His name, and where His honor and glory dwelleth.

The churches of Christ, considered severally and individually, stand for all the Son of God stood for, each in its own place and always for the same thing. Changing countries and centuries make no difference here. Changes come, of course, in methods of work and in environment, but never in the essential and basal purpose of the church. Those churches whose life is recorded in the New Testament all stood for one and the same thing. And so it is today, and in this sense surely we are their successors, if our churches are moving in their appointed sphere and in fulfillment of their high function.

Churches Stand for Christ

They stand for Christ and all that He is and has done. The church, like the individual Christian, is the salt of the earth; is the light of the world; is a city that is set on a hill and cannot be hid; and has the glorious privilege of letting its light so shine before men that they may see the good works and glorify God. We have never yet realized the full meaning, or the honor and distinction, or the responsibility and opportunity of membership in the church of Christ. We need to walk humbly here, and yet with our faces to the stars. It is this membership which we are to make worthwhile, and which by our very life must be commended to men everywhere. We honor Christ by honoring His church. We bless the world in making a membership that is commensurate with its high station.

God's Voice in the World

A church stands for God in Christ and for the kingdom of God among men. This is distinct and basal in its very structure. Nature is a revelation of God. But in the church, in His making of the church, there is additional revelation of Himself. This revelation in a way is of higher order, of clearer and greater fullness of meaning. Herein is His personality seen. Herein also are clearly seen the greater wonder of His being, His love and mercy, His pardon, and the marvelous working of His grace in saving sinners and making them fit subjects for the heavenly courts.

The stars shine in splendor with His glory. But in the church, made up of those redeemed by the blood of His Son and rich in the experience of His saving grace, may be seen "the manifold wisdom of God," and the revelation of "the mystery of His will." The church, individually or collectively, is not the custodian of grace, nor the dispenser of grace, and yet is itself a wonderful exhibit, repeated over and over again through the centuries, of the actual working of God in giving His Son for the world's redemption. And in this sense the church outshines all the splendors of the firmament in declaring His glory, and in bearing testimony for God among men.

Its members were dead in sin. But God made them alive again and raised them up with Christ, making them sit together in heavenly places. They are new creatures—a new creation indeed in Christ Jesus—God having made them anew in the working of His grace; "for we are His workmanship, created in Christ Jesus, unto good works, which God hath before ordained that we should walk in them."

Moreover, "he that cometh to God must believe that He is, and that He is a rewarder of them that diligently seek Him." This great foundation truth has constant and tremendous emphasis in the services of the church. Its worship is the worship of God, who is glorious in holiness, fearful in praises, doing wonders. In receiving members the church declares what God hath wrought in the working of His grace; in its ordinations, whether of deacons or of preachers, while imparting nothing of grace or gift, the church yet recognizes God's choice and declares His call of these men. Its very house of worship has become the house of God. Its ordinances are declarative of what God has done. Its preaching of the gospel is but proclaiming the kingdom of God as His mighty witness among the nations of the earth. These things in its life and work and ordinances, make the church a voice for God. They are the people of God, having their church home in the house of God, and are serving for His honor and glory.

The Church and Its One Book

A church stands for the Bible as God's Book and the embodiment of Christ's teaching. It is a revelation of Himself, and here as our only source of wisdom we learn His will and ways. We need diligently to study the church and its Book—the Bible, the Holy Scriptures. As viewed by the church in its belief and life, the Scriptures were written by men divinely inspired; have God for their Author, salvation for their end, and truth without mixture of error for their matter; are the true center of Christian union, and the supreme standard by which all human conduct, creeds, and opinions should be judged.

The church is itself an interpretation of the Scriptures. A Baptist church is the Baptist interpretation of the Scriptures, especially of the New Testament, and is at once both a result and support of that interpretation. Christians differ in the matter of interpretation, and as a result there are different denominations. But the Scriptures, as one may read and study for himself, are the only sufficient and satisfactory basis to determine his church relation and membership. Holding a Baptist interpretation as a personal belief justifies and requires membership in a Baptist church. I have said the New Testament especially, not as against the Old Testament in any sense, but simply because the church is an organization exclusively of the New Testament. And concerning the church as to its nature, ordinances, missions, members, and indeed for everything pertaining to its life, the New Testament is our only guide and our one authority.

Loyalty to the Scriptures

Loyalty to the Scriptures is of supreme moment both with the church and with the individual Christian. Loyalty is a composite thought or sentiment—love and law—the law of love and love under the regulation of law. Loyalty to Christ means loyalty to the things which are His—His teaching, His church, with its ordinances, mission, and ministers. It means loyalty to the New Testament. And true loyalty to the New Testament means loyalty to Christ.

We know nothing of Christ historically except as we know Him through the Scriptures, and especially the New Testament, directly or indirectly. In the name of our God we lift up our banner, and our banner is the Word of God. Wherever you find a church, this is what it stands for, whether now or in the New Testament period, whether at Ephesus or in some modern city or village or country retreat. We do well to insist on this, and make our loyalty known to all men.

A church stands for saving the world. Christ saves men individually, then groups them into churches, and sets them to save the world. This is its high mission, and everything must be subservient to this. Our Lord said to His Father, "As Thou hast sent Me into the world, so sent I them into the world." To His disciples He said, "As the Father hath sent Me into the world, so send I you into the world."

Final Triumph in Redemption

Like the Lord and Savior Himself, the church gives itself for the world—not to the world, that would be for the marring of the one and the ruin of the other, but for the world and for the world's saving. The church in its highest mission is a rescue party, a life-saving service. That church is mightiest which excels in evangelizing the world. While a church wishes a preacher with converting power, the preacher also wishes a church with converting power. There is general need for converting power in the pulpit, but converting power also in the pew.

This gives a church preeminent distinction. It stands for the work of redemption, for the cross, and the crucified One. Its mission is to carry the good news of salvation to the uttermost parts of the earth. The members having themselves been saved through riches of grace, the church sets itself to the glorious purpose for which Jesus died—the saving of lost and ruined men for the kingdom of God.

Final Triumph and Glorious Consummation

A church, moreover, stands for final triumph and glorious consummation—the triumph of saving the lost, the consummation of bringing in the kingdom of our Lord. The church is an ever-abiding prophecy of coming coronation, and will not be hushed in its song. It is at once a standing protest of the deadly work of sin, and a declaration of coming redemption and freedom in Christ Jesus.

The church declares life for the dead and resurrection for the buried. In the final triumph there shall be no more death and no more dying. Death, contrary to the seeming, is no challenge or mockery of the church; but the church in its might and courage, with its house of worship standing near where the dead are buried, boldly proclaims the coming end of death. Oh, the heroic daring and faith that cuts into the very rock which marks the grave, the everlasting words of the everlasting King! "I will raise him up at the last day." The very funeral itself, for which the church assembles in sorrowful memory of those who die in the Lord, is a prophecy of the final funeral when death, the last enemy, shall be destroyed and there shall be no more dying—the funeral of death. There shall be a new heaven and a new earth with Christ as King of kings and Lord of lords.

The church sings its songs of victory even when and where the battle is fiercest. Defeat today will only mean triumph tomorrow. Death today means life and resurrection tomorrow. This is the word that is ever going forth from the church of Jesus Christ. The church militant is the promise of the church triumphant, the potency and power of the coming kingdom.

Such is, somewhat, the meaning of the church, and surely it gives distinction to the house, however humble, as the place where we meet and worship. There should be with us a feeling of care and concern for the church home which is our Bethel, and which itself stands for all we hold dear in its high and glorious service as the meeting place for the saints of God. Mount

Vernon, the shrine of human liberty, shares the renown of the nation's greatest chieftain as the Washington home. Why may not our church home as the place of worship share the distinction of the church which gathers there and for which the Lord of glory died? It was this double thought that created the great church hymn:

> I love thy kingdom, Lord,
> The house of Thine abode;
> The church our blest Redeemer saved
> With His own precious blood.

> I love Thy church, O God,
> Her walls before Thee stand,
> Dear as the apple of Thine eye,
> And graven on Thy hand.

> Beyond my highest joy,
> I prize her heavenly ways,
> Her sweet communion, solemn vows,
> Her hymns of love and praise.

Behold, the heavens, and the heaven of heavens cannot contain thee; how much less this house which we have builded! And yet, surely God is in this place, and this is none other than the house of God, and the gate of heaven.

CHAPTER SIXTEEN

The Church in the Thought of God

Where did the church come from? This question points to the beginning of individual churches, not of "The Church" as the phrase goes, and which is purely a growth in history much this side of the New Testament period and contrary to both the teaching and spirit of the New Testament. The question of when the church began is similar to the question of the beginning of the family. Where did the family come from—as to its starting, its nature and plan, its purpose and history? Where did the stars come from? and the flowers? and the fields? These all have a common source and a common answer in the opening verse of the Bible—in many respects the most remarkable single statement in human speech—"In the beginning God created the heavens and the earth."

The church is here because, like the family, God thought it, planned it after His own choosing, commanded it through His own appointed agencies, and set it for the high mission of working out His providence and grace. God's appointment of agencies in His moral government is, perhaps, even more conspicuous and commanding than the creation of material things and His direction of their course by established laws. Like a building in the thought of an architect prior to its erection and prior even to its appearance in drawing on paper, so the church was in God's mind before its operation or even appearance among men. This fact gives emphasis and dignity to its character, and shows its true place and rank among the forces which make for righteousness.

God Thought . . .

God thought the stars, and the stars emerged, coming in glory and studding the heavens as sentinels of the night. God thought the flowers, and the flowers emerged, coming through seed and soil. God thought the family, created man in His own image as a living soul, gave to him a helpmeet, commanded, and the family emerged with the solitary set in families for the blessing of the race. God thought the church, and in the fullness of time Christ came, as the unspeakable gift of God's love for man's redemption from the ruin which sin had wrought. The church emerged, began its blessed career surcharged with the mighty force of God, was greatly multiplied from one to many, and to this good day, has held its glorious mission and commission for saving the world.

It is entirely scriptural, and accordant with all the facts, to count the church as emanating from the creative energy of God. Concerning the mountains and the stars and all created things, God spoke the word and it was done. So concerning the church, as concerning the family also, God commanded and these came into being—the family first in point of time and then the church taking its place as God's creation and appointment for the good of mankind and His glory among men. "For we are His workmanship, created in Christ Jesus unto good works which God hath before ordained that we should walk in them." And, "If any man be in Christ, he is a new creature (or a new creation); old things are passed away; behold, all things are become new."

The Coming of John the Baptist

The coming of John the Baptist marked a turning point in the affairs of men, and in the history of the human race. He was the immediate forerunner of Christ as others had been more remotely. His preaching prepared the way of the Lord for the coming of the church. When he began his preaching in the wilderness, there was no church. There had been no church. He faced a world without a church. God from the first, indeed, had not left Himself without a witness in the world and witnesses. There was the individual, men and women, who honored Him in their devotion and worship. There was the family, multiplying and succeeding each other throughout the centuries, in which His name was written and where His glory dwelt. There was the nation also whose people were His chosen people who served Him with ever-varying moods and conditions, and who worked out His purpose among the nations of the earth. There was all this, and with a meaning of tremendous moment, but no church.

A Part in God's Great Plan

The coming of the church as a distinct movement of God's grace was reserved until the coming of Christ. He brought in the new dispensation, and with Him came the new order of things—the outgrowth and fulfillment of the old. He stood at the new opening in the highway of human history and spoke that creative word of assertive power and prophetic vision, "I will build My church, and the gates of hell shall not prevail against it." The Old Testament period was behind Him with all its manifest marks of God's presence and care, but our Lord was bringing in a new period, and setting in operation new forces, and making new history which would make possible and necessary the New Testament.

He entered His public ministry through an ordinance new then, but thenceforward to be perpetuated among those who love Him—the ordinance of baptism, as seen in His immersion in the Jordan. When He began there was no church. No church at Jerusalem, nor in Judea, nor in Asia, nor in Europe, nor anywhere in all the world. It was His to build, and He did the building. He found no church here, but left a church behind Him, which He Himself had founded and entrusted with His truth and ordinances, and which He commissioned with the mighty task of giving the gospel to the world, and of making His name great among the nations of the earth. He has continued His church just as He made the one at the first, by saving men and gathering them into churches, for the fulfillment of His mission and the inbringing of His kingdom.

The Plan of Human Redemption

So surely as God planned the heavens and set the stars in their places, whether fixed or moving, so surely did He devise and has in process of execution the plan of human redemption. He chose the gospel as His means and the church as His instrument, and He Himself in the person of the Holy Spirit is ever present as the efficient cause in saving the lost. He draws men unto Himself, makes them willing in the day of His power, and works in them to will and to do according to His good pleasure.

When God created the universe He did not retire and leave the universe to run itself. Everything moves at His bidding as everything came into being at His call, whether the lily that blooms in the field, or the tiny sparrow that feeds from His hand and has His care in its fall, or the stars marshalling in splendor to the music of the spheres around His great throne. And as He is ever present in nature, guiding things after the ways of His will, so also in the saving of men He works out the wonders of His purpose through riches of grace in Christ Jesus.

This is the meaning, at least in part, of those mighty words of inspiration. In their sweep of thought and expression they encompass the ages. They look backward to the first movements of His grace, and forward to its finished work and final consummation. "For God, who commanded the light to shine out of darkness, hath shined in our hearts, to give the light of the knowledge of the glory of God in the face of Jesus Christ." "He hath delivered us from the power of darkness and translated us into the kingdom of His dear Son"; "that in the dispensation of times He might gather into one all things in Christ." And whom He did foreknow He did also predestinate, and call, and justify and glorify. And He who hath begun a good work in you will perform it until the day of Jesus Christ, in whom we have redemption through His blood; that in the ages to come He might show the exceeding riches of His grace toward us through Christ, in whom also we have obtained an inheritance among the saints.

The Wonderful Word

This is the teaching everywhere throughout His Word as to the fullness of His plan and the working of His purpose. Note the wonderful word which He has left upon record for our instruction:

> God according to His abundant mercy hath begotten us again unto a lively hope, . . . to an inheritance incorruptible, and undefiled, and that fadeth not away, reserved in heaven for you, who are kept by the power of God through faith unto salvation ready to be revealed in the last day.

> The God and Father of our Lord Jesus Christ hath blessed us with all spiritual blessings in Christ; according as He hath chosen us in Him before the foundation of the world, that we should be holy and without blame before Him in love.

> I was made a minister, according to the gift of the grace of God, . . . to preach the unsearchable riches of Christ, . . . to make all men see what is the fellowship of the mystery, . . . to the intent that now unto the principalities and powers in the heavenly places might be known, by the church, the manifold wisdom of God; according to the eternal purpose which He purposed in Christ Jesus our Lord. . . . Unto Him be glory in the church throughout all ages.

Surely it becomes us, much more than is common, to think largely of God, to follow in our thinking back to His thinking, to recognize His abiding presence and preeminence in redemption.

For as He hath set the solitary in families, so also He hath set the saved in churches, and made the church the embodiment of His work of grace and the expression of His kingdom among men.

The Price Which God Paid

Nor is this all, for there is yet another view which shows the surpassing greatness of the church in the thought of God, and emphasizes its distinctive character as God's chosen method and instrument: its purchase price. Its cost was infinite, but was freely paid. When creating the world, or even when constructing worlds and systems, there was on God's part only the expenditure of power coupled with infinite wisdom. But there is an amazing difference when He planned to create men anew and redeem them from ruin. This involved much more and required infinite demand on the infinite richness of His nature, and represents the price which God paid for human redemption in Christ.

For God so loved the world that He gave His only begotten Son; and God commended His love toward us in that while we were yet sinners Christ died for us. Herein is love, not that we loved God, but that He loved us, and sent His Son to be the propitiation for our sins; and we are accept in the Beloved, in whom dwelleth all the fullness of the Godhead bodily, and who of God, through His death on the cross, is made unto us wisdom, and righteousness, and sanctification, and redemption. For it pleased the Father that in Him should all fullness dwell, and we are complete in Him.

Such Is God's Plan

Such is God's plan, and such also the outworking of His purpose and the fullness of His saving grace. Having given His Son to die on the cross, God also raised Him from the dead by the exceeding greatness of His power, and set Him at His own right hand in the heavenly places. He gave Him also a name above every other name as the one only Savior of lost men; put all things under His feet, and made Him to be the head over all things to the church which is His body, the fullness of Him that filleth all in all.

Herein is the preeminent distinction of the church on earth, because of Christ's preeminent distinction in the heavens, and also because of His own exalted personal relation to the church even as now operating through men and among men. What Christ is to the church and in the church makes it today what it is, both to God on the one hand and to men on the other.

For this reason, too, the church even now, as with the church at Ephesus, is called the church of God which He hath purchased with His own blood—the house of God, the church of the living God, the pillar and ground of the truth; and is also called the church of Christ which He loved and for which He holds the scepter of righteousness that He may present it to Himself a glorious church.

God's plan and purpose named the purchase price, which Christ freely paid in the shedding of His blood on the cross. This price is of infinite worth and of unwasting fullness.

> Thou dying Lamb, thy precious blood
> Shall never lose its power
> Till all the ransomed church of God
> Be saved to sin no more.

Such is the confident song of the redeemed, both on earth and in heaven, the boast of their faith and the joy of their hope. The glory of Christ is upon the church—upon the church of today as upon the church of God which was at Corinth or Ephesus. It is the glory of the crown, and has the renown of the cross, the crimson flow of whose fountain is for redemption and cleansing. And what the church is to Christ makes it inexpressibly great, gives it a singular rank among men, and commands of us the best we can give of honor and praise and service. We honor Him in doing honor to what is His. We magnify and glorify Christ in magnifying and glorifying His church, which He hath purchased with His own blood.

Emphasizing the Individual Church

Other considerations could be presented which would show further the greatness of the church in the thought of God. And these, too, would again indicate the worth and force of church membership, and should quicken our devotion and loyalty. But leaving these for future discussion, we press the importance and urgent need of giving fresh emphasis to the individual church and the individual member. Consecrated individuality is a mighty power for God, whether the one church or the one member. The church is for the saved, and is their opportunity to cooperate with God in saving the world. One may so make his church life a service for God, that his church life in turn will crown him with the blessing and the glory of God.

The church, as God's chosen method of operation, is for the making of a kingdom—a kingdom not of this world though in the world with Christ as King. This is the office and function of every church wherever located. And every member has a place of rank and efficiency in the fulfillment of this great mission. With every church and with every member there is the hindering or helping, the marring or making, as each one may choose for himself. It is for him if he will to share in the glory of the coming kingdom and in the coronation of the King.

Divine Institutions

It is not "The Church," mark you, whatever that term may mean in common use, that does this mighty work for God, but the church which we almost belittle by calling it the "local church," but which God has made great as His chosen instrument and endowed with power to this high end. There is much need that we reconstruct our use of words and make them conform to the New Testament meaning and usage.

The family and the church have much in common as divine institutions, and are used in Scripture to illustrate each other. The family had its rise in Eden, is of God's appointment, and stands to this day for His moral government among men. The church had its rise with the coming of Christ and through His death on the cross. It, too, is of God's workmanship created in Christ Jesus, and stands now, as it has always stood, for the kingdom of His grace in the world. It abides through the centuries, and will yet abide, as an institution with a membership of the saved and set to save others. And so its building goes on from one to others with the passing years.

The word "church," like the word "family," has specific meaning, but also a generic sense and a generic use. An individual church, like an individual family, may pass away—many thousands of them have passed away when their work had been finished, and are among the things that were. But the church, like the family again, is God's institution, and remains because God has given it remaining power. With Him is its increase and growth, whatever human agencies He may use. He brings on new forces, as when Paul plants and Apollos waters, and new churches follow in the place of those passing away and in further conquest for Christ. In this way the line has been unbroken, and from the first until now the Lord has added unto the church those who are saved. The local and incidental will pass away, but the essential is permanent and will stand until the end comes.

Made to Persist Through His Keeping

The persistence of the church commands our attention and awakens our song. The church persists because of the keeping power of God, and is in line with the fulfillment of His promise. The saints persevere, but God preserves. Persistence of the church and preservation of the saints are from God. And this word "persistence," as describing the life of the church, is preferable in my judgment to the words "succession" and "perpetuity"—the persistence of the church through the ages. This word has the basal and essential meaning of the other words, but is free from historical entanglements and present-day misconceptions.

Centuries have passed and yet, like the family again, the church is here, and still stands along the way of triumph, regardless of local failures and human perversion and corruption of the truth as it is in Jesus.

God set out to make His church, and through His church to make a kingdom. He hath wrought continuous deliverance, and has promised deliverance which shall be complete and permanent. In Him is final triumph, to be consummated in the glorious destiny of the church. God is in the midst of her and she shall not be moved. God shall help her and that right early.

> Thy saints in all this glorious war
> Shall conquer though they die;
> They see the triumph from afar,
> And seize it with their eye.

> When that illustrious day shall rise
> And all Thine armies shine,
> In robes of victory through the skies,
> The glory shall be Thine.

This is the triumphant sentiment and song which the devout have sung through centuries. What hath God wrought for those who love Him! And the crowning day is yet to come, both for the individual Christian and for the church of the firstborn, whose names are written in heaven. That day of glorious destiny for man redeemed by the blood is fixed in the calendar of God, and standeth sure. Thy kingdom shall come. The coronation of the King shall follow. God will show what He hath wrought in Christ for human redemption, and there shall be a new heaven and a new earth for the mighty throng of blood-washed and glorified.

The Chief End of Man

The Presbyterian catechism has the question, "What is the chief end of man?" And gives the great answer: "The chief end of man is to glorify God and to enjoy Him forever." How true this is! And yet, when one knows through blessed experience the saving power of God's grace, and contemplates the glorious destiny into which He brings the redeemed, and considers all that God has done for human redemption, the thought is overpowering, and we almost venture the word, that the chief end of God is to glorify man, and to enjoy him forever. Such is the glory of the church as the workmanship of God, and like the starry heaven in declaring His glory—glorious now, but more glorious far when the work of grace is done.

CHAPTER SEVENTEEN

The Church and Its One Book

The story of Sir Walter Scott, one of the world's great authors, though worn threadbare from use, is still of common interest and point among the thoughtful, because of its fundamental truth. When dying or in a sickness which was unto death, he called for the Book, and wanted someone to read to him from the Book. In answer to the question, "Which book?" the charming writer of books made answer: "There is but one Book." They brought him the Bible, and read to him from the Bible, as the one Book in all the world's great kingdom of literature, that could suffice for the pressing emergency of life and for the infinite need of light on the darkness which lay beyond.

Queen Victoria, who came to England's throne a young, unseasoned girl, but developed into one of the noblest of women, made a rule for that great empire unexcelled by any predecessors. Her reign for more than half a century is marked as the Victorian Period in English history. It was the period of England's greatness, and she made herself a blessing to her own subjects in both the empire and the colonies, and a blessing also to the whole world. She was asked for the secret of her successful reign and of the prosperous condition of her dominion. In answer and from her throne she held up the Bible as being in its great principles and forces the cause of England's greatness and the one secret of success in her sceptre and crown—that the Bible maketh for righteousness and righteousness exalteth a nation.

Essential to the Church

This thing which is true and essential for the individual and for the nation is also true, and essential out of all comparison, to the church. For the church certainly there is but one Book. That one Book is the Bible, the Scriptures of the Old and New Testament wrought into one as the Book of books of all the ages; and by the church is meant the one definite specific church, like the church of God at Corinth, local in character and organic life, though worldwide in its mission and operation. The Bible is indispensable to the church as its guide and its one source of infallible instruction. The physical, mechanical book is a necessary piece of furniture in the church home, and the Bible itself as the Word of the Lord, is to the church in no mean sense its life and light and salvation. It is the "inspiration of God, and is profitable for doctrine, for reproof, for correction, for instruction in righteousness; that the man of God may be perfect, thoroughly furnished unto all good work," and also that the church in its organic life and ministration may be a blessing to the world, an honor to God, the entrance of whose Word giveth light.

The Coming of the Book

When the new dispensation came there was no New Testament. Its Scriptures had not yet been written and its history had not yet been made. The Old Testament, about as we have it now, was the Hebrew Bible—the one Word of the Lord in the possession of men. It lay as the foundation of the New Testament, or as the seed planted by the divine hand, out of which the New would grow. The fulfillment of its prophecies furnished the material and made possible the writing of the New. The Old, with its revelation and inspiration, found its completeness and crown of glory in the revelation and inspiration of the New. Taken together, they make the one Book, "the Holy Scriptures which are able to make wise unto salvation through faith which is in Christ Jesus."

The Old Testament as the Hebrew Scriptures was Christ's Bible—His only Bible. It foretold His coming and found fulfillment in Him. It was in the Old Testament Scriptures that He was taught and trained in the Hebrew home, as He "increased in wisdom and stature, and in favor with God and man." It was the Old Testament Scriptures, also, which He used with such fine effect, whether in His private life when resisting the devil, or in His public ministry when teaching the people. That mighty Word of His—"it is written" as the Word of God—was His one rock of defense, His one sword for aggressive warfare. "Search the Scriptures," was His word of instruction, "for they testify of Me, and in them ye think ye have eternal life." Moses and the prophets was a final appeal, the end of controversy between God and man.

The Old Testament

The Old Testament entered also very largely into the life and labors of the apostles and those early preachers of the gospel. The words of the old prophets became the text of the new preachers. They learned their lesson from their Lord, and right well did they use the Scriptures as the Word of God, being matched and fulfilled in the things which had lately come to pass. This Word of prophecy, with a new power of experience in the heart, and touched afresh by the Holy Spirit, and with a new meaning from new events, became the gospel of the kingdom. That Word—"according to the Scriptures"—was the keynote of the preaching, whether with Jew or Gentile, whether in rehearsing the wonders of God in former years, or in unfolding the greater wonders of Christ and Him crucified, of His resurrection from the dead, and of the future resurrection of those who are His. It was the conquering Word wherever it went, and so the kingdom of Christ was established among men, and His churches coming into existence in many places bore testimony to His saving grace.

The history of Christ and of His disciples—of His life, death, resurrection, and His work of redemption, of their labors in suffering and in bearing the good news of salvation to the lost world—all this history put into written form by holy men, chosen and guided by the Spirit of God, added the New Testament to the Old. The Bible was made larger, and even richer, since to Moses and the prophets were added the four Gospels as the biography of our Lord, the Acts of the Apostles, showing what God's Holy Spirit had wrought among men, those wonderful letters from men of God to the churches and to the saints scattered abroad everywhere, and finally the Revelation of John, in which on the Isle of Patmos God vouchsafed to him, and through him to us, a vision of the future triumph of the kingdom and the coronation of the King.

Wrought by the Providence of God

This one Book of the church, therefore, our Bible of today, consists of the Old Testament Scriptures, together with the New Testament Scriptures, wrought into one by the Providence of God as His Word forever and ever. We do not discriminate between the Old and the New as dividing their authority or significance, but hold them together, as they have come down to us the one Book—the Book of God, the Man of our counsel, and the lamp to our feet.

So it comes to pass that we have more in the way of the Bible than Christ had, even more than His apostles had, and are richer in the enlarged and enriched Word of God. We have more in the Christian Bible for instruction in the home than the Jews had in their Hebrew Bible. The church has more in its Book than the temple had in its Scriptures. They had the tree. We are rich in the beauty of its foliage and in the ripeness of its fruit. Our light is greater, and also our privilege and our responsibility.

A Book of Divine Authorship

This Book of the church, like the church itself, has God for its Author. It is the Book of God for instruction in the church of God. When Paul remained for a year and six months with the church at Corinth, he "taught them the Word of God." He, no doubt, opened to them the Old Testament Scriptures, as the Master had done with the two disciples on the way to Emmaus when their hearts burned within them under His gracious words of exposition. But Paul, no doubt, also was adding to the Scriptures of the Old something of the New which he had received of the Lord and which later he committed to writing. But it was "the Word of the Lord," and he was God's messenger, with God's message—the Word of God preached in the church of God as it is to this day.

Inspiration

There is no intention here to make technical discussion of any theory of inspiration. It need not concern us as to how God inspired men, or how God created the universe. Suffice it, that God spoke the Word, and it was done. And God breathed upon the mind and heart of men, and they in speech or written word "spake as the Spirit gave them utterance" concerning the wonderful work and ways of God. Each writer wrote for himself, preserving his own individuality, and yet wrote for God as God would have him write. A man's individuality under the power and spell of inspiration was no more interfered with than when he is the subject of regeneration, which is of the same power, and is even more radical and revolutionary in heart and mind.

Whatever theory we may have of inspiration or of how God gave the Bible to men and through men, it must be at once large enough and exclusive enough to leave the authorship unquestioned. There can be no abridgment of God's authorship of the

Bible, working through such channels and by such methods as please Him. So long as God is doing things through men, there will be more or less of the human element both in the doing and in the product. But we should not go too far in trying to separate between God and man in producing the Bible, just as we should not try to point out the human and the divine in Christ; at any rate, it is safer and in better keeping with the mystery and majesty of the question, not to minify but rather magnify the divine element. Holy men of old spake and wrote for God as the Spirit moved them, and gave them utterance. Their words were the very Word of the Lord, which endureth forever.

Revelation and Inspiration

This mighty fact is true both for the revelation and inspiration which enter into the making of the Bible, and gives it a name and place above all other books. Revelation is the uncovering and making known things which man could not know of himself, and such as God in His grace has revealed to him—the deep things of God, the mystery of His will, the great and wondrous doctrines of His grace and of His love in redemption. "Eye hath not seen"—human eye hath not seen—"nor ear heard, neither hath entered into the heart of man, the things which God hath prepared for them that love Him. But God hath revealed them unto us by His Spirit; for the Spirit searcheth all things, yea, the deep things of God." This is revelation, and without it men would have been in the dark forever—as the world would be, and even worse, if the sun should not rise tomorrow morning.

Inspiration, on the other hand, is God's special work in the writer to guarantee the writing in making the record which God would have written. It comes by virtue of God's breathing His Holy Spirit upon the human heart and mind, as one tells of the revelation which God has made and how God manifested Himself in history. We know not the movements of the Holy Spirit in the new birth or in that sanctification which comes by the Holy Spirit through the truth. Nor do we know of His movement in the special work of inspiring men to write in such way as to leave the writer free in his own individuality, and yet they gave us

God's thought in God's words. And because of this work of the Spirit, the writing bears the heavenly imprint, "it is written"; it has the fragrance of the heavenly fields and the flavor of the heavenly fruit.

Both Old and New Testament

Revelation and inspiration both appear in making both the Old and the New Testament. Together they make the Holy Scriptures, which claim to be of God, and vindicate their claim. They hold the unique place of single and supreme authority in doctrine and life. They are that Word of the Lord which He compares to rain and snow, coming down from heaven and not returning to Him void, but fulfilling their mission and prospering in the thing whereunto He sent it. And for us today the Holy Scriptures are the burning bush in which God appears and speaks to us as He did to Moses; or the pillar of cloud by day and of fire by night in which God appears as He did to the children of Israel; or as Jacob's ladder which he saw in vision at Bethel, with angels ascending and descending, and with God revealing Himself in the open heavens. Surely the God of the Bible is our God, and the Book is His message which He will have us hear.

The New Testament Added

The New Testament came several hundred years after the Old Testament. Its coming marked a new and mighty period in the world's history when God and men were again coworkers, both in making history and putting it in written form. There is no need for discussion here as to how the New Testament came, or how it grew through passing years, and finally became coequal with the Old Testament Scriptures in inspiration, dignity, and authority.

Dr. Albert Henry Newman writes:

> It may be taken for granted that from the apostolic time onward each church in general had for use in public service at least one Gospel containing the life and words of the Master, and some of the

apostolic epistles, especially those addressed to themselves and to the churches in the same region.

A highly-appreciated apostolic writing possessed by one church in a given region would soon come into the possession of most or all of the churches. Such apostolic writings as could be conveniently procured were possessed by the various churches and were freely used for reading in the church services and as material for the literary and oral discourses of the Christian teachers.

From the close of the apostolic age, or even earlier, most of the books that were afterwards accepted as canonical were in use in greater or smaller collection in the various Christian churches for purposes of edification, and were reverenced because alike of their apostolic authorship and of the authoritative account which they contained of the life and Word of Christ and of the apostles.

An August Movement in the Literature of the World

The making of the New Testament as an addition to the Old Testament was an august movement in the literature of the world. The Book is here and speaks for itself; and speaks now, as its writers spoke, in soberness, with heavenly wisdom, and in the demonstration of the Spirit and of power. The churches, out of whose history it grew as cause and effect, may have failed in their succession, but the Book in unbroken continuity is here with us, having the freshness and fragrance and power of the morning of the first day.

First came the Epistle of James, named for its author, who was the brother of our Lord, and subscribed himself, "a servant of God and of the Lord Jesus Christ." It was written while he was serving the church at Jerusalem as bishop or pastor. Then came the letters to the Thessalonians. They were written by Paul from the church at Corinth, and addressed to the church at Thessalonica, then lately established. The opening salutation is of peculiar interest as being among the first words written for the New Testament, and the second record in writing of the new forces which had been introduced into the world's movements, and which had made the new dispensation: "Paul, and Silvanus, and Timotheus, unto the church of the Thessalonians, which is in God, the Father, and in the Lord Jesus Christ."

Then came the letters to the church of God at Corinth, written by the same writer, but while he was serving the Ephesian church. The gospel had produced the churches, and now the churches are the occasion at least of putting into written form for all succeeding ages the gospel of the grace of God, with its wonderful history among men. The Book grew in its several parts and the churches became custodians of the new treasure, and passed down the line until it became just as we have it now. It has passed through fiery trials unscorched, has met all the demands of his friends, and for many centuries has been the light and joy of all who will walk in its light or live in its joy.

Our Guide in the Study of the Church

It is the New Testament especially which must be our guide in the study of the church, and must determine all questions of church life, whether of creed or conduct. For the church is distinctly of the new dispensation; and whatever pertains to the church, as to who shall be members, as to its officers and government, as to its ordinances and service, as to its character, life, and mission, must be learned and settled from the New Testament. That is the one touchstone of all church creed and conduct, and cannot be asserted too strongly or followed too closely. What the New Testament rules out is ruled out, whether in precept or in practice. What it commands is commanded, is the end of controversy, and requires obedience, with the promise of reward.

There is need for this one standard in our church life, and without it there is uncertainty and discord everywhere. In a large jewelry store there may be five hundred watches and clocks, but the workman at the bench, as he sets your timepiece, looks at the regulator as it hangs on the wall and marks the hour of day. So in our belief and practice, even with our convictions and conscience, we must look away from ourselves to the one standard of authority. The Scriptures alone can be this one rule of faith, and their authority is final. No human authority will suffice. We must look to the Word of God and measure all by that Word as the one standard. If the Scriptures, for example, require infant baptism, then we must have infant baptism. If the Scriptures restrict baptism to believers, and place that ordinance before the Lord's Supper as prerequisite, then the restriction must stand. If the Scriptures command sprinkling for baptism, so it must be. If the Scriptures require immersion as the one form of baptism to the exclusion of sprinkling, then the requirement must stand, and we must do as we are commanded.

The more completely we are mastered by the one standard, and the more devoutly we recognize the one authority in belief and practice, the more nearly will we come to the mind of the Lord and in conformity to His Word. There are no substitutes. There can be no division of authority, neither division of obedience and loyalty. There is no room here for a divided heart or a divided life. "The Bible, and the Bible alone, is the religion" of those who will serve God in His church according to His Word and His plans.

God's Authority in the Written Word

The Scriptures hold this commanding place of authority as the expression of the will of God. The Bible is more than regulator or referee, more than a set of rules or a code of law. It is no fetish to be worshiped in blindness and ignorance; nor a power in itself to have as a charm on the person or in the home. As the living Word of the living God, it is a guide to be trusted and followed, an authority to be known, honored, and obeyed. We serve and worship not the Bible as a book, but the God of the Bible as our light and salvation, as our Father to whom we should give living obedience—giving a free obedience with an obedient liberty.

This is the recognition of God's authority in the Scriptures, and obedience to Him is not bondage to a book. We recognize His dominion in heart and thought and life, but that is not slavery of soul, nor has it any kinship with slavery. It makes rather for the larger freedom. God's call is indeed imperative; but imperative as meeting man's deepest needs and as opening the way to the larger life. The call of a father to his child crying in the dark is a call for deliverance. Prayer, study, interpretation for oneself, personal obedience—"these are mutually dependent, and form an invisible whole," as the best method of handling the Word of God. "If any man will do His will, he shall know of the doctrine whether it be of God."

Holding Supreme Sway in the Church

The Book—this Book which holds supreme sway in the church—meets a great and pressing necessity. Man is blind and in the dark for the things which concern him most deeply. Whether for men individually, or for any number of men, as in the aggregate of church membership, there is imperative need for an authority and a light outside themselves. No light from within will suffice; whether mind or heart or reason or consciousness, or all of these combined. These themselves will need to be tested over and over again, and must be regulated by the standard which is higher and supreme in authority. For this high function God in condescending grace has given His Word. It is man's prerogative to search the Scriptures for himself, and in searching may find himself in his relation to God, and find also his salvation through faith which is in Christ Jesus.

We cannot exaggerate our dependence upon the Scriptures as the Word of God, or their supreme place in the churches and in our church life. Here and here alone can we know the mind of the Lord, His will and ways concerning us. Here and here alone is our only safeguard, our light and joy in serving Him in the things which He has commanded. The transforming of God's Word into life and action through His Spirit, into human words and deeds, is the noblest life before men, and the most acceptable to God. It makes the vital and necessary connection between belief and practice, between creed and conduct. Without God's Word the foundations are all gone. But with it the building of God standeth sure, and we are safe in Him.

The Book alone, moreover, reveals both the God of our salvation and the salvation of our God. Nowhere else can these mighty things be learned, whether in the wonders of nature or the greater wonders of Providence. Grace is not made known in the stars, nor His infinite love in the planets. And the great doctrines of the Bible, as to man's origin and nature, his ruin by sin and his redemption by the cross, his salvation now, and his destiny hereafter—these things of tremendous moment can be learned nowhere else except in the Book of the church. From its wonderful pages come the light which shines on the darkness, gives cheer and comfort, opens the way of the heavenly walk, and by foretaste and forecast makes known the joys and glories which shall follow.

Without the Bible, too, we know nothing of Christ—the historic Christ; nothing of His life, nothing of His wondrous nature, suffering, death, and resurrection; nothing of His wonderful love and gracious words; nothing of His churches as to their origin or character, nothing as to His ordinances as to what they are or what they require or what they mean in their great message to men; nothing as to our life in the church of Christ as to its blessing and lofty walk, nothing as to His own saving grace and kingly power. All this comes alone from the Bible, either directly or indirectly. By its pages alone can we get back to the Christ of history who came to save, and who saves us through the blood of the everlasting covenant. Loyalty to the Book is loyalty to Him. It reigns without a rival in its own great domain of truth; it is forever supreme in the church, and for the individual has undivided command in precept and practice. It is the Book of God, the one Book of the church—God's message to men, and man's mission for God.

CHAPTER EIGHTEEN

The Confession of Faith

It is quite the fashion now to knock the orthodox with adverse criticism. But the word "orthodox" is one of the noblest words in our language, and comes directly from the richest language spoken by man. It describes one of the noblest acts of the human soul, and means "right thinking" as a process or "right thought" as a result. Why take part in murdering or in the effort to besmirch a great word? You can hardly make the word suffer without the thing for which the word stands also suffer. This matter has wide application, and should elicit our concern, for there is kinship throughout the whole realm of truth.

Right Thinking

Right thinking about flowers makes the orthodox botanist and gives fellowship with kindred minds. Right thinking about the stars in their courses makes the orthodox astronomer, and creates companionship along the highway of the skies. Newton and Kepler were orthodox in their great kingdom of thought when, thinking God's thoughts after Him in the course of the universe, they discovered the law of gravitation and the three imperial laws which govern the movement of the heavenly bodies. Right thinking in nature makes the orthodox scientist. Right thinking about God gives right views of His being and nature, goodness and love, holiness and power. It makes one orthodox in the science of theology. Right thinking in the Scriptures gives right exegesis, right interpretation. It makes one orthodox in the Word of God and possesses him with an orthodox confession of faith.

The Nobler the Subject of Thought . . .

the nobler also the act of thinking. Hence the apostle's great exhortation for the orthodox: Hold fast the form of sound words, as essential to right thinking and expression of doctrine. And that other lofty word: "Whatsoever things are true and honest, whatsoever things are just and pure, whatsoever things are lovely and of good report, if there be any virtue, and any praise, think on these things"—be orthodox in them. This is not straining the word in its significance and use, but only an effort to let it out into its own wide free realm, and a plea that it be not stricken in the house of its friends.

It is loosely said that the gospel is a life and not a doctrine or system of doctrines, a service and not a belief; that our times call for the "man of deeds and not a man with a creed." Some are even bold in saying it makes no difference what one believes, if only his life be right; that the confession of faith is of little or of no concern, if only we have right service. But this is a manifest fallacy and thoroughly wrong. Right thinking and right living go together. One may possibly sometimes be better than his creed, but his life and character are in what he thinks. For as a man thinketh in his heart so is he, and out of his heart are the issues of life. The orthodox heart and the orthodox life are as the fountain and its stream. Words and actions depend on character. They are powerful in their reflex influence on character, and character depends upon what one thinks and believes, and also upon the great and eternal things in which faith anchors itself, and in which thinking finds its largest range and most rapturous exercise. The man who would live godly must first be godly. The water which flows over the iron bed in the hidden secrets of the earth is chalybeate when it puts out at the spring. The gospel is both life and doctrine, and finds expression in both Christian doctrine and Christian service.

"Dead Orthodoxy"

Much has been said adversely also about "dead orthodoxy," and perhaps it deserves all that has been said. But why not consider the orthodoxy that is living as to its value and power? When discussing man as our subject, we do not take a corpse as an example, nor is the corpse mistaken for a man. The Westminster Confession of Faith was once like molten lava fresh from burning hearts and minds. If it be otherwise now, whose fault is it? Why not take an example of living dogma? When Luther on the stairway at Rome found his new experience of grace in one of the greatest of all the dogmas, he became a new man in the realm of truth, an orthodox man with a new creed, and forthwith made a new confession of faith, and found a new power in which he moved the world. It was the power of living dogma. We complain for the want of better living; possibly the deeper want is a better believing—a living faith that is anchored in the deeper, greater, better things. Herein the soul through the Spirit of truth gets its connection with the sources of life and power, and finds its largest freedom in the liberty wherewith Christ maketh free.

For this reason, a recent writer in philosophy, when speaking of science and dogma in a friendly way, but expressing a psychological necessity, said, "A religious society cannot dispense either with doctrine or doctrinal teaching. The more moral (or rather the more spiritual) it is in character, the more it needs a dogmatic symbol which defines it and explains its raison d'être. It will have its teachers as well as its pastors and missionaries."

Surely this must be true of the church—especially today, when there are contrary voices with contrary views. One's Christian confession of faith, which determines his own doctrinal life and his church relations, is the product of what he finds or thinks he finds in the Scriptures. It is his interpretation of the Word of God, an expression or statement of what he believes the Bible teaches. The days of doctrinal conception and experience are always days of might within the individual soul and in the history of any people.

The Supreme Test of All Creeds

The place we assign the Scriptures in our confession of faith is decisive of nearly all other questions of belief and practice. This is especially true concerning the New Testament and our church life. One may "possess an inward rule of conduct, and along with this a principle of free judgment." Of course, he may and must, but his inward rule will need light from without, and his free judgment will need guiding, will need oftentimes curbing and correcting, a mastery, indeed, from another hand than his own—such a guiding mastery as he may find in the Word of God. A single look outside of self—to the heights above, to the depths beneath, through other standards than his own, will cure or modify many misconceptions and serve to set one in the right course. Measuring ourselves by ourselves is seldom edifying.

Were you ever puzzled when lying in your sleeper berth at night in trying to decide which direction the train was going? A light in the berth even gives no light on the question, but one look out of the window gives the decisive answer. Or were you ever puzzled even to being deceived when, sitting at the car window, your train standing still while another train was passing, you thought yourself moving—saw it with your eyes and felt it down in your being? But one look through the opposite window out in the open breaks the illusion, undeceives your eyes and feeling, and shows the inner error and folly.

So it is in the larger and higher sphere. Man in his best estate needs the light from without, and a standard of measurement other than is possible within his own little sphere, or from the consensus of all that has gone before, apart from the Word which God has furnished and which shineth as a light in a dark place. Conscious of his need, man cries out of the dark and out of the storm for the rock that is higher. The answer is in the Scriptures, not simply as a Book, but in the revelation and unerring Word which are able to make wise unto salvation. Especially and preeminently is this true in matters of Christian doctrine and life when one wants and the soul is crying for certainty and for certitude.

If the Scriptures are not an authority, then we are left without authority in our church life. It is not the case of the Scriptures plus something else, or the Scriptures versus something else, but the Scriptures or nothing. This is not a question of individual right of private judgment and interpretation. That with everyone for himself before God, is his inalienable privilege and imperative obligation. But while we may differ in exegesis and interpretation, yet when the meaning is once determined and agreed upon, that is the end of the controversy, and acceptance, belief, and practice is the imperative course if our hearts be loyal and our lives obedient to what God has written.

The Inevitable Law

This comes not as an arbitrary edict, but lies deep in our very nature and situation as the inevitable law. It is God's gracious provision for man in his deeper needs. We cannot refuse to eat in answer to the law of hunger. We dare not throw ourselves contrary to the law of gravitation. Why then refuse the light of the sun, turning the day into night, and then lighting our candle as our guide in the most momentous concerns? There are deeper laws than edicts. They are the laws of heart and mind, of conscience and character, of life and destiny. They are imperative in their demands, and carry within themselves their own terrible penalties for infringement. Putting the hand in the fire violates the law in the physical kingdom, and the penalty goes with the act. So surely do the laws in the kingdom of mind and heart have in themselves power to avenge their breaking. We follow nature's laws for the larger service they can render, and count them not hard but rich in physical good. God appeared in His Word, reveals Himself to men, and opens the way to the best He can give. It is the offer of His grace and love.

Concerning and According To

In formulating, therefore, our doctrinal statements for belief and practice, there are two basal words: first, "concerning the Scriptures," and second, "according to the Scriptures." Considering the confession of faith in the figure of an arch, these two words in their full meaning are the foundation on either side of the arch—what the Scriptures are in themselves and what they teach for belief and observance. Baptists at different times in their history, and to meet impending claims and conflicts, have issued their confession of faith, and have always given this primal and decisive place to the Word of God as their one authority. This is the bedrock of their faith, the one rule of their practice. None of these confessions were authoritative as a creed, in the sense of dominating others in conduct or belief; but all of them more or less were authoritative as statements of their own agreement as to what they themselves believe—not authoritative, perhaps we should say, but representative of their faith concerning the Scriptures and according to the Scriptures. And this they apply to the whole round of Christian doctrine and practice, as expressed in their church life, and in their efforts to serve God on God's plan.

And to this end they have insisted upon right translation, right interpretation, and right observance of the Scriptures as the threefold necessity in church life, whether of doctrine or practice. Concerning the Scriptures, and according to the Scriptures—this has been their battle cry in all ages. If this is not sufficient, then we are helpless and in the dark. If it is sufficient, then disobedience and disloyalty are our shame, and we suffer in our own wrongdoing. To the law and the testimony, our people make their final appeal, and to the more sure word of prophecy:

> For the prophecy came not in olden times by the will of man, but holy men of God spake as they were moved by the Holy Spirit . . . .

All Scripture is given by inspiration of God, and is profitable for doctrine; . . . that the man of God may be thoroughly furnished unto all good works. . . . Thou hast known the Holy Scriptures which are able to make wise unto salvation through faith which is in Christ Jesus. . . .

Take heed unto thyself, and unto the doctrine; continue in them; for in doing this thou shalt save both thyself and them that hear thee. . . . For I delivered unto you first of all that which I also received, how that Christ died for our sins according to the Scriptures; and that He was buried, and rose again according to the Scriptures.

In these several declarations, two New Testament writers give us a comprehensive statement as to the origin and character, the purpose and value of the Scriptures—the Old Testament certainly, and possibly the New Testament also, so far as it had then been written. The word "moved" used here by the apostle Peter is very strong and significant. It is used in two other places: When Paul's ship was caught in the storm and was going to pieces, they lifted anchor and "let her drive"—the same word, and the ship was driven under the power of the cyclone on the sea. And then with the coming of the Holy Spirit on the day of Pentecost, there was "a sound from heaven, as of a rushing mighty wind"—rushing is the same in the original as moved and driven—and the disciples were filled with the Holy Spirit and began to speak with other tongues as the Spirit gave them utterance. Peter was in that cyclone at Pentecost, knew its power, and said it was so when in the olden times men of God spake as they were moved by the Holy Spirit.

Paul, on the other hand, emphasizes the authority of the Scriptures in his statement of doctrine, basing all on this, according to the Scriptures. He takes Christ's death, burial, and resurrection

1. as matter of history;

2. in their doctrinal significance as the atonement for sin;

3. in their relation to us as having been in our stead;

4. and all according to the Scriptures, he admonishes to care and concern for doctrine and commends the Scriptures

- as being holy,

- as coming through men under the inspiration of God,

- as being sufficient for doctrine and conduct, and

- as being able to make wise unto salvation through faith in Jesus Christ.

The Need to Show What We Believe

So we have the inspired writers themselves to furnish this two-fold standard, which is of as much value and is deeply needed now as then—perhaps even more needed. And Baptists, whenever they have issued a statement of doctrine or declaration of principles, have followed their example, and applied the standard to the whole round of Christian history and doctrine—first concerning the Scriptures, second, according to the Scriptures. In what is generally accepted as their confession of faith, there are some twenty or more separate articles of belief and practice, but every article throughout the whole confession represents what they believe the Scriptures teach. It is not enough in this day for either a person or people to say, "The Bible is our creed." For immediately come the two imperative questions: What is believed concerning the Scriptures, and what according to the Scriptures? And the answer to these questions makes the confession of faith.

Articles of Faith and Practice

During the war with Spain an American fleet was sailing for Cuba. As the men of war were passing the South Carolina coast a large ocean steamer sailed out from Charleston harbor, headed for the open sea, but without a flag at her mast. She was signaled to run up her flag, but refused. A cannon shot was sent across her bow. Then she hoisted her colors as the symbol of her nationality. It was worthwhile in those war times to learn who she was, where she was going, what cargo she had on board, and what business she had at sea and in these waters. The confession of faith is something in the nature of a people's banner or symbol or colors, showing to all who may need to know, or who care to know, who they are and what they are concerning the Scriptures and according to the Scriptures.

Baptists agree with other denominations in many of the great fundamental doctrines, but part with them seriously when we come to other articles of faith and practice. The basal and most imperative need is agreement without equivocation or reserve as to the place which the Word of God shall have in the making of our creed. This would well-nigh settle all other questions, if admitted and worked to its full limit. In the early seventies, Christian union was much discussed—some people being clamorous for it even to using hard words against those who could not accept their view. My father, one of the earlier preachers of Kentucky, was much interested in the subject from the Baptist standpoint. As the discussion went on and waxed warm, he developed three rules not as the basis of union, but as a guide in forming that basis. In all good faith and in a fraternal spirit, he proposed these three rules as the Baptist challenge to other denominations, as they laid their several creeds and confessions of faith side by side in comparison for comparative study, as follows:

1. Agree to adopt and practice whatever we mutually believe that the Bible teaches.

2. Agree to give up, and strike out of our respective creeds, whatever causes division and which we ourselves do not regard as essential to truth.

3. Agree to give up, and strike out of our respective creeds, whatever causes division among us and for which we cannot give a plain precept or example in the Word of God.

These rules concerning the Scriptures as a basis of agreement were to make in their application a confession of faith according to the Scriptures. Standing in the line of these rules, Baptists, while holding many great fundamental doctrines with others, yet stand aloof in certain other vital matters, and follow the lead of God's Word as their own distinct principles and emphasis. For example, take these items of Baptist faith which they show as their banner before all the world:

- the sufficiency of the Scriptures as the Word of God, and our loyalty to them in belief and obedience;

- individual responsibility and freedom of conscience in the service of God;

- separation of "church and state" in all matter—"a free church in a free state";

- a converted church membership of only such as profess a saving knowledge of Christ as their personal Savior;

- congregational and local self-government in the churches;

- independence and cooperative right of the churches—each one in itself;

- baptism with immersion as the only form, and believers as its only subjects—believers being those who, with personal trust, have accepted Christ and personally confess Him as their Savior and Lord;

- the Lord's Supper within the church and for church members;

- the purpose of the church to evangelize the world for Christ in the saving of men and the building of the kingdom of our Lord.

A People with Definite Belief

Baptists are not "The Church" with a people, but are a great and glorious people with churches. These distinctive principles root themselves back into other principles more profound and even more important in relation to God and His work of human redemption. At the same time they branch out into other and more or less minor items of faith and practice. But all of them are related to each other as one complete and consistent system of truth, are fully-comprehended and made clear in the Scriptures. This is expressed sometimes in their confession of faith, sometimes otherwise—never authoritative but declarative and representative of what they believe the Scriptures teach and command in precept and example.

In View of Present Church Conditions . . .

it is worthwhile to consider from this standpoint the place of baptism and the Lord's Supper in the Baptist confession of faith as compared with what others believe and practice. This should be done, of course, in becoming spirit, and for better understanding and larger fellowship. Other denominations admit the belief and practice of believers' baptism, but depart from the Baptist view in the additional practice of "infant baptism," holding that infants also are to be baptized. They say "believers and their children." Baptists say, only believers. And finding no word for "infant baptism" in the New Testament, and that it contravenes the very nature of the ordinance as the very command of our Lord, they leave it out of their confession of faith. And so the divergence comes as to the subjects of baptism.

Baptism

Other denominations admit also that immersion is baptism, and that the immersion of the believer as baptism is valid and scriptural. Indeed, they practice this in a way and upon occasions, and will receive into their churches and fellowship any who have been baptized in Baptist churches. But here again they make divergence from the practice of our people in the additional belief that sprinkling equally with immersion is "a mode of baptism." Baptists say only immersion, the others say immersion or pouring or sprinkling. But neither sprinkling nor pouring appeared in the New Testament as baptism, and utterly fail to represent the great ordinance as commanded by Christ and practiced by His early disciples. So these are not given a place in the Baptist confession of faith, and mark further divergence between Baptists and others in their church life.

The Lord's Supper

Furthermore, and with hardly a dissenting voice, the other denominations also agree with Baptists that the Lord's Supper is a church ordinance for church members, and that in the appointed order baptism comes first and is a prerequisite to the communion service. This principle, however, others do not follow to its legitimate conclusion, for it justifies and requires the practice in Baptist churches of restricting the communion to those of like faith and order, and who as church members have fellowship in the ordinance. Fellowship in baptism comes first, and is essential to fellowship at the table of the Lord. Baptists concerning the ordinance stand by the rule according to the Scriptures—following their confession of faith, but seeing first that the confession of faith follows the Word of God—going with others when they can, but standing apart when they must in faithfulness to the New Testament.

Immersion, therefore, as the form and believers as the subjects of baptism, having the requisite scriptural authority, must be classed among the universals of Christian belief and practice. Sprinkling, on the other hand, as "a mode of baptism," and infants as subjects of baptism, fail of New Testament authority, and for this reason fail also to have any place in Baptist church life—are not among the universals of Christian belief and practice, but on the contrary have been to this day chief factors in dividing the hosts of the Lord. This is a vital issue, and not "a question of mere mode," as is sometimes said, but of the form and subject of baptism, and involves the very meaning and life of the ordinance. Infants are not believers. There is no proxy in obedience and no proxy in the New Testament. Form is not mode and can have no substitute. We must adhere to the original form and require subjects according to the Scriptures, otherwise there is disobedience and disloyalty. We might surrender "mere mode" in the interest of larger fellowship, but not the form or the subjects. These must remain without addition or taking away.

It is a question for settlement by the New Testament, and according to the Scriptures. These great principles which are common to all should not be violated in the interest of some, and in sacrifice of allegiance to our King. They rest on the authority of God's Word, and are for the conservation of His truth and of His ordinances as He has commanded and set them in His church for observance. The Baptist confession of faith is their banner for the King. His call is personal and imperative. Our answer must be in person and in joyous obedience. To follow Him where He calls—to follow where the banner leads, if only it be the banner of the King—is the crowning glory of discipleship, opens the way for larger achievements in His service and for everlasting renown.

CHAPTER NINETEEN

The Church and Its Public Services

There is nothing of the Star Chamber in the church of Christ, or in its services. Its foundations were laid in the open, and nothing was done in a corner. This has always been true of the church of God in its service and worship, except when the church, hunted down and persecuted by "The Church," hid itself away in mountains, or worshiped in caves and dens, or such other places as offered them safety. There is here, from the very nature of the church and its service, no secret confessional between priests and either penitent or the coverer up of crime. The "Confessional" is out of place in the church of Christ, though it may become "The Church" in its method and spirit, in its pretension and purpose.

The Uniqueness of the Church Assembly

We need to give fresh emphasis to the unity of the church, its uniqueness and marked distinction when assembled for public service. Unity of the church is more than unity of believers, and fellowship in church life and membership is something more and additional to the universal brotherhood of those who believe in Christ as their Savior. There is here an element all its own, a power in whose magic workings the many are wrought into one—many members but one body. The church is a people, born each one from above, born not of blood, nor of the will of the flesh, nor of the will of man, but of the Spirit of God, and made one in Christ Jesus. It is the individual, local church of which we are speaking, and which, being complete and independent in organic life and structure, is a people who are wrought into marvelous oneness of body and unity of spirit.

Bonds of Fellowship

Its members are made one in the noblest bonds of fellowship. The membership, however small or however large, is yet one—as the flower in its several parts is yet one in structure, symmetry of form, in beauty of color and fragrance. "The body is one, and hath many members; and all the members of that one body, being many, are one body. For by one Spirit are we all baptized into one body, whether Jews or Greeks, whether bond or free; and have all been made to drink into one Spirit." We have lost sight largely of the unity of the church, partly because of so much indefinite thought about "The Church," and partly because we have failed to appreciate the dignity of character and loftiness of purpose, the supremacy and sovereignty of a single, individual church of Jesus Christ.

Those Great Words of the Apostle Peter . . .

were written not of a local church as such, but of disciples at large, as being saved and in their relation to Christ, yet those very words describe to the letter the people who make up the membership of such a church—of the churches of Christ wherever found. The church, and we wish to write it down with all emphasis, is of "a chosen generation, a royal priesthood, a holy nation, a peculiar people; that they should show forth the praises of Him who hath called them out of darkness into the marvelous light; which in time past were not a people, but are now the people of God." And God is not ashamed to be called their God, because He hath prepared them a city. Such, indeed, is the church wherever found, when in life and spirit it is commensurate with its unique nature, with its lofty purpose, with its noble and mighty mission, and shines in the darkness as a light for Jesus Christ and His glorious work of grace. This may be ideal, but it is nevertheless true, and gives definiteness to the real, with efficiency and glory to the practical in church life and church service.

Christ Himself placed on His church the badge of supremacy and sovereignty in its relation to all other organizations. And its coming together in public assembly is one of its distinct and essential marks. Herein is almost its very heart and life. Its membership as individual believers may of course be widely scattered, and yet come together as one in the public service. And the church assembled in such public service is unlike all other gatherings as to character and purpose, as to privilege and spirit. It assembles primarily to worship God and to honor Jesus Christ as King in Zion and the Lord of all. And to this assembly of the saints in their fellowship and communion is given the special distinction with its special privilege and even blessing: "If two of you shall agree on earth as touching anything that they shall ask, it shall be done for them of my Father which is in heaven. For where two or three are gathered together in My name, there am I in the midst of them."

Our Lord on previous occasions had emphasized the importance and reward of praying in secret—within the closet and the door shut; and His precept in this regard had the emphasis of His own personal example. And He does not here weaken, or discount, or disparage in any way the blessedness and necessity for worshiping in private. But as something additional, He takes notice of the coming together of His people, and promises something extra in the fullness of privilege and blessing—puts Himself among them, marks their agreement in prayer, and commends their assembly for worship. Have we yet learned, or will we be always learning and even then never coming to know, the full significance and power of the church in prayer, as at Pentecost, or on the night of Peter's deliverance from prison and from the watching soldiers? "Satan trembles when he sees the weakest saint on his knees," but much more when the multitude turn as one to the throne of grace with agreement of heart in purpose and petition. It is a symphony of immeasurable power, for a church in prayer has connection with the throne and is in touch with God.

Public Worship

Count this a true and practical thing when the church assembles in public worship, when there is agreement in prayer. Viewed in this light and from this angle of vision, the midweek prayer meeting takes on new meaning and becomes of tremendous import. For that is the church assembled in prayer—the coming together of two or three in Christ's name with Him in their midst—distinctly the prayer service with songs of praises. This word "agreement"—symphony—is very significant. There is in figure of speech the thought of tuning and keying and bringing into harmony two or more instruments of music. As a great orchestra with many instruments, but all striking the same key and the same note in their symphony, will stir the soul, and move us with marvelous strains of music. That is the harmony of many voices, the agreement of many instruments, the symphony of sound, but oh, what is this compared with the agreement of hearts, the symphony of desire, and petition before the throne?

It is like the symphony in the singing of angels, the richest music on earth. Here is where heaven and earth touch. Heaven comes down our souls to greet, and glory crowns the mercy seat. Oh that wonderful, wonderful Word, let it be learned over again and made familiar with every heart and in the church life of every member: "Where two or three are gathered together in

My name, there am I in the midst of them. If two of you shall agree touching anything they shall ask, it shall be done of My Father which is in heaven." And this is the midweek prayer meeting, where Christ is in the midst of His church, and out of which come the energies and power for blessing beyond anything we have yet dreamed. It may well be called the power house in our church life, whether for the individual member or the church as a whole. Here we find the storage battery, which means increased energy and effectiveness in service for Christ, and for the extension of His kingdom among men.

The Set Day for Church Worship

But Sunday, by common consent and for nearly two thousand years, has been the great day for the churches and their public service. This came not so much by command as by concord of circumstances and fitness of forces making it the day of all other days. This is the memorial day, occurring and recurring every week, of the resurrection of Jesus from the dead. Every Sunday is a new celebration of that glorious triumph over death and the grave, and shall ever stand as the greatest of all days with the followers of our Lord—not, of course, to either the exclusion or prejudice of other days and other services, but as having special mark and emphasis and fitness.

Because of Resurrection Morning

On that wonderful morning—the first day of the week—Jesus our Lord, who had died on the cross and been buried in the new tomb, reappeared as the risen Christ before His disciples, who were gathered together in one place. Then again, eight days later—on the first day of the week again—He found them assembled in the one place. From that time on and until now, the first day of the week stands separate and apart. Other days may equal it in sacredness and even in service, but it stands alone in its marvelous significance. What a day it was at the first—that first resurrection morning! And from that time to this good hour, the first day of the week has held the chief place in the calendar as the

Lord's day, the lordliest day of all the seven as they come and go with alternating light and darkness. It set aside the Jewish Sabbath as a distinct victory in the world's timetable, and took rank all its own, marking a new date in the calendar, as the resurrection of Jesus had marked the world's history with a new and startling wonder.

> This is the day the Lord hath made;
> He calls the hours His own.
> Let heaven rejoice, let earth be glad,
> And praise surround the throne.
>
> Today He rose and left the dead,
> And Satan's empire fell;
> Today the saints His triumphs spread,
> And all His wonders tell.
>
> Hosanna, in the highest strains,
> The church on earth can raise!
> The highest heaven in which He reigns
> Shall give Him nobler praise.

This is the universal song of the redeemed host of the Lord. And now, this first day of the week has come and gone for nearly one hundred thousand times. With its every return the Lord's people somewhere around the world have marked its coming as the coming of the Lord's day—the memorial of His resurrection, a fresh coronation of the risen Christ, now enthroned at the right hand of the Majesty on high as King of kings and Lord of lords. There are no better words in which to greet the return of this day, than the words of Thomas as he met the risen Christ on that second Sunday morning: "My Lord and my God." And our Lord's response through all the centuries is new and fresh as the morning of springtime: "Thomas, because thou hast seen Me, thou hast believed; blessed are they that have not seen, and yet believed."

And Sunday—there need be no objection to calling it Sunday. This very name itself came as a trophy and testimony, won by the cross and the resurrection power from heathenism, the noblest and brightest day in all their calendar of worship and far away longing—the forecast indeed of our Lord's final and universal conquest of all the empires of darkness. And Sunday finds its new and fullest meaning, its crown of glory in being emphasized as the day in which the church assembles for worship, and has its preaching service, and its teaching service in commemoration of its Lord's resurrection. Would that this exalted notion of the day and of its glorious service could once get full sway over the hearts of the people! It would master them, making them strong and joyous in the kingdom of the Lord, and would bring fresh honor to His name, and mightily augment the power of the church for the conquest of the world.

Preaching is not worship, listening to sermons is not worship, but they contribute in marvelous fashion to the noblest and loftiest worship. A thousand hearts—thousands of thousands, will bear testimony to this. Right preaching—the man of God, the man sent of God and bearing God's message to the people—is the most dynamic power in the world. And when the Lord opens the hearts of those who hear that they attend to the things spoken, then heaven and earth are in conjunction. Preaching is the first and highest on the list of things which men can do for God. The preacher is Christ's ambassador, and in Christ's stead pleads with men for God, as indeed through Christ he pleads with God for men. "After that in the wisdom of God, the world by wisdom knew not God, it pleased God by the foolishness of preaching to save them that believe." And the preacher, endued with power from on high, in his great message and in the rapture of his heart may lead his people to the very portals of the heavenly, and awaken in them songs like the angels sing. Then the preaching service becomes a season of worship devout and rapturous, and refreshing for the days to follow.

The Sunday School

And the Sunday school, moreover, as the teaching service of the church, is becoming more and more a distinct and powerful factor in church life. As an institution it is a church school, when in operation a church service. Under our Lord's great commission as the Christian's program, the church must be evangelistic and missionary but also didactic—teaching observance of all things which He hath commanded. The Sunday school as a service for teaching the Word of God is putting new emphasis upon the teaching function of the church, and day by day is adding new power with the members for bringing in the kingdom. The church is coming to its own in this matter of teaching the Word of God, and teaching also the observance of His commandments—and that, too, without priest or prelate, but by the blessed leadership of preacher and pastor. There is no need to talk of changing the name. Let it be Sunday school for Bible study in church service, for having the membership better trained, made more efficient and more true in their church life.

The Beauty of Ceremonial Services

We must mention in this connection the ceremonial services of the church, as deserving special emphasis, namely, the administration of baptism and the Lord's Supper as ordinances of the Lord's house. The one reproduces in a manner the scene at the Jordan when John baptized our Lord, and shows with realistic power the empty sepulchre in the garden, that people may see afresh the place where the Lord lay and get anew the inspiration of His resurrection from the dead. The other brings Calvary and the cross into the service; and with such vividness as to awaken all the pathos, love, and devotion of the believer's heart. As often as repeated, the Lord's Supper shows the Lord's death on the cross—the love of God for lost men, the gift of His Son as their atonement and redemption from sin, the exalted relation and glorious privilege of the believers in Him—as if He would have His church live always in sight of the cross, lest it forget and lose hope and heart for its mighty mission in the world.

Baptism, the Beautiful Ceremony

And what shall we say for baptism, that beautiful ceremony, so full of meaning in its double picture of burial because of death, and of resurrection because of life in Christ Jesus. Both ordinances are witnesses, and both are on the witness stand before the world for God and for Christ. Their testimony is practically the same, the one supplementing and strengthening the other. But oh, the baptismal scene, how many times and with rapturous power has it stirred the hearts of God's people when gathered for worship in this ceremonial service! It matters not whether they assemble on the banks of a beautiful stream like the Jordan, or around the pool in either the open field or shady grove, or before a baptistry built on purpose in the house of worship as an open sepulchre in the house of God—the meaning is always the same. Its beauty and the power of its message come home to the heart of all who will hear, as the believer in Christ is buried with Him in baptism, and is raised up again with Him to walk in the new life.

But what does baptism say for God in this ceremonial service? This question of rich and momentous import has been overshadowed by the question of what the ordinance may do for one who is baptized. We have been so much concerned about what baptism does for man that we have almost lost sight of the larger question and failed to hear its voice for God. Surely it speaks for Him as did the cloud in the temple when the house of the Lord was filled with the glory of the Lord. God appeared to Moses and made Himself known in the burning bush. God appeared at the Jordan and made Himself known through the opening heaven in that audible approval of the baptism of His Son. So in this ordinance or ceremony which He Himself has set in His church for glorious purpose, He reveals Himself, speaks His Word, and in symbol, makes known His work of grace in saving men.

Buried and Risen

Imagine yourself in a baptismal service. The man going down into the water as the Ethiopian did, and coming up out of the water as Jesus did at the Jordan, is a believer. He has made public profession of his faith in Christ as his Savior, is here obeying his Lord's commandments and following his Lord's example, is buried in baptism, and is risen again with Christ to walk in newness of life. Mark the simplicity of the act. Witness the significance of the form. See the burial and resurrection. And listen for the voice of God.

> In Thy name, O Lord, assembling,
> We, Thy people, now draw near.
> Teach us to rejoice with trembling,
> Speak and let Thy servant hear—
> Hear with meekness,
> Hear Thy Word with godly fear.

I Am That I Am

The voice of God at the Jordan finds its counterpart somewhat in the baptism of every believer. God is present in this ceremony as the cloud was the symbol of His majesty and presence in the temple worship of the Jews. In the burning bush God's presence was manifest, and He announced the unity of His Being—I AM THAT I AM. Baptism goes further in the revelations of His grace:

- It says for God that He is present in this ceremonial service as in the scene at Horeb and the Jordan;

- It declares for God the Trinity of His Being—Father, Son, and Holy Spirit;

- It says for God that He gave His Son to die as an atonement for sin, and sent the Holy Spirit to make His work effective in the hearts of men;

- It declares for God the believers' adoption into the divine family as His Son through faith in Jesus Christ—saying this is My Son in whom I am well pleased;

- And in a figure of marvelous beauty and force, baptism declares for God a threefold resurrection as the product of His power:

  —the resurrection of Jesus from Joseph's new tomb,

  —the spiritual resurrection wrought in the believer's heart by the Spirit of God when He raised Him up with Christ,

—and the final resurrection of the dead when at the last day the trumpet will sound and all that are in their graves shall come forth.

These are the things, at least some of the wonderful things, which baptism says for God. The glory of heaven is upon this ceremony, while again and again with its every return, God's voice is heard as through the open heaven with the same message of His grace. This is in part at least a sublime meaning of this ceremonial service of the church, and should subdue our hearts as we look on and listen.

So Simple but So Glorious

This service, so simple, yet so august and glorious in meaning, holds the devout attention of all who fear God and keep His commandments. It appeals to our hearts with pathos and power. It is the witness on the witness stand for God, and for Christ in all that He did for human redemption. The service is full of the things concerning God, and voices what He is ever saying to a lost world, and has in it the flavor of heaven. The followers of Christ in times past have died for this ceremony in their devotion to Him, and sealed their vows with the blood of martyrs, to keep this ordinance sacred and true. It is worth dying for, and worth living for, too. It makes death heroic and honorable. It calls for the cleanest, noblest living, and makes life beautiful in its testimonies of love and loyalty.

Our bearing in this ceremonial service may be the test of the real heart condition toward God, toward Christ, toward His church, and His commandments. One may of course make much ado about baptism—ready to fight for it, ready to burn others at the stake for it, possibly even ready himself to die for it—and yet lack the lofty conception as to its spirit and meaning, even be without the heart condition which baptism requires, and without the character and life which baptism professes. This is a fearful incongruity, and yet possible, and full of danger and warning. But on the other hand, in this ceremonial service there may be the noblest exhibition of allegiance and loyalty. It calls for right spirit and form and purpose in the keeping of the ordinance. It calls for great earnestness and seriousness in its observance, and in what we ourselves do concerning it. We need, like Moses, to pause before this baptismal scene, "put off our shoes from off our feet," uncover in its august presence, and listen to what is said for God in this ordinance of His house.

The Fulfillment of Its High Mission

The church with its enduement and equipment is commissioned to high service. And in the assembly of the saints and in its public service the church finds largely the fulfillment of its mission. In every one of these gatherings for worship, there is the emphasis severally and distinctively of the unity, equipment, and enduement, the function, mission, and fruitage of the church. These services make for its edification as a body, and for the edification also of its members in their individual church life. The church is self-edifying, builds from within, as the human body or the oak tree builds from within. Its equipment and enduement, as well as all its public services, are for this very purpose, and "maketh increase of the body unto the edifying of itself in love." These things all work together in beautiful harmony and glorious purpose, "for the perfecting of the saints, for the work of the ministry, for the edifying of the body of Christ, till we all come in unity of the faith, and of the knowledge of the Son of God, unto a perfect man, unto the measure of the stature of the fullness of Christ."

Outside of the church, also, and as augmenting its power for good, these services are of surpassing worth to a community and thence to the world at large. No one can estimate the worth and far-reaching power of Sunday in the nation's life, with its public services in thousands of churches throughout the length and breadth of the land. They are the salt of the earth, and the salt also in the nation's life—its salvation, if its salvation shall ever come. They are for the glory of God, too, in the world, and for the advancement of His kingdom among men. They were for the honor and glory of Christ in showing what the gospel can do in its power to save through the riches of grace in Him. In these services, moreover, there is the communion of saints. Here they sit together in heavenly places in Christ Jesus. And in this blessed fellowship and common experience of grace they get foretaste of what shall be hereafter:

> The hill of Zion yields
> A thousand sacred sweets,
> Before we reach the heav'nly fields,
> Or walk the golden streets.
>
> Then let our songs abound,
> And every tear be dry;
> We're marching thro' Immanuel's ground,
> To fairer worlds on high.
>
> Come, we that love the Lord,
> And let our joys be known,
> Join in a song with sweet accord,
> And thus surround the throne.

The church here is promise for the consummation of the church hereafter; the assembly here for the assembly hereafter; the church militant for the church triumphant; the services here for the services hereafter—when we shall "come unto Mount Zion and unto the city of the living God, the heavenly Jerusalem, and to an innumerable company of angels, to the general assembly and church of the first-born whose names are written in heaven," where congregations ne'er break up and Sabbaths have no end.

CHAPTER TWENTY

Your Membership in the Church

How is it that you are a member of the church? And how about your church life, in its relation to the cause of Christ, and to your position and influence in the community? These are personal questions of much moment, to be laid on the individual heart, to be confronted and answered by each one for himself. And yet your answer greatly concerns others, because you do not stand alone, and no man liveth or dieth unto himself. Your membership in the church came by your own choice, and by your individual, voluntary act. But it came also by the welcome consent and vote of others, who were already members, and established for you new relations with new privileges and obligations.

None but Christians should unite with the church—only those who are Christians professedly and at heart. Being in the church, therefore, presupposes that one is a Christian; that he has accepted Christ as his Savior, committed himself to Christ as his Lord, has appeared before others somewhere in a public profession of faith, and told of the work of grace in his heart. This marks in a formal way your connection with the church of Christ, and shows outwardly and visibly your place in His kingdom. It is the outward expression among men of the kingdom of God in your heart. If, therefore, the outward be true to the inward, you have already come to a position of honor and eminent distinction.

A New Birth

Becoming a Christian is a new birth, a birth into the family and kingdom of God through the Spirit of God. This, however, though momentous and of infinite worth, is not a finished condition—a commencement, indeed, but not consummation.

In its very nature and purpose, the new heart contemplates and requires church connection, and has the promise of church life. If these do not follow the profession of conversion as opportunity may allow, there is something incongruous and wrong—some failure through want of right instructions, or some shortage in the conversion and the profession of faith.

It is in the heart of the newly-saved and of his very nature—the cry of the child for the mother's care is not more natural—to seek consort with the people of God and companionship among the followers of Christ as they associate themselves in the church and in church life. On the one hand, grapes in the market presuppose the vine and vineyard, but on the other hand, the vine and the vineyard have in them the potency and promise of life and leaf, of foliage and fruitage. The fountain demands outlet in the stream, and greater fullness in the fountain gives also greater fullness in the outflow. Church membership is the fruitage of the Christian life, the outflow of the new heart, the response to the call from within, as baptism is the answer of a good conscience toward God. The grace of God in the heart must have its outlet in church life, in forms of public profession of Christ, in the loyalty of keeping His commandments, and in the noble purpose of living to His honor and of magnifying His saving grace.

Setting a High Standard

The purpose of this chapter is to apply these great fundamental principles to the individual; and to emphasize the individual character and worth of membership in the church, and the individual activity and energy in church life. It is a personal matter throughout, though the one be associated with the many. It involves tremendous issues which you must settle for yourself. If you are not a Christian, you should not be in the church, but if you are, then you will not stay out of the church nor stay away from the church. Contentment out of church connection is inconsistent with the grace of God in the heart, and will surely discredit all your professions, however sincere they may be. This must be so; otherwise we would question our Lord's wisdom in His provision of the church, and challenge His call to follow Him and keep His commandments. The outward in Christian living must match the inward of Christian experience. This gives emphasis to the worth of church membership for the individual, and demands a church life commensurate with the new and exalted relation.

Church Privileges

Having become a member, you have been admitted to all church privileges. You have been baptized upon a profession of your faith, as your Lord was baptized before the beginning of His public ministry. You have come to the Lord's table with His people, and in symbol of your union with Him and of your life in Him, you have partaken of the sacred emblems in this holy service. This is unspeakable honor, and puts a line of demarcation between you and the outside world, as surely as the crown and royal robe separate between the king and the people. It calls for the best possible life, a life becoming the gospel of Christ. One may be a better church member than he is a Christian, but his best attainment as a Christian will find noblest and most complete expression in his church life. For in this he is not only serving God, but serving on God's plan and fulfilling His call and purpose.

This requires the highest and best that is in you, with something always above and beyond. Surely every member should make the best member possible for himself, and should have it as the mastering ambition of his heart to give, both to the church and to the world, the best church life. Why be satisfied with the good if the better is in possible reach? Why be satisfied with the better when you may reach that which is best? "I count not myself to have apprehended," wrote a great master in Christian living, "but this one thing I do, forgetting those things which are behind, and reaching forth to those things which are before, I press toward the mark for the prize of the high calling of God in Christ Jesus." Here is a life with the individual personal element which masters all else, and sweeps everything before it like a cyclone in the forest.

An Example to Others

This is setting a high standard for ourselves, and puts before the church member of today an example before which the best might well stand abashed. And yet this man in his example and life is worth our study, if only we may discover the source of his power and the mainspring of his action. We come at once in our inquiry upon his experience of grace, his doctrinal life in its mighty force and energy, his ever-abiding sense and conviction of being saved and called of God to save others, his over-mastering, all absorbing purpose to honor Christ and have Christ glorified in himself—these were the elements that made his life great, with Christ as the all and in all.

He was Christ-centered, and therein was the mighty source of his power. "The love of Christ constraineth me," he wrote; "neither count I my life dear unto myself, so that I might finish my course with joy; yea, doubtless, I count all things but loss, for the excellency of the knowledge of Christ Jesus my Lord; with all boldness Christ shall be magnified in my body whether by life or by death, according to my earnest expectation and hope." So he wrote and uncovered the mainspring of his choice and championship. He had met Christ on the way to Damascus, and surrendered all to Him—his heart with its motive, will, and mighty impulse, his intellect with old belief passing away and new belief coming in with power, his purpose in life when all the high ambitions became set for the coronation of the newfound Lord. Such was his surrender, and Saul of Tarsus came out of that experience with a view of the Lordship of Jesus of Nazareth, that never once in all after life did he get from under its spell and power. It breaks out again and again in his writing and oftentimes becomes a rapturous song—the Lord Jesus, and Jesus the Lord, and Christ Jesus the Lord, until the end came. And then in realization of his hopes, he finished his course with joy, and received his crown of righteousness from the Lord, the righteous Judge.

Expressing Experience and Belief

In the case of Paul, also, you have a new view of doctrine as to its essential value and practical worth, and you may readily discover at least the possible place and power of doctrine in your own church life. His doctrinal power was unsurpassed by any other element in his character in determining his conduct or in the settlement of great questions. His doctrinal convictions were his creed—melted and moulded in his own heart experience, and his creed was largely the making of his character, and was in his teaching and conduct like the granite and iron in a great structure. "Take heed to your doctrines" was his earnest admonition; "take heed unto yourselves that you may adorn the doctrine of God our Savior in all things;" hold fast the form of sound forms, and let no man take your crown. And this is but another form for the Master's great word: Let your light so shine before men that they may see your good works—the beauty and power of your doctrine as shown in your life, and glorify your Father which is in heaven.

A Person's Church Life

The church life of a person should be at once the embodiment and adornment of his church doctrine; and his member-

223

ship in the church, in the fullness and richness of its meaning, is the expression not only of the experience of grace, but also of his doctrinal character and life. His church convictions tell, or should tell, what he believes, while his church life shows the manner of his believing and the power of his doctrine in his own conduct. Christian life means a creed, more or less comprehensive, but clear and powerful. The necessity and demand are very urgent that your church life should be the expression of your church creed. Especially is this true in this present time of so much looseness and indefiniteness of faith. If one is a Methodist, then let him be a Methodist in the doctrine which he advocates; if a Presbyterian, then let him be true to his Presbyterian creed—by all means let his life be in keeping with the doctrines of his heart, then people will know where to place him. A Baptist in heart and belief is honor bound to be only a Baptist in his church connection and church life; otherwise he is untrue to himself and to his own convictions. It becomes him to adorn the doctrine in all things, and to show its beauty as the doctrine of God.

Sincerity and faithfulness in doctrine are basal in Christian character and find their exemplification in church life. And in the very necessity of the case neither church life nor church character can come to its best, except there be a doctrinal basis. If you shall ever come to the highest life, there must be the doctrinal character with the doctrinal conduct, and the doctrinal conviction with the doctrinal conquest. There is nothing higher for us in this particular than to adorn the doctrine of God in Christ Jesus. It makes us strong and we can make it beautiful before the world. And yet men have decried doctrine, have talked much against it, have even said there was no difference in doctrine, no difference in churches; and that one doctrine is as good as another, and that it makes no difference "what we believe, or what church we join, so the heart is right."

But those who say this fall much short of the great apostle. He was a powerful and vigorous contradiction to all this, both in his teaching and in his manner of life before men. How he did adorn the doctrine, but not until the doctrine, through the Spirit of God, had transformed and glorified his character. The great doctrines as he believed them, and experienced them in his heart, were the granite in his character and the iron in his blood. His faith and creed were experiential. They burned in his life like the bush at Horeb on which the glory of the Lord had fallen, and in which God appeared and made Himself known. Paul was what he was, largely because of his doctrine—a living system of truth—systematic theology vitalized and aglow in the richest experience and profoundest convictions. This made his life glorious for the King, finished his course with joy, and won him the prize of the crown.

A Personal Asset with Individual Power

Returning to your membership in the church—how does it compare when measured by these high considerations, and by your own possiblities? What is your membership worth as an asset in your character, and as a force in directing your conduct among men? And your church life, how does it stand as to its influence on others for the cause of Christ, and what are you doing for its cultivation and enrichment? These questions are not asked as being adverse, or for your discouragement. But they deserve your attention and may lead on to high and nobler things, for with the best members there is yet something for richer attainment, and in the best church life there are possibilities for yet larger things and better living in the kingdom and service of our Lord.

Paul first gave himself to Christ, in all that he was and in all that he could do. This was the secret spring of his life, and points out to us the line of our possibilities. It is with you to do what he did—first give yourself to Christ, make your life render its full measure to His service for His honor and glory. This is something more, and far more important, than the giving of money. Withholding this, you can give Him nothing. But with this being given Him, all else will follow. The purpose to make Christ first in all things is a practical possiblity, and interferes with none of the right affairs of life. It rather ennobles and

225

enriches the life in every direction; the giving of a cup of water—if given in His name and in consideration of Him—at once becomes an act which angels might do. The self-centered man is the opposite of all that is best in Christian life. The Christ-centered man, with Christ enthroned in his heart and crowned in his life, is everywhere for Christ, lives under the banner of the King, and leaves no question as to his attitude in the great cause of God.

With this fixed as a principle in the heart, then the settlement of other and minor matters comes easily as a matter of course— as the solid block of ice would melt and disappear under the blaze of the summer sun. Christ Himself is the settlement of most questions, and is Himself the answer of many problems in life. The purpose to glorify Christ is far better than attempts to imitate Christ. The one is outward and may be mechanical, the other is inward and of the heart, and works as an engine of power both for impelling and for direction.

Take two social matters, for example, and view them alongside this principle, and in relation to your church membership and church life. A young man, who was a professing Christian and worthy in many ways, came to me as his pastor with the question whether I thought there was any harm in dancing. This is a frequent question and tries the conscience of many young people who are members in the church. In answer to my question as to why he wanted my opinion and whether that would decide his own course, he replied that he could not say as to that. But my final word with him, speaking as his pastor and from a desire to serve him and lead him on to better things for God, I said about this, calling him by name: "I will give you the privilege, so far as I have the right to give you the privilege, to dance as much and whenever you please, on only one condition." He caught at this, and awaited the condition. "You first make out of yourself the best Christian and the best church member possible to you, and then you may dance all you please." His countenance changed, and his eyes dropped, as he responded, "But, then, I would not want to dance." Precisely so, and that settles the whole issue. It is a choice between one of two courses.

Putting Christ First

The other matter is even more serious, and yet can find settlement by the same general principle of putting Christ first, and making the church life mean something in the social life. In the cities, and more or less in the village seeking to imitate the city, the young church members and all have changed Sunday evening into a social service for the parlor and made it a set time for calling. Some have gone even further, and made it the occasion for the social function in the community. The last is thoroughly ungodly, robbing God of His day, and borders close on to the vicious in its general and hurtful influence upon character and life. And even the first comes from low views of church obligation, or want of concern for church life—a lack more or less of loyalty to Christ, and of genuine concern for His honor and as to how He is represented by their conduct in the social circle. This is where the test comes, and many who would be true to Him as martyrs fail utterly in these open hours of pleasure.

To live for Christ is sometimes more severe and more trying than to die for Him. Herein are severe perils for your membership in the church and for your church life. Why not be a social power for Christ? Why not bring on His coronation in the social realm? Is there any greater glory for the parlor than its dedication to Christ in all of its mighty influence in home life and business life? The parlor for Christ is a noble motto to which the best may well set their best abilities and energies. So in every other department of the home and in the business world. Why be a master of finance in the markets, and practically worthless in the management of your church finances and in directing things for the glory of Christ? If church membership is worth anything, its worth must hold good everywhere. If church life is a beauty and power at all, it must be seen and felt in the whole range of conduct and association. One of the greatest needs of the church of Christ today is that the business sense of the men and the social power of the women shall be consecrated and centralized in His service. These two things, combined in any community, would command and control for His honor, and set everything on a higher and nobler plane.

An Open Door for Usefulness

This opens exceptional and increased opportunities in church life that are almost immeasurable in far-reaching power for God. The one, by his association with the many, becomes mighty in the many. One strand does not make a cable, but the cable is made up of single strands wrought into one. Church membership is associated units, each of which has in it an element of divine power. Church life has in it the power and advantage of association. It is a combination of many wrought into one by the Spirit of God, to serve God on God's plan for the making of His kingdom among men.

It is a great moment in life when one unites with the church and takes his place among the people of God as one of them, and yet back of that is the greater event, the supreme moment in the soul when God touches the heart, opening up its hidden sources, and faith emerges, and the light of the knowledge of the glory of God shines in. Old things have passed away. All things become new. And the man himself is a new creature in Christ Jesus. Christ is in him the fullness of grace and the hope of glory. It is an experience one never forgets, and the results of whose coming shall outlast the stars, growing brighter and brighter unto the perfect day. This is the beginning of his church life, which will become richer and more fruitful with the passing years.

Somehow, if one may tell in print his own simple story, I am writing now with a boy in mind, into whose heart God came, and in the recollection of the blessed day when grace began its work. It was with the Cane Run Baptist Church in Kentucky—if the reader will pardon the putting of its name on record. A meeting was in progress, the sermon had been preached, full of pathos and moving power, the people were singing

Amazing grace! how sweet the sound,
That saved a wretch like me!
I once was lost, but now I'm found,
Was blind, but now I see.

With the opening of the second stanza, the boy started for the front to offer for membership, and to ask for a place among the followers of our Lord. What a time it was, and how it all comes back to him now as he writes and the tears run down. Blessed people they were, and many of their kindly words spoken that night linger with me to this day.

A Few Years Later . . .

my father changed his pastorate to the New Liberty Baptist Church in Owen County, of the same state. In this church, and as the result of a meeting of refreshing power and great ingathering, there came a fresh awakening with a larger and more intense spiritual life, which became more definite and more insistent in seeking to honor the Lord. It seemed to me then, and seems to me now, after the years have passed, that God went beyond Himself—if one may dare to say so—in a further work of grace, and in condescending love, and in an unusual display of His providence which led the young man out into the open and set him to his life's work. Among these people and in this church came the sense, so new and startling, yet so clear and irresistible, that God would have him preach. It seems strange even to this day, but so it was. He called, and I followed on. He touched me, and I ventured on the task. And in great kindness and forbearance, these people voted in church meeting, so some of them told me, to give their consent for "the young brother to exercise his liberty of exhortation," and so it came to pass. These people, too, like the others, live with me in grateful remembrance.

The two houses of worship—the one a country church, the other a church in a small village—may bear their silent testimony for the people who lived and wrought and worshiped there in other years. And there, within those sacred walls, the two churches still have their homes, and worship, serving God in their day and generation much as their predecessors did in the time gone by—doing honor to Christ in maintaining the worship and faith of their fathers. People come and go, but the song is unbroken, the chord and sentiment remain unchanged among the people of God: "The Lord is my strength and song, and He is become my salvation; He is my God, and I will prepare Him an habitation; my father's God, and I will exalt Him."

CHAPTER TWENTY-ONE

The Church of Your Membership

This chapter, like the last, is individual and personal in subject and treatment. It deals with a specific church in the aggregate of its membership, rather than the individual member. There it was you and your church, but here your church and you—the church of which you are a member. It is more to you than any other, than all others, and your membership should be kept alive, active, and growing. Much depends on you as to what the church is, and much depends on the church as to what you are in character and life. There is here powerful reflex action one on the other—far more than is generally supposed.

A specific church, like a person, or school, or business house, has its individual character and reputation—character being what it really is within itself, reputation what it is reputed to be among those on the outside. And these, of course, vary in different churches, as the churches themselves vary, and often in marked way, in the aggregate of its membership and in its conduct as a body. This is true even of "The Church" in its several forms or "branches" as they appear among us today. They are but historical remnants of "The Church" in its first departure and mongrel growth from the church of Christ, which was local and individual at the first according to His appointment. But we are speaking here of local churches, some of which are better than others when measured even by proper standards—some Baptist churches, I mean, are better than other Baptist churches.

This was true of the churches in the New Testament period, and is manifest from comparative study of their several records—just as some men are better than other men, some Christians better than other Christians. "We have this treasure in earthen vessels," and the treasure is always the same, but its manifestations vary—shining now with more light, and now with less. It follows, therefore, that your church is largely what you make it, in a threefold way—in its character, in its reputation, and in the fulfillment of its mission. Its character is a composite character, and its life a composite life, made up of the aggregate character and life of its members. The community will read you and your life, and from them will make up its judgment as to the church of your membership.

This magnifies both church and member. It places responsibility on the member in what he shall do for the church, and responsibility even more pressing possibly on the church as to what it shall do in training its members in character, in doctrine, and in service. A church is known by its fruit, as much so as a fig tree or fir tree—as much so as the saloon, if the opposite poles of the earth may be set in comparison. Its fruit consists of what it does in the making of homes, in the making of character, in the blessing of the community, in fulfilling the function and mission of a church of Jesus Christ. It is a severe test, but after all it is the test of a standing or falling church.

The Standard of Measurement

Some people, of course, have very inadequate and even improper ideas in judging as to either what a church is or should be. Their praise may be no compliment for the church, while their censure and adverse judgment may be for its praise and honor. So there is need for a standard of judgment—a standard both for yourself and others in judging your church. To this end we will name here for study and comparison the specific case of a New Testament church—the church at Ephesus, together with individual connection and responsibility in its life and work. Read these Scriptures as if they were fresh from the pen of their author, and were written to you and to the church of which you are a member.

> Take heed unto thyself, and unto the doctrine; continue in them; for in doing this thou shalt both save thyself and them that hear thee.

> Take heed therefore unto yourselves and unto all the flock over which the Holy Spirit has made you overseers, to feed the church of God, which He hath purchased with His own blood.

> These things write I unto you, . . . that thou mayest know how thou oughtest to behave thyself in the house of God, which is the church of the living God, the pillar and ground of the truth.

> I am Alpha and Omega, the first and the last, and what thou seest write in a book, and send it unto the seven churches. . . . He that hath an ear let him hear what the Spirit saith unto the churches.

Commanding and August Words

These are commanding and even august words. They have the stamp and authority of Him who liveth and was dead, who holdeth the seven stars in His right hand, and walketh in the midst of the seven golden candlesticks. There is no reason why these words of Scripture should not apply to you and to the church of your membership. They are full of meaning and responsibility for members in their relation to the church, and for the church in its relation to the members both as individuals and in the aggregate of its membership. Transferring the emphasis from Ephesus to a specific church of today, like the one in which you hold membership, we may follow these words as guide and standard to determine what that church should be in its modern environment and with its modern problems.

In relation to its officers and members—to its organic government and the administration of its affairs. This is simple but basal to all else. Take heed to thyself; take heed to yourselves; the many are wrought into one, while each retains his individual person and place; all on the same basis, all dealt with in a uniform way; all equal and coequal with one another, with behavior becoming those who have in hand the management of the affairs in the house of God; and all, too, under the Holy Spirit who dwells within the church as a body, renewing and guiding, endowing and enriching; the simplest of all organizations and yet the most effective, choosing its own officers and directing its own officials, whether pastor or deacon, and seeking always the honor and glory of its one sovereign head, in loyalty and devotion to the Lord Jesus Christ.

In relation to God. The church of God, which He purchased with His own blood in the person of His Son when dying on the cross; the church of the living God—the organic body in which the Spirit of God is active and powerful; the house of God—the inward and invisible find expression here in the outward and visible; the house standing for the body that worships within; and the body of believers standing for the unseen kingdom—the simplest expression of the mightiest and most glorious reality. This is the basal element in church character, the universal and supreme standard for its testing and measurement.

Its relation to doctrine. What it believes and teaches—the pillar and ground of the truth. The truth equals the truth as it is in Jesus—the doctrines of the gospel. The church is made custodian of the gospel, and is entrusted with giving its facts to the world with what these facts mean in the way of doctrine. The falling apple, for illustration, was fact in nature, but the mighty law of gravitation was its truth—the meaning of the falling—in the system of the universe. The death of Jesus was fact in history, but its meaning or doctrine is the atonement which came by blood. The church holds within itself as its entrustment the purchase price both of its own making and of human redemption. The church of which you are a member, like the church of the New Testament, stands for doctrine—the doctrines of the New Testament—the doctrines of the grace of God. It makes a tremendous difference as to the doctrine which a church holds and gives out to the world. Take heed unto thy doctrine.

The relation which the church holds to the community—to government, whether city or national. This, too, is of great importance. It shows what a church is, and opens the way for the fulfillment of its mission. The church—your church through its members and its aggregate membership as a body—must never fail of this. It is the light of the world, the salt of the earth, a blessing always to municipality and commonwealth—saving the nation by saving men.

This outline as a brief unfolding of the Scriptures quoted above represents in a moderate way what the church was in the city of Ephesus—a church complete and independent, operating its own affairs within itself, standing for God, for Christ, and for the doctrines of the gospel. It shows the character of that church and the elements of its power, together with the lines of its activity and operation. Quietly, but powerfully, it wrought, with its influence permeating the city life and undermining the mighty reign of gods and goddesses, until the business of making idols was gone, or about going, and the great traffic itself was brought into disrepute, and even the great goddess Diana was about to lose her prestige. It was a struggle between church and temple, with the gospel coming into the ascendency.

This serves as a standard as to what should be the church of today—the church of which you are a member—and points out clearly what must be the elements in which there should be the training and care of its membership. If the church is to have a membership of power, it must come through training; and this training is the business of the church itself, each church training its own members, and cannot be entrusted to another—though in many ways help may be called in from the outside from those of like spirit and purpose. This is basal and imperative, essential alike to the highest attainment in church character, and to the fulfillment of the lofty task to which it is called in the world. God has wonderfully endowed and equipped the church to this very end, as the human body that converts bread and meat into bone and muscle, or the great oak whose every leaf is a lung and whose roots draw up nourishment from the great depths of the earth, and yet for itself builds within, making fiber and bark, growing in stature and strength. It is with the church to make of itself a glorious structure for the King, a fit temple for His indwelling.

A Converted Membership Necessary

The church, in order to the training of its members, must maintain the principle and policy of a converted membership—receiving as members only those who have made public profession of faith in Christ as their personal Savior. For only those who have an experience of grace can be cultivated in the fruit of the Spirit. Only those with a Christian experience can be trained in Christian character and in the richness of Christian service. This is fundamental and as fixed as any law in the physical world. Things are trained and grow along the line of their nature, and bear fruit after their kind. Only the new heart can be trained in the line and fruit-bearing of the new heart.

"Church Culture"

"Church culture" is a term just now coming into use among us, and stands for real need and promises large possibilities. Why not this for renewed hearts, as well as culture of the field, or the culture of the flower garden in beauty and richness, or the growing of the vineyard, or the training of the vine to fullness of fruit bearing? There are certain fundamental laws which are common in both spheres and which will yield as much in the church as in the field. Church culture is in a sense self-culture. The training of its members is largely self-training, as has been said; the church sets itself to the training of its members, to the strengthening and enriching of its membership in the aggregate.

But there must first be the Christian, else there can be no Christian culture, and there can be no coming to the full stature of manhood in Christ Jesus, with the individual until there first be the birth of the Spirit, or with the church unless there first be the membership of those whose hearts are renewed in the regenerating grace of God's Spirit. Men can be grown only from children: "You cannot gather grapes of thorns; or figs of thistles;" the Christian character and life come only with the Christian; and church culture and training require the regenerated membership, as God has emphasized in many ways.

Training the Membership

In training its membership, whether as individuals or in the aggregate, the church needs for itself at least a threefold emphasis and a threefold culture: in character, doctrine, and service. These three are closely related and largely interdependent. Taken together they make the member what he should be in his church life; and taken together again in the aggregate membership, they make the church what it should be in spiritual life, doctrinal character, and in its active ministries—cultured in Christ Jesus, trained for God in the line of His purpose and for the fulfillment of its mission in the world. Surely this is a great task, and lays upon the church itself tremendous responsibilities and opens to the future a large and glorious usefulness.

Church doctrine, the training in church doctrine, deserves and requires all possible emphasis if it be the New Testament doctrine. The church is here for that very purpose; that in part at least is the essential business of the church, also its strength, and gives to the church definite meaning and teaching power. All that was said in the preceding chapter concerning doctrine in relation to the individual should be said with increased emphasis for doctrines—the doctrines of the gospel—in relation to the church as a body, and in the training of its membership. What the church stands for in doctrine is the test of its character, a measurement of its worth as a mouthpiece for God, and in bearing witness for His grace in Christ Jesus. A church which stands for "nothing in particular," as with an individual, has nothing in particular to stand for, is without doctrinal character among men, and has no mission in the world. It is like the chaff before the wind or floating trash on the sea.

The church of which you are a member necessarily finds its essential self in its doctrinal character, for here you come upon its very life and heart and power. As with the one member so with the church in the aggregate of members—and even more powerfully—the doctrine is the metal in the blood, the iron and granite in the great structure. What is it that makes the red rose red as it blooms in your garden? What is it that gives the dog fennel the odor of that weed in the field? It is that indescribable something which by strange process enters into the very life, flows through their very veins, and shows in stalk and fiber, in color and fragrance, making one flower to differ from another flower in both field and garden. So it is with doctrine in the church of Christ; it gives it doctrinal character, gives it a color and beauty all its own, enriches its flavor and fragrance, and gives it inner strength and withstanding power—in the one case like the rose in the garden, in the other like the giant oak in the forest. Doctrinal character means doctrinal power, and where there is doctrinal power in the gospel of the grace of God, there is also efficiency in the building of His kingdom among men.

Choosing Its Agencies for Training

It is with the church to choose its agencies and methods for training its membership. It has both privilege and obligation to organize its own forces within itself for greater efficiency in the kingdom of Christ. The question of method is optional, but the doing of the thing is imperative. Fields and flower gardens yield the best returns when best cultivated, and this again calls for the best implements and the best approved methods. There must be training in the church if the greatest and best attainments come; the church itself must train its members for God, and so momentous and important is the undertaking that the best members may well afford to give their best energies for devising the best methods—and even they themselves will reap largely from such efforts for general betterment.

The churches themselves have been very slow sometimes in making this provision for self-improvement and greater efficiency, sometimes not even giving recognition or thought to the need, or possibilities, or obligation—failing to see their high mission or to hear God's call for the rising opportunity of a new hour. It is a sad fact that many of the great movements for the kingdom of Christ were begun and carried forward, not by churches as such, but by a few members of the church, who, working patiently and faithfully, came finally to enlist the church for its furtherance. Churches, like persons and nations, may fail to see their day, or hear when God is calling to new and larger things.

Modern Missions

It was so with modern missions. Carey, though stirred within himself with the Spirit of God, could yet get no following, and even met with opposition in his purpose to evangelize the world—as if the church had any other business, or God any other plan for making known the gospel of His grace. It was so also with the Sunday school. Within the easy memory of men still living, churches voted to tolerate the new movement, and to allow some of the members to use the house of worship for such schools in the teaching of God's Word. It is a fearful thought and fact that a church, the noblest of all organizations in its nature and purpose, may yet, like field and garden, go utterly to waste for failure to do what God intended should be done.

The same course has followed also, as a thing still not worked out among us, concerning Christian education, and the training of young people in our churches. But it is coming to pass with these movements as with the others; and yet still others will come in the forward movement of the kingdom of God. At the first a few members gave themselves to these objects, and finally churches, as such, were enlisted, and set heart and hand to make good the purpose of its being. Once when pastor, I proposed a special work for the young people in the church, but the deacons deemed it not wise. I submitted, but said, very well, brethren, and now, leaving this method aside, what will you do or propose for the training of our membership? And that is the imperative question in the churches of today, and must be answered before God. Will the clock strike twelve and leave the question unanswered?

I am pleading with the church and for the church, the specific church of which you are a member and for which you are largely responsible. It is an effort to magnify the church in the mission which it was set and sent to do, to have to come to its own in privilege, power, and blessing. The waste places will bloom as the garden of the Lord, and in fields now barren there will be the golden harvest, and the joyous song of the reapers as they gather in the sheaves. A golden day of serving and seed sowing in the church will surely bring a glad and golden day of gracious ingathering.

Three Agencies the Church Can Use

It is in mind and heart to mention here, with strong and specific emphasis, three agencies or methods which the church can use within itself and of itself, for the training of its membership in greater efficiency: the Sunday school, the B.Y.P.U., and the Laymen's Movement. The first is older, of more general use, and has come to its place of power. The second is slowly but surely coming into use, and showing itself well adapted as a church agency for church culture. The Laymen's Movement is but starting with men as church members feeling themselves called of God to high purpose, showing their own membership worthwhile, and making their own church mighty for God in the world's redemption.

Sunday school and B.Y.P.U. training join in one purpose, as a joint church effort to make better members and a better church condition. In both, the teaching function of the church is emphasized for the furtherance and fulfillment of the Christian's program; the one in teaching the Word of God, the other for teaching church doctrine and training in church service, but both for the enrichment of the spiritual life of its members; both also aiming to make the members more efficient in their church life, more competent, active, and true in the management of the affairs and in the care of "the house of God," which is the church of the living God, the pillar and ground of the truth.

The Pastor in Leadership

In the matter of church training, the pastor holds the place of leadership, as a place of honor and responsibility. In the organic life of the church as Christ established it in the world, this is his place by divine appointment. This is his office, with its twofold function of preaching and teaching, of feeding and caring for the flock, "the church of God which He hath purchased with His own blood."

But specifically, and with a particular church, the pastor comes to his high office first by the choice and voluntary vote of the church, and second by his voluntary acceptance of the pastorate. It is a question of serious moment and must find settlement between him and the church—a solemn, sacred trust offered and accepted. It is not to be governed or guided or interfered with by anyone on the outside, whether Conference, or Bishop, or College of Bishops. It is the sovereign act of an independent church, seeking divine guidance, and choosing a pastor in the fear of God as leader in its service and efforts for the kingdom. It is a severe moment for a church, and they should seek such a pastor as will come to them as one sent of God and in the fullness of the blessing of the gospel of Christ.

But while a great honor, the highest honor indeed among men, this office in the church imposes a responsibility and care that might well make angels hesitate; and surely it should be accepted only in obedience to God's call. God chooses men for fields and fields for men, and the pastor comes to his office as the anointed of the Lord.

> 'Tis not a cause of small import,
> The pastor's care demands;
> But what might fill an angel's heart,
> And filled a Savior's hands.

Being intrusted with such a charge, the pastor comes to it called of God, not to lord it over God's heritage, but to serve in

His strength for leadership in the church for larger things. His ministrations in the pulpit, his care for souls among his people, his organizing the force for better service, his training of the membership in character, doctrine, and church life—these are the lines of his operation as he leads his people for the furtherance of the gospel and the building of the kingdom. The church in the exercise of its own choice has set him for its leader in teaching and training, and his leadership for God will be for him as a crown of glory.

Whatsoever a church sows, that shall the church also reap; this law so mighty and inevitable in the kingdom of nature stands fast also in the kingdom of grace—alike for the one and for the many. Neglect and indifference and failure in teaching and training will surely bring forth fruit after its kind. Church culture, gaining in character, doctrine, and service, will give everlasting life in the church—in the church of your membership, with ever-increasing power for the fulfillment of its mission in the world. A better church membership will surely give a better church life to you and others; and this in turn will mean a fresh coronation for the King in Zion and more joy for His people.

CHAPTER TWENTY-TWO

The Baptist Art of Living Together

A recent book called *The Christian State* defines government as "the art of living together." It is a fine designation, and concerns alike the county, the village, the town, the city, the state, the Federal Government, and every form of human society—becoming more delicate, more difficult, and more important as it involves a larger territory with a larger number of people. This art of living together is the basis, and is at the very heart, of the Commonwealth. As a principle and policy, it has universal application.

This high art is essential in the family where association is closest, and where the bonds are the strongest and most tender. Without it there can be no peace or prosperity or happiness. It goes also to the very heart of the membership of a church, and determines its character, condition, and efficiency, as Christ's chosen instrument and method of advancing His kingdom among men. It is of the essence of the gospel, that this art of living together is made possible, and actual even under adverse circumstances. The apostle emphasizes the fact that in the church of God at Corinth, Jews and Gentiles, bond and free—the most unlikely extremes of race and social conditions—are yet brought together, and are made one through the work of the Holy Spirit in the individual heart and through the larger dispensation of His grace in the organic life of the church. This indeed is the cause and consummation of church unity.

The Key to Success

This art of living together is also the key to the success of a great army, whether in training, or mobilizing, or for efficiency on the field of action. Without this there can be no "esprit de corps." This is the meaning and purpose of all the tedious drill for the soldiers, the army regulations, equipment, and movements. Keeping step on the drill ground may determine success on the battlefield. A whole year's drilling and training in camp may be essential to success in one great decisive battle. Government in an army is the art of camping together, marching together, fighting together, winning victories together—or perhaps if need be taking defeat together. It requires masterful training and masterful generalship for an army to keep step in defeat and retreat. This is the high art of high caste soldiery—camping together, marching together, fighting together, winning victories together, and is the "esprit de corps" of the highest order. There must be no fighting among themselves, no shooting down of their own men, or hindering one another either in the camp, or on the drill ground, or on the battlefield.

The Army of the Lord

All this applies with remarkable force to our great Baptist hosts as the army of the Lord, whether of America or throughout the world. This "Baptist Art of Living Together" should be written large and made the word of conquest throughout our Southern Zion. More depends on that, humanly speaking, than on any other one thing as to what our people shall do for the cause of Christ, and for the extension of His kingdom to the uttermost parts of the earth. There is no drill master for this, and there can be no drill master except as each one shall master himself for the honor and glory of Christ. Consideration for one another, the recognition of the rights of one another, these are essentially Baptist principles and are at the very core of the Baptist art of living together in fellowship and efficiency for the gospel.

At a great dining of notable men some years ago, Dr. John A. Broadus sat beside Dr. John Hall, the distinguished Presbyterian preacher of New York. In their conversation Dr. Hall expressed surprise that Baptists kept together with such force and efficiency when they are held by no ecclesiastical bond, "but simply by a rope of sand." Dr. Broadus replied, "That rope of sand is what holds them and is the mightiest bond if you will look into it more closely." How true this is! Baptist fellowship is unique, is their bond of union, and is their art of living together. Fellowship in its highest form is an affinity—and affinity means an inherent, inevitable coming together of like seeking like, and forming the union of many into one. Baptist fellowship is a kind of fourfold affinity—a fourfold cord or bond of union, at once their bondage and their liberty, their life of service and their crown of rejoicing. The fourfold elements may be enumerated somewhat as follows:

1. *Fellowship in conversion*: spiritual affinity, a common experience of grace through the Spirit's work in the heart, and the one sure basis of all Christian fellowship and church association.

2. *Fellowship in doctrine*: doctrinal affinity, oneness of creed and confession of faith, as the expression of personal conviction concerning the fundamental doctrines and policy of the Scriptures, especially of the New Testament.

3. *Fellowship in the ordinances*: ceremonial affinity, oneness of view concerning baptism and the Lord's Supper, as to their spirit, form, and purpose.

4. *Fellowship in service*: affinity of common interest and aim as coworkers with God, and as having fellowship with Him and with His Son Jesus Christ.

These are the mighty elements in Baptist fellowship, and make them one as a great people, and create among them the Baptist art of living together, and of working together in churches, in associations, and conventions. With these rooted and grounded in the character and life, there is yet left large room for individual views and private interpretations, and yet with royal regard for Baptist loyalty and Baptist liberty. There is in this the high art of at once holding fast all we count dear while at the same time we give and receive liberty of conscience and freedom of choice. Surely this is possible with a people who live in the fellowship which is outlined above.

The Baptist Situation in the South

For twenty years now I have studied the Baptist situation in the South, and I honor and love our people as a great people more and more as the years go by. My supreme desire for them is that they should do their best for the glory of Christ, and show themselves a mighty brotherhood in His service. I do not see among them the differences which are often mentioned and sometimes, as seems to me, are emphasized out of all proportion. Some years ago I ventured to express the conviction that it is possible to gather up the views of our people from over even a wide extended territory, and so to formulate them into one statement as to win almost unanimous consent among the Baptist hosts of the South. Someone thought it worthwhile to answer the suggestion with a laugh of scorn. That, however, did not disturb me, and my conviction still abides. The Baptist agreement in fundamentals is so large and strong, so comprehensive and definite, so unencumbered with details, that it affords ample room for our private views and personal notions concerning many other matters. By this means our people have come to what they are, and by this means, too, they shall come to yet larger things in the kingdom of God.

Enjoyment of Baptist Fruitage

The Baptist art of living together has already been at work for years, and we are in the enjoyment of its fruitage. It is our exalted privilege, not to use the word "duty," to cultivate it in our hearts, and to illustrate it in our lives. Surely it is worth being made the watchword in our Southern Zion. It will give our people the place of prestige and command in the future ages. We have in the territory of the Southern Baptist Convention over twenty-one-thousand churches with a membership of largely more than two million; and every one of these two million made a public profession of faith for himself before some Baptist church, was voted a place among its members, was buried with Christ in baptism, and raised up again to walk in newness of life. What a host they are, and by what mighty bonds they are held! Thinking of them as a vast army for God, what can they not accomplish for Him when they are trained in the art of camping together, marching together, fighting together, winning victories together—united in one mighty effort and purpose for the world's conquest, and for the coronation of Christ as King in Zion! This is our hope, our inspiration and joy.

CHAPTER TWENTY-THREE

Baptism in the Christian System

The whole Christian world will come in this lesson to the baptism of Jesus; will stand again at the Jordan, and witness afresh His immersion in the swiftly-flowing stream of that sacred river. It is an excellent opportunity, and brings imperative obligation, to study the great ordinance anew, both as to its beautiful significance, and its exalted and even commanding place in the Christian system.

The Baptism of Jesus

His immersion in the Jordan was at once an act of humiliation, and yet one of the most august and significant scenes in the life of our Lord. He walked sixty miles or more from His home at Nazareth, to be baptized of John as a man sent of God to baptize. It was the gateway to His public ministry, and at the same time foreshadowed His death on the cross and His resurrection from the grave. He had the approval of His Father, and the glory of heaven was upon His pathway—upon His pathway then into the Jordan and through the Jordan, as afterward upon His pathway into the garden and through the garden. It put the stamp of His example upon the great ordinance and gave it dignity and glory forever among those who love Him. "The dignity of this act is worth the audience of kings and princes," and no doubt that angels looked on with wondering gaze, as the heavens opened on this new scene among men.

The Task of Interpretation

The mighty task of its interpretation falls in this lesson to the lot of Sunday school teachers; and with them rest the privilege and responsibility of saying what it means. Here they will speak for God, and for the sublime act of His Son as He made this new and startling advance in His purpose to fulfill all righteousness. In our interpretation there is always danger lest we fall below the mighty ideal presented in the baptism of Jesus, and the momentous act has found scant treatment from many who have undertaken to write the story of His life. We are confronted here with a solemn and pressing duty, and should meet it as those who speak for Him.

The scholarship of the world, regardless of denominational connection, but speaking as scholars and leaders of Christian thought, hold with remarkable oneness and even emphasis that the baptism of Jesus was His immersion in the Jordan, and that John sent of God to baptize fulfilled His mission by immersing those who came to Him. And thus the great ordinance came, and found its place in the new dispensation as a ceremony in the gospel system. Christ put upon this ordinance the emphasis of His example, and later the authority of His commandment, and so it was to stand for all time as a thing to be done by those who love Him, and to be done in the way of His example, and in the spirit and purpose of His commandment. And our bearing in this impressive ceremony of baptism may become a test of our allegiance in His kingdom and our loyalty to Him in His service.

A Beautiful and Powerful Symbol

Our Lord's baptism in one phase of its meaning, prefigured in beautiful and powerful symbol His "being plunged under penal judgment," as described by a distinguished Episcopalian, and also His resurrection and risen life—all of this in one glorious picture, as He was laid beneath the yielding wave and raised again from the watery grave. Standing midway between the Jordan and the garden, to be followed by His crucifixion, and manifestly holding in comparison the two startling and tragic events, Jesus said, "I have a baptism to be baptized with," "an immersion to undergo," as translated by an able and honored Presbyterian, "and how am I straightened till it be accomplished." He was looking forward to His baptism of suffering, the overwhelming sorrow and anguish of soul that broke over Him in the garden and came to its floodtide on the cross. Oh, that cry of His heart in advance, as already He saw its coming—"how am I straightened till it be accomplished."

The first baptism and the second baptism stood one over against the other in His vision, the one a figure and shadow, but the other an awful reality and substance. The shadow of the cross was upon the Jordan, but also the glory breaking from the open and empty sepulcher. And in His baptism He set us a glorious example, indeed, but went far beyond that to set out beforehand the mighty work of His atonement for sin through the shedding of blood for sin's remission and human redemption.

The Believer's Baptism

The believer's baptism—our immersion, whether in pool or river or baptistry—bears close relation to our Lord's baptism in the Jordan. As He looked forward, so also we look backward to Calvary and His open grave. In our baptism we not only follow His example set us at the Jordan, but declare in figure our

personal faith in Him as our Lord and Savior, and in His atoning death on the cross and His resurrection from the grave
with power as the Son of God. In the sublime act we declare in
bold and beautiful figure that "we believe on Him that raised
up Jesus our Lord from the dead, who was delivered for our
offenses, and was raised again for our justification."

The baptism of Jesus, therefore, fixes the great ordinance in
the Christian system, and gives us the key to its wonderful meaning and message. Baptism is best seen in its relation to Christ's
redemptive work, and as declaring our personal belief in Him
and our allegiance and loyalty to Him. This is strongly stated by
Dr. Sanday, of the Church of England, and one of the foremost
scholars of the day. When commenting on the expression, we are
buried with Christ by baptism, he says of baptism:

> It expresses symbolically a series of acts corresponding to the
> redeeming acts of Christ:
> Immersion = Death;
> Submersion = Burial (ratification of death);
> Emergence = Resurrection.

This states the case with rare beauty and force, and its meaning cannot be either missed or gainsaid. Baptism is for saved
people, and the occasion of their rejoicing as they walk in the
ways of the Lord. It has no meaning for others, but holds exalted
and glorious rank in Christian belief and practice. We follow
Christ in baptism as we follow Him in other things. It is wrong,
surely it must be wrong, even seriously wrong, to profess our
love and obedience in everything else and then refuse to follow
Him in the great ordinance in which He sets the example. The
beautiful song we sing takes on new meaning by a slight change
in a single word, and gets a touch of the heroic, especially as
referred to the ordinary duties in our church life:

> I can hear my Savior calling,
> I can hear my Savior calling,
> I can hear my Savior calling,
> "Take thy cross and follow, follow Me."

I'll go with Him thro' the garden,
I'll go with Him thro' the Jordan,
I'll go with Him thro' the Jordan,
I'll go with Him, with Him, all the way.

Where He leads me I will follow,
Where He leads me I will follow,
Where He leads me I will follow,
I'll go with Him, with Him, all the way.

Why not the Jordan as well as the garden? He met the one in fulfillment of righteousness as He endured the other with sorrowfulness of soul. He was as heroic and lofty before God in the one as in the other. Why not follow Him in life's ordinary duties as well as in life's trials and sorrows? Why not follow Him in baptism—buried with Him unto death and rising again to a new life with Him? There is nothing higher or more heroic than the keeping of His commandments and the walking in His ordinances. To obey is better than sacrifice, especially when the obedience is of love and loyalty. Herein is the very heart and beauty and power of all Christian living. It is our joy and His glory to go with Him, with Him, all the way.

Questions for Group Discussion and Personal Reflection

Chapter One

1. R. M. Dudley writes: "The exercise of religious liberty is subject to two very important restrictions." What are those restrictions? Explain them.

2. What does Dudley say is the "subject of a serious misapprehension"? Discuss.

3. Ponder the quotes the author uses by Dr. Gotch, Dr. Armitage, and Dr. Pendleton. Why do they "come short of the full truth"?

4. What is the "bedrock on which the denomination rests"?

5. What is "close communion"?

6. What did Luther say about baptism?

7. What did Calvin say about baptism?

8. Discuss the following statement: "Baptists do not yield their position about baptism because it is the surface indication of a great underlying principle."

9. What do Baptists believe about "infant baptism"? Why?

10. According to Baptists, what is the purpose of the Lord's Supper?

11. Why does Dr. Dudley write that he is a Baptist?

Chapter Two

1. What are the three reasons Dr. Eaton gives to answer the question proposed in his chapter title?

2. Discuss some of the testimonies given by "great thinkers."

3. What are the other standards offered that the author lists?

4. Ponder the quote cited by Kant.

5. Discuss the quote cited by Herbert Spencer.

6. Contemplate the following: "Outside the Bible we can learn of God's power, of His wisdom, of His glory, but only here can we learn of His love and of His mercy." What does this statement mean to you?

7. Describe the statue of Luther.

Chapter Three

1. The author writes: "The question, Why immersion and not sprinkling or pouring? may be answered in the light of three considerations." What are these three considerations? Discuss each.

2. Would you agree or disagree with this statement and why? "We can handle the Bible better with immersion as our act in baptism than we can with sprinkling or pouring."

3. What did Dean Stanley write in 1879 about baptism?

4. When and why was sprinkling or pouring practiced?

5. What does the *Didache* explain about baptism?

6. Describe the baptism of Novatian in the third century.

7. What is the "pronouncement of Liddel and Scott" regarding *baptizo?*

8. Do you think Dr. Stakely makes a good argument for baptism in light of Baptist belief?

9. What did baptism mean in the days of the New Testament?

10. Why is "the thought of a sprinkling or a pouring . . . so utterly incongruous as to be inadmissible"?

11. What is the difference between "an immersion" and "an emersion"?

Chapter Four

1. According to the author, what is the purpose of Sunday school?

2. Why does Dr. Broughton insist that we need a "training school"?

3. Discuss the comment made by Thomas Jefferson in his discussion with Daniel Webster. Could that statement be made today? What difference would it make if today's children could be taught "to love the Savior"?

4. Who was Robert Raikes and what did he do?

5. What is the difference between preaching and teaching?

6. Name the three reasons why teaching is commanded.

7. In what four ways can we extend the work of the Sunday school? Discuss each way listed, and add your own ideas.

Chapter Five

1. Why is "the verdict of the ages" "My Lord! and my God!"?

2. Discuss: We are "world-missionary and not anti-world-missionary because our Master has commanded His people to be so."

3. Ponder the following statement: "If missions did not 'pay,' if not a single heathen ever believed, if all alike refused to become disciples, to go and teach would still be but to obey the command."

4. Discuss the following: "Jesus came not to save people from a place called hell, but from a state of being and character, and a course of conduct called sin."

5. "Depravity is a historical fact as well as a Bible doctrine." Why is this statement true? Discuss.

6. How does Dr. Harris answer the question he poses: "Can it be possible that God will condemn people for rejecting His Son, when they have never heard of Him?"?

7. Do you agree with the author's argument? "Unbelief or the rejection of Christ is a sin and augments the already existing sin whose penalty is death." Why or why not?

8. Why is this statement true? "But the very unity with Christ which makes us saved people at all, which makes His death our death, His life our life, His place our place, His wealth our wealth, makes His work our work."

9. Why is "the believer's unity with Christ . . . spiritual as well as legal"?

10. Why are Baptists world-missionary in our faith, and trying to be in our practice?

Chapter Six

1. What four words sum up the essentials of evangelical Christianity and why?

2. What is the meaning of "regeneration"? How does it prepare us for the service of Christ?

3. What does the author mean by this statement: "There is no distinction between work for Christ in the home church and on the foreign field"?

4. What do you think of this statement: "An anti-missionary Baptist then is an anti-Christian Baptist, and from all such may the church of Christ be delivered"?

5. Who are the "Omissionary Baptists"?

6. According to the author, why should "Baptists ought to be the best and most effectual servants of God in all the world"?

7. Why is "to be omissionary is to bring ourselves into judgment"?

8. What is the "sin of omission"?

9. Why is to be "omissionary is to imperil the destiny of millions"?

10. Consider this statement made by Robert P. Wilder: "Religion is the only commodity, the more of which we export, the more we have at home."

11. Why is to be "omissionary is to fail to glorify God"?

Chapter Seven

1. J. P. Greene writes that "it is a good thing to educate [the children] in our own historical traditions." Do you agree? Why?

2. Consider and respond to this statement: "Every young American should get his college education in America, among his own people. It is a great mistake to take him abroad for his early training. So it is a mistake for a Western boy to go East for his college training." Do you agree or disagree? Why?

3. "In the college our young people become acquainted with denominational enterprises," writes the author. Why is this true? Do you agree?

4. Why is "the college course . . . a good schooling for church work"?

5. Do you agree with this statement: "When we educate our young people in our own colleges, we secure their influence to our denomination"?

6. Why is it "absolutely necessary that our young ministers be educated in Baptist colleges," according to the writer?

7. Ponder this statement: "Young preachers also need to be educated in a spiritual atmosphere. While they are growing in knowledge they should also grow in grace." Why is this true?

8. What is the main reason given for having our own colleges?

9. Considering the following statement was made almost one hundred years ago, what would you say today about public schools? "Most of our children get their primary training in our public schools. These are not Christian, but they are not un-Christian. Our public school teachers, as a rule, are Christian men and women. They come out of our best homes, and are in sympathy with our pious wishes to bring up our children in the Lord."

10. Why should the college "be an evangelical agency—a missionary institution"?

11. "Soul-winning is not generally recognized as a part of college work, but it should be." Do you agree with this statement? Why or why not?

12. Why should "the Bible be taught in the college"?

Chapter Eight

1. In your own words, tell the experience of the baptism of David M. Ramsey.

2. Why did Ramsey's father object to his baptism?

3. Describe the experience of Dr. Ramsey's mother's death. How did it affect him as a six-year-old child? What did he most vividly remember about his mother and their time together?

4. How did Dr. Ramsey answer the question he posed in his chapter title "Why Become a Baptist"?

5. Describe the moment of his baptism. With what event does he compare it?

Chapter Nine

1. What is the New Testament ecclesiastical unit?

2. Discuss the following: "Christ is the only sovereign, and His churches are His executives, acting under His law and guided by His representative on earth, the Holy Spirit."

3. What are the two general theories to which all Christendom holds?

4. Explain the first theory.

5. What is the second theory? Who holds this theory?

6. What does a convention add to a church?

7. Why have a Baptist convention?

8. What is the purpose of a convention?

9. What does Dr. Gambrell mean when he writes, "Boards are channels, not fountains"?

10. What is the purpose of the Home Mission Board, the Foreign Mission Board, and the Sunday School Board? How do they work together for the common good of Southern Baptist churches?

11. Discuss the following: "Unified, sympathetic movements, running, perhaps, on different lines but in harmony, always tend to economy and the highest efficiency."

Chapter Ten

1. How does the author answer his own question: "What then is meant by 'use,' 'money,' and 'the cause of Christ'?"

2. Ponder the meaning of the following: "No thought, sensation, desire, or volition is possible without the loss of blood in repairing the waste of nerve tissue."

3. What must we do to help toward the coming of the kingdom?

4. The author poses this question: "Why should a Christian employ as an instrument for advancing the kingdom of God the wealth into which a part of his life has been transmuted?" How would you answer it?

5. How can we become "coworkers" with God?

6. Does God really need our money? Why or why not?

7. Could God achieve His purpose without our aid?

8. What are the five reasons cited that we should give our money to the cause of Christ in the world?

Chapter Eleven

1. What is the Sunday school of today? How has Sunday school changed since Dr. Frost's time?

2. Tell the history of the Sunday school's beginning and growth.

3. Who was Robert Raikes?

4. Who was William Fox?

5. Who was Benjamin F. Jacobs?

6. What is the purpose of the Sunday school in the local church?

7. What work does the Sunday school do in regards to the church?

8. Why is this work important to the church?

9. Ponder the thoughts quoted by Dr. William E. Hatcher of Virginia.

Chapter Twelve

1. Describe the teacher as "God's interpreter."

2. What are the three elements cited in teaching?

3. What are the "synonyms" of teaching and why are they important?

4. Describe Christ as our "model interpreter."

5. Ponder Jesus' skill at teaching. What kind of teacher was He?

6. Who is the Sunday school teacher's audience?

7. Why is the teacher's job to "interpret God and His Word"? In what ways can this be done effectively?

Chapter Thirteen

1. What was the reason for establishing the Sunday School Board?

2. What were some of the conflicts and arguments that plagued the beginning of the new Board?

3. Describe the former Sunday School Board. What happened to it?

4. What was *Kind Words* and what impact did it have on Southern Baptists?

5. When did the Home Mission Board move from Marion, Alabama, to Atlanta?

6. Describe the part the author played in the establishment of a new Board—the Sunday School Board.

7. What happened in Birmingham, Alabama, in 1891, regarding the new Board? Describe the unusual actions of Dr. Broadus.

Chapter Fourteen

1. What is "the word" that Dr. Frost gives to the denominational leaders?

2. Discuss the "lack of doctrinal conviction."

3. Consider this statement: "We need to give emphasis to creedal character and doctrinal conviction as having practical virtue and value in everyday Christian living."

4. Do we, as a Convention, need to heed closely the words of Dr. Frost in our own age? Discuss.

Chapter Fifteen

1. What does Dr. Frost suggest will be the aim of this chapter?

2. How would you describe Paul's letter to the Ephesians?

3. "The church home may emphasize in powerful and glorious fashion what the church people stand for." Why is this statement true?

4. Contemplate the following: "The church, like the individual Christian, is the salt of the earth; is the light of the world; is a city that is set on an hill and cannot be hid; and has the glorious privilege of letting its light so shine before men that they may see the good works and glorify God."

5. Discuss God's revelation of Himself to us. In what ways does He reveal Himself?

6. What elements make the church a "voice for God"?

7. How does the author describe God's Book?

8. Why is "the church . . . itself an interpretation of the Scriptures"?

9. Why is "loyalty to the Scriptures" so important?

10. Discuss: "Christ saves men individually, then groups them into churches, and sets them to save the world. This is its high mission, and everything must be subservient to this."

11. What is the meaning of the following statement: "Like the Lord and Savior Himself, the church gives itself for the world—not to the world, that would be for the marring of the one and the ruin of the other, but for the world and for the world's saving"?

Chapter Sixteen

1. Comment on the following: "It is entirely scriptural, and accordant with all the facts, to count the church as emanating from the creative energy of God."

2. Why is this true: "The coming of John the Baptist marked a turning point in the affairs of men, and in the history of the human race"?

3. What was "a part in God's great plan" as described by the author?

4. What is God's plan of human redemption?

5. What does this statement say to you: "The church is for the saved, and is their opportunity to cooperate with God in saving the world"?

6. Why has the church remained?

Chapter Seventeen

1. Why is the Bible essential to the church?

2. Describe the "coming of the Book."

3. What "Bible" did Jesus use and quote?

4. Consider: "Whatever theory we may have of inspiration or of how God gave the Bible to men and through men, it must be at once large enough and exclusive enough to leave the authorship unquestioned."

5. What is the meaning of "revelation"?

6. As He did to Moses, as He did to the children of Israel, as He did to Jacob, how does God speak to us today?

7. Why was the making of the New Testament "an august movement in the literature of the world"?

8. Tell in what order the New Testament came to be written.

9. Why must the New Testament be "our guide in the study of the church"?

10. What is meant by the "new dispensation"?

Chapter Eighteen

1. What is the meaning of the word "orthodox"?

2. Discuss what the author means by "right thinking."

3. Consider: "Man in his best estate needs the light from without, and a standard of measurement other than is possible within his own little sphere, or from the consensus of all that has gone before, apart from the Word which God has furnished and which shineth as a light in a dark place."

4. What happens to the church if the Scripture is believed not to be the authority?

5. What is the "inevitable law"?

6. What is the "purpose" and "value" of the Scriptures?

7. Discuss the word "moved" as suggested by the author.

8. Ponder in detail the following:

   "Paul, on the other hand, emphasizes the authority of the Scriptures in his statement of doctrine, basing all on this, according to the Scriptures. He takes Christ's death, burial, and resurrection

   1. as matter of history;

   2. in their doctrinal significance as the atonement for sin;

   3. in their relation to us as having been in our stead;

   4. and all according to the Scriptures, he admonishes to care and concern for doctrine and commends the Scriptures

   • as being holy,

   • as coming through men under the inspiration of God,

   • as being sufficient for doctrine and conduct, and

   • as being able to make wise unto salvation through faith in Jesus Christ."

9. What is a "confession of faith"? Why is it important?

10. Explain: "Baptists are not 'The Church' with a people, but are a great and glorious people with churches."

Chapter Nineteen

1. According to Dr. Frost, what is the church? Would you add anything else to his description? If so, what?

2. Fill in the blanks:

   "The church is a _____ generation, a royal _____, a ____ nation, a _____ _____; that they should show forth the _____ of Him who hath _____ them out of _____ into the marvelous _____; which in time past were not a _____, but are now the _____ of ___."

3. What is meant by the term "assembly of the saints"?

4. What does the author write about the praying church and its power?

5. What does Jesus tell us about agreement in prayer?

6. Why do we worship in a congregational service on Sundays?

7. Would you agree or disagree with this statement: "Preaching is the first and highest on the list of things which men can do for God"?

8. What is the unique and beautiful symbolism of baptism?

Chapter Twenty

1. Why is the following statement true: "Becoming a Christian is a new birth, a birth into the family and kingdom of God through the Spirit of God. This, however, though momentous and of infinite worth, is not a finished condition—a commencement, indeed, but not consummation"?

2. Discuss this statement: "If you are not a Christian you should not be in the church, but if you are, then you will not stay out of the church nor stay away from the church. Contentment out of church connection is inconsistent with the grace of God in the heart, and will surely discredit all your professions, however sincere they may be." Do you agree? Why or why not?

3. What does the author mean by this statement: "Having become a member, you have been admitted to all church privileges"?

4. Describe the change that came when Saul of Tarsus became Paul the apostle.

5. Why should a person be true and faithful to his particular doctrine/denomination? What reason does the author give?

6. Answer or ponder privately the questions J. M. Frost asks of his readers: "Returning to your membership in the church—how does it compare when measured by these high considerations, and by your own possiblities? What is your membership worth as an asset in your character, and as a force in directing your conduct among men? And your church life, how does it stand as to its influence on others for the cause of Christ, and what are you doing for its cultivation and enrichment?"

7. Ponder this: "To live for Christ is sometimes more severe and more trying than to die for Him."

Chapter Twenty-One

1. How is this statement true? "Your church is largely what you make it, in a threefold way—in its character, in its reputation, and in the fulfillment of its mission."

2. What is the standard of measurement for a church?

3. With what does this chapter deal?

4. What responsibility should the church take in educating its members?

5. Discuss the church in relation to its officers and members.

6. Ponder the church in relation to God.

7. Talk about the church in relation to doctrine.

8. Describe the relationship between the church and its community.

9. Tell in your own words the qualities of the church in Ephesus.

10. Give your opinion of this statement: "If the church is to have a membership of power it must come through training; and this training is the business of the church itself, each church training its own members, and cannot be entrusted to another—though in many ways help may be called in from the outside from those of like spirit and purpose."

11. What is meant by the term "church culture"?

12. What is the meaning of "doctrinal character"?

Chapter Twenty-Two

1. Why is this "high art" of "living together" so essential? What does the author mean by the term "the art of living together"?

2. Discuss the following statement: "Without it [the art of living together] there can be no peace or prosperity or happiness. It goes also to the very heart of the membership of a church, and determines its character, condition, and efficiency, as Christ's chosen instrument and method of advancing His kingdom among men."

3. Describe the situation and tension between the Jews and the Gentiles in biblical days.

4. How does the author compare the art of living together with that of a successful army? Do you think his analogy communicates effectively?

5. Contemplate the discussion between Dr. Broadus and Dr. Hall.

6. Why is Baptist fellowship unique?

7. What does "affinity" mean and how does the author use it to describe Baptists?

8. How is Baptist fellowship a "fourfold affinity"?

9. According to Dr. Frost, what was the situation of Baptists in the South in his day? Is his assessment true today? Why or why not?

10. What does the following statement say to you: "The Baptist agreement in fundamentals is so large and strong, so comprehensive and definite, so unencumbered with details, that it affords ample room for our private views and personal notions concerning many other matters"?

Chapter Twenty-Three

1. Describe the baptism of Jesus.

2. Why is His baptism considered the "gateway to His public ministry"? What else is considered in His baptism?

3. Discuss the following: "Christ put upon this ordinance the emphasis of His example, and later the authority of His commandment, and so it was to stand for all time as a thing to be done by those who love Him, and to be done in the way of His example, and in the spirit and purpose of His commandment."

4. What is the symbolism of baptism, and what does it mean?

5. Why do Baptists practice immersion and not sprinkling?

6. What is meant by the "first baptism" of Jesus and the "second baptism" of Jesus? Why is one called a "figure" and the other a "shadow"?

7. What does the "sublime act" of believer's baptism declare?

8. Discuss Dr. Sanday's statement.

Name Index

Subject Index